In more than fifty years of teaching History of Religions, from both Harvard and Chicago roots, I have never before encountered a work that shines with such authoritative and insightful scholarship, as well as methodological maturity, in two radically different traditions—indeed two civilizations. The mastery of primary languages and texts alone, in their social settings, is astonishing. But this book affords more than portraits of two towering figures in their full-bodied uniqueness. As their presence requires, it is finally an original perspective on faith, carefully developed theme by theme, which compels the reader to seek afresh, with awe and delight, One whom the author quietly names "an open-hearted God, in an open-ended universe."

—Harmon Hartzell Bro, Ph.D., theologian and former graduate dean, author, *A Seer Out of Season*

A fascinating book; less the usual introduction than an in-depth study of Qur'anic themes. Combing years experience, piety, scholarship, and appreciation for things Islamic, the author offers personal and creative insights that help illuminate the landscape of Muslim-Christian dialogue. His view that the Qur'an was formulated by Muhammad enables him to portray the Prophet in very human terms and to read the Qur'an as he would the Bible, a text rich in themes both divine and human. It is an excellent resource for graduate and post-graduate students and others interested in enlarging their understanding and appreciation of Islam.

—Harold Vogelaar, Ph.D., teaching scholar in residence for Christian–Muslim relations, Lutheran School of Theology

I read through your book with great enthusiasm. It is an honest, courageous, and well-researched study of a religion that is more than any other calling for our attention. It is honest, as you combine your Christian faith with an eminent scholarship concerning Islam. It is courageous, as you are one of the few theologians who study Islam as a theologian; that is to say, you give Islam a place within the dealings of God with humankind within the history of salvation. You combine islamology with theology in liberating vision. It is well researched, as you give a proof of a life-long study of Islam, of mastering the most recent literature and of being fully informed about tragic and rather recent events concerning human rights in Turkey.

—Arnulf Camps, O.F.M., past president, International Association for Mission Studies

I am favorably impressed by the contribution this books makes toward increased mutual respect and fuller understanding among Muslims, Jews and Christians.

—Rev. Durwood A. Busse, Wordwide Ministries Division, Presbyterian Church (U.S.A.)

Also by R. H. Drummond

A History of Christianity in Japan

Gautama the Buddha: An Essay in Religious Understanding

Unto the Churches

Toward a New Age in Christian Theology

A Life of Jesus the Christ

A Broader Vision: Perspectives on the Buddha and the Christ

Understanding Muhammad and the Koran

ISLAM
for the
WESTERN MIND

Richard Henry Drummond

HAMPTON ROADS
PUBLISHING COMPANY, INC.

Excerpts reprinted with the permission of Scribner, an
imprint of Simon & Schuster Adult Publishing Group,
from *The Koran Interpreted* by A. J. Arberry.
Copyright © 1955 by George Allen & Unwin Ltd.

Map inside front cover:
The Spread of Islam and Christianity © 2005 Maps.com
Map inside back cover:
Muhammad's Missions and Campaign to 632 © Cartographica Limited.

Hampton Roads Publishing Company, Inc.
1125 Stoney Ridge Road
Charlottesville, VA 22902
434-296-2772
fax: 434-296-5096
e-mail: hrpc@hrpub.com
www.hrpub.com

If you are unable to order this book from your local
bookseller, you may order directly from the publisher.
Call 1-800-766-8009, toll-free.

Library of Congress Cataloging-in-Publication Data

Drummond, R. H., 1916-
Islam for the Western mind : understanding Muhammad and the Koran / R.H.
Drummond.
    p. cm.
Summary: "Surveys the life and times of Muhammad and the rise of Islam,
including the prophet's visions and the politics that shaped his message"--
Provided by publisher.
Includes bibliographical references and index.
ISBN 1-57174-424-X (5-1/2x8-1/2 tp : alk. paper)
1. Islam. 2. Murhammad, Prophet, d. 632. 3. Islam--Doctrines. I.
Title.
BP161.3.D78 2005
297--dc22

                            2005015508

                ISBN 1-57174-424-X
                10 9 8 7 6 5 4 3 2 1
            Printed on acid-free paper in Canada

To Pearl, who has walked with me
on this way to a broader vision.

Contents

Preface

No serious book about Islam could properly be written in these days without reference to the tragic events of September 11, 2001, and their aftermath. Readers will recall that 19 Muslims of Egyptian and Saudi Arabian background hijacked four American passenger planes. Three of them wrought very great loss of life and destruction of property, two of them upon the World Trade Center in New York, the third upon the Pentagon in Washington, D.C. The fourth plane crashed in a meadow in Pennsylvania, killing all on board. The shock of these events—the first overt large-scale attack on the continental United States since the War of 1812—was very great both within and without the United States. Out of this has come widespread knowledge of a worldwide network of Muslim terrorist activity, called al-Qaeda (the Base), aimed at the United States and, more generally, the entire Western world. (The capitalized word "Western," it should be noted, is here to be understood in a cultural and religious sense rather than a geographical one.)

The leader of this network was found to be one Osama bin Laden, a wealthy, charismatic former citizen of Saudi Arabia. This man has come to be seen as a Muslim singularly devout in his own interpretation of Muslim faith, a faith at least in part influenced by the harshly puritanical Wahabi sect of his home-land. Bin Laden and his colleagues in their worldwide network were seen at first as the primary culprits in aggressive activity, and the war in Afghanistan was the result. This military effort, widely supported throughout most Western lands, was designed to overthrow the Taliban Afghan government that was providing training grounds and otherwise safe haven for Osama bin Laden and his growing number of followers. This military effort largely succeeded, but from this there developed the American decision to invade the neighboring and populous country of Iraq, which was highly civilized, although ruled by a ruthless and corrupt dictator, Saddam Hussein. This invasion, largely the result of unilateral American decision-making, found the United States with substantial support only from the United Kingdom, token support from a number of other nations, and often strong opposition from countries such as France and Germany. It seems that the general populace of most countries in the Western world oppose the American-led invasion/intervention. All in all, as the war, now a kind of guerrilla war, drags on, there seems to be a crisis in leadership styles, largely, I believe, owing to inadequate understanding of the world of Islam, its faith (in all its varieties), and its practices (in all their varieties).

This book was begun more than a dozen years ago in a more peaceful era, a labor long in years but rich in growth of understanding. The purpose of this book is not to provide policy-makers with specific programs or solutions to current problems but to furnish background materials and a broader vision for intelligent persons to work with. Islam is stated by some to be a religion of peace. Actually, over its long centuries of expansion, it is not. But neither is Christianity, except possibly for its first three centuries until it became the state religion of the Byzantine Empire.

Yet there is a great deal of quiet goodness among ordinary people in both the Islamic and Christian traditions. It is very largely unknown in the Western world that a central element of Muhammad's preaching and teaching was that God (Allah), the Lord of the Worlds, leads unto goodness. That is, to ethical goodness, both individual and corporate, both interior and exterior. During the first 13 years of his prophetic ministry in Mecca, Muhammad's demeanor, both public and private, was peaceful. In the latter ten years of his life in Medina, where "the preaching became policy" and he emerged as the leader of armies and probably the greatest statesman of his time, he always preferred negotiation to violence.

This is not to whitewash anybody or anything. But the fact that history's Islam has a spotty record in following the example of Muhammad does not alter the very high significance and very great value of that example, any more than the spotty record of historic Christianity in following the example of Jesus alters the very high significance and very great value of that example. Both examples have inspired, motivated, and moved millions—indeed, billions—of human beings in the direction of better, nobler modes of human living and relationships.

In any case, we have got to get along. This book aims to contribute to that.

This book is also intended to combine perspectives with fair and judicious balance, in quest of truth. I do not believe that any of us are in a position to lay hold of absolute truth, but I am strongly convinced that we profit by a sincere *quest* for truth. This study seeks the truth with regard to both Muslim and Christian Scriptures. However, Oliver Cromwell's advice to some of the ardent divines of his day, "Remember, you may be mistaken," is still advice worth pondering.

I am a specialist in the history of religions. For more than 50 years, I have studied, taught, and written about Islam and Buddhism, and, with less intensity and depth, other world religions. But I do not write as a so-called secular historian of religions. Indeed, I am inclined to think of such terminology almost as an oxymoron. I do not see how a person can properly and responsibly study or write about religion without some measure of personal participation and commitment. I do not mean participation and commitment to some kind of amorphous "religion in general," but participation and commitment to a particular mode of religious faith and practice that allows—nay, requires—empathetic attitudes and approaches to other modes of religious faith and practice, yet retains the right and means of critical discernment of one's own stance and that of others.

I write as a Christian. But this does not mean that I view other religious traditions with antipathy or denigration. Quite the contrary, like major theologians in the early Christian Church, my own understanding of and commitment to Christian faith and practice led me to see the wider presence and work of the living God in the world. Such understanding, I believe, leads to discovery of both truth and goodness—surely, in many cases, of divine origin—outside the ranges of historic Christian or Jewish faith, and within them.

With reference to my dislike of the term "secular historian of religions," I wish to add a few words. I understand the term "secular" in this case to mean that the historian is operating entirely, by intent, on the plane of history on this planet. This posture presumably also means confinement of human perceptions of reality to what may be perceived by the five physical senses. Religion should, of course, be concerned with reality, persons, and events on the plane of human history and with the perceptions of the five physical senses, for "God is with us." But it is inescapably concerned *also* with dimensions of higher consciousness and "location." I regard, for instance, Jesus' use of the phrase "Our Father who art in heaven" as indicative of the "location" of the Maker of this cosmos in a place where the entire universe of God's making and loving concern can be superintended. Such "location," of course, does not confine the Divine to a place outside this world. In keeping with the Logos theology of the early Church, I believe the Spirit of the living God to be present and working throughout the whole of creation, in all times and places.

This language inevitably leads us into theological discourse, and I do not wish to develop the theme further. I only wish to affirm that the historic religions of humankind have almost without exception believed in a multitiered universe, with some measure of communication between the Divine and the human, and the possibility of higher levels of human consciousness than those stimulated by the five physical senses.

This way of understanding enables me to say that I regard historic Islam as authentic religion. I regard the Prophet Muhammad, the Founder of this massive and highly significant movement in human history, as primarily a religious figure, worthy of deep respect and appreciation by persons of Christian or Jewish faith.[1] I fear, however, that my attempts at rapprochement will be unacceptable to many contemporary Muslims, primarily because I am in conscience compelled to make use of historical/critical methodology in religious studies, including the study of Scriptures.

Contemporary events in the Middle East have created a heightened and at times intense focus or interest in those lands among peoples all across the world, both east and west—and have revealed an astonishing degree of ignorance of Islam's religious, historic, or cultural manifestations on the part of most of the cultural or political leaders of the world. This ignorance naturally leads to ignorance of Islam's relationship to economic and political developments. There is clearly need for a book that aims to further an understanding of Islam based on knowledge, proper perspective, and balance. My intent, therefore, throughout this book is to be fair, honest, and, as much as humanly possible, factually correct.

I write this as a Christian believer, and I intend this work as a contribution to contemporary religious dialogue. I intend to be respectful, conciliatory, and appreciative, even if at times critical—a critical stance that I also take with my own faith, its primary documents, and its historic manifestations.

I am a Christian believer who claims to participate in the developments in Christian theology that now seem to characterize the growing edge of such theology in every major tradition of that faith: Eastern Orthodox, Protestant, Roman Catholic. These developments signify a fresh openness to other religious traditions that can be critical, yet appreciative, even generous, in its appraisals. This generous appreciation, I would contend, is not a trivial product of twentieth-century "cultural liberalism," but has solid roots in both the Bible and the mainstream of early Church theology.[2] This life context can provide a fresh approach to understanding Islam that may contribute to calming tempers, healing wounds, and building and crossing bridges, all to the end of creating truly significant areas of mutual cooperation and mutual respect.

The major factual content of this book is the life of the Prophet Muhammad and the teaching of the Koran. These are the primary data of history, the primary source materials that continue to feed and motivate the inner and outer lives of Muslims across the world. No meaningful conversation between Christians, Jews, and Muslims can take place without due consideration of these data, just as Christians expect due consideration of the life and teaching of the Pioneer and Perfecter of our faith, and of the Scriptures of our own tradition. Today the Western world needs a fair and balanced presentation of the life of Muhammad and the prophetic content of the Koran, illumined by a judicious use of the *hadith*, the body of extra-Koranic recorded sayings and deeds of the Prophet that, as we shall see, require far more careful scrutiny as to their historical authenticity than is the case with the Koran.

At this point, I would like to give a brief explanation regarding the meaning of the phrase "the prophetic content of the Koran." For most contemporary Muslims, such language would be understood to mean that God (Allah) himself is the sole author of the text. This is to say that the Prophet Muhammad, as my friend Dr. Wanis A. Semaan, who is of Lebanese-Christian and Arabic-speaking background, has put it in a very helpful letter to me regarding current Muslim beliefs, "was merely the means of conveying God's message to people: warning, guiding, teaching, and so forth." I do not intend to deny the religious authenticity of Muhammad as a Prophet of the Word of God. I would hesitate, however, to use the qualifying adverb "merely" to express my own understanding of the role of Prophet—whether in the case of Muhammad, or of the Hebrew Prophets, or of Jesus himself. I believe that the Prophet has a participatory role in the larger prophetic experience and process. The Prophet's total life experience, larger cultural and religious background, and personal consciousness inevitably play a role in giving the message its particular coloring. This is not to deny the religious authenticity of the message as "revelation," that is, its possible ultimate source in God. It is intended primarily to remove the discussion from the context of consideration of verbal inerrancy or similar claims of "fundamentalisms," whether Christian, Jewish, or Muslim.

Muhammad evidently had a sense that the language he was able to pass on as that of God in his native Arabic was distinctly more exalted in content and style than was commonly the case with his own speech or that of his compatriots (K 10:38–39; 2:21). But he ordinarily does not use the terminology associated with modern fundamentalisms. Just where he claims that his teaching from the Book Sublime is without falsehood, he states that the content is naught but what has been given to God's Messengers before him (K 41:41–44). To my knowledge, only once in the entire Koran does Muhammad use language that seems to claim he is proclaiming God's Word in a verbally inerrant form. This is a passage in an apparently early Meccan sermon. Muhammad is telling his compatriots of what was evidently his initial vision on Mount Hira, of his call to a prophetic ministry (actually through the agency of the angel Gabriel, "one who is powerful and mighty," although not named in the passage). The context is that of a response to his fellow Meccans who are questioning the religious authenticity of his vision.

Muhammad insists that his own heart tells him he does not lie, an insistence that seems to claim that his own inner awareness and personal integrity were realities well known and acknowledged by the Meccans. In this context, Muhammad proclaims, evidently swearing by the Evening Star: "Your compatriot is not in error, nor is he deceived! He does not speak out of his own fancy. This is an inspired revelation" (K 53:1–12, N. J. Dawood's translation).

Actually, as I discuss in more detail later, Muhammad was

more concerned with the "Essence of Divine Communication" than with niceties of form. Indeed, his mode of proclamation was such that I believe I can describe it as showing freedom from legalistic or overly rigid fixation with verbal precision or even accuracy (as in the case of the Divine Abrogation of verses). I venture even at times to speak of his style as open-ended and pragmatic, as indeed I could speak also of the Prophets of the Hebrew Bible. Such language on my part is by no means intended to be disrespectful. It is certainly not intended to deny that "Divine Revelation" is being communicated, albeit colored by the total personhood of the Prophet. The Prophet himself or herself believes that s/he is speaking the Word of God in its essential Truth. This is the primary reality. The form or format is secondary, although important.[3]

Acknowledgments

I wish to express my warmest thanks to a specialist in Islamic studies who graciously read my manuscript, Dr. Wanis A. Semaan, formerly director of Christian-Muslim relations at the Evangelical Lutheran Church in Bavaria, Germany. I have greatly profited from his comments, suggestions for improvement, and corrections. I am very grateful to Dr. James L. Bailey, New Testament professor at Wartburg Theological Seminary in Dubuque, Iowa, for his kind reading of my manuscript and for his helpful comments and suggestions. I wish also to thank most sincerely my older son, the Rev. Donald Craig Drummond, for his work in preparing the bibliography and index of this book. Long pastor of Christ Presbyterian Church in San Francisco, he served as an educational and field missionary in Japan for ten years and has worked widely in the whole area of history of religions.

I wish to thank most heartily two specialists in Armenian studies who have kindly read the last chapter of this book with its rather extensive consideration of Armenian-Turkish relations over the past century. They are the Rev. Giragos H. Chopourian, Ph.D., of Havertown, Pennsylvania, and Dr. Richard G. Hovannisian, professor of Near Eastern studies at the University of California, Los Angeles. I have been greatly helped by the comments and suggestions of these two fine scholars.

I wish especially to thank the Rev. Dr. Donald K. McKim, long-time friend and colleague in theological studies, who kindly and professionally read my manuscript and made exceedingly helpful comments. I wish also to thank most warmly another friend, the Rev. Durwood A. Busse, who graciously read my manuscript and offered a number of suggestions. Rev. Busse and his wife, Barbara, served as Presbyterian missionaries in Tehran, Iran, and in Pakistan for 19 years. They have been serving since 1999 as partnership consultants for Central Asia, based in Tajikistan.

I wish to thank also most warmly two other specialists in religious studies. One is the Rev. Dr. Arnulf Camps, OFM, longtime professor of missiology at the University of Nijmegen, in the Netherlands. A friend since 1974 and with a rich background of missionary service in Pakistan, Professor Camps has offered most perceptive and helpful comments. The next, a newer friend, is Professor Dr. Harold Vogelaar, Resident Scholar in Christian-Muslim Relations at the Lutheran School of Theology in Chicago. Professor Vogelaar has long served with distinction in Egypt and elsewhere in the Middle East and has written comments of great value to me.

I wish to express my deep thanks to Mrs. Linda Hall and Mrs. Luann LeConte, the two faculty secretaries of our school who have done the typing of this manuscript over its years of preparation. They have been accurate and most helpful.

I wish to also thank Frank DeMarco, chairman of Hampton Roads Publishing Co., and Sarah Hilfer, managing editor, for their fine editorial skills. The experience of working with them has been a happy one for me at every stage of the process of publication.

I

AN OVERVIEW OF ISSUES

I begin this treatment of the issues leading to proper understanding of Islam with a quotation from the American heartland.
Leighton Ford was a long-time associate of Billy Graham in various Christian evangelistic ministries. He may properly be
called a conservative evangelical Protestant, of moderate and
irenic stance (that is, concerned with securing Christian unity),
and, with Billy Graham himself, may be classified as a person of
the highest integrity within this tradition of Christian faith and
practice.

In these days of very great concern for the events and persons
of the Middle East, Leighton Ford was trying to build bridges of
understanding, especially among his own constituency of supporters. He writes, in the modest report-periodical regularly sent
out to these supporters, as follows:

> In truth, we who follow Christ have more than we realize
> in common with Muslims and Jews. Our faiths were born in
> the Middle East. We all believe in one God. And ... we all look
> to Abraham as one of our great spiritual ancestors. Not only

is Abraham the father of believers, in the New Testament he is strikingly called "the friend of God" (James 2:23).[1]

So far, so good. But then Leighton Ford goes on to do what many in Western lands have long been accustomed to do, move into a kind of "put-down" of Islam based on incorrect information. Ford continues:

> Few Muslims, however, would call themselves God's "friends." For the Muslim Allah is totally apart from sinful humans. In contrast, the God of the Bible is not remote but one who has drawn near.[2]

Are these latter statements correct? Not entirely, not even for the Bible. We must remind ourselves that the Bible itself is by no means a seamless robe of monochromatic sameness in moral and spiritual content or tone. Taken as a whole, the Bible shows us images of God our Creator, now near, now far. So does the Koran, the Holy Book of Islamic faith.

Now, the content of the Koran, its nuances of style, and its religious emphases are both similar and dissimilar to those of the Bible. It is not easy to make comparative statements about these two great collections of religious faith and affirmation. But in the tenth chapter, or surah, of the Koran, significantly entitled "Jonah," we find a striking affirmation that believers—not just Muslims in the historical sense but apparently all authentic believers in one God—are friends of God:

> Surely God's friends—no fear shall be on them, neither shall they sorrow. Those who believe, and are godfearing—for them is good tidings in the present life and in the world to come (K 10:64–65).[3]

The Koran is an exceedingly practical book, vitally concerned from its earliest materials with the whole life of humans in this world. It puts that life, however, in a transcendent setting and makes its primary orientation the fact of God, the Creator, the Merciful, the Compassionate, and of the reality of the unseen world. We may even note at this point that, for all the Koranic emphasis on the unity and uniqueness of God (called by the ancient Arabic word for "God," *Allah*), it portrays an unseen world replete with angels and archangels, with *jinn, shaytan,* and other spirits, not to mention the spirits of humans after physical death on earth. For Muhammad, the spiritual world was richly peopled and was, like the world on the plane of human history, under the lordly control and providential disposition of the Maker of all, the Lord of the Worlds.

The Koran, however, is also concerned with aspects of intimate personal religion. We find many verses that express a vivid sense of the presence of God. These verses seem to have had central meaning for Muhammad himself in his personal life as a religious man and in his public role as God's Messenger and Prophet. God is indeed cited as "the Protector of the believers" (K 2:258).[4] But a verse that is frequently recited by devout Muslims is the famous pronouncement: "We [Allah] indeed created man: and we know what his soul whispers within him, and we are nearer to him than the jugular vein" (K 50:15).[5]

We are reminded of Alfred Tennyson: "Closer is He than breathing, and nearer than hands and feet."[6] Another Koranic verse of similar import is "He [Allah] is with you wherever you are" (K 57:4).

But the text that has appealed to devout Muslims in a special way, to those in particular who may be classed as participating in that great stream of Muslim spirituality known as the Sufi movement, is the Koranic verse that reveals God's great goal to bring forth "a people He loves and who love Him" (K 5:59).

Admittedly, the Koranic term (*hubb,* or the *mahabbah* of the Sufis) that is commonly translated into English as the word "love" is not totally consonant with the nuances of meaning of the New Testament terms for love (*agape, philia*). It often seems to emphasize approval from God's side and, from the human side, is more akin to "adoration" (*ibadah*). As Frithjof Schuon has put it, the essential virtues of the ideal Muslim life of faith are rooted in a blending of fear, love, and knowledge of God.[7] Indeed, Islam itself claims to be a "manifestation of truth, of beauty and of power." But Islam is more than the religion of the Absolute, and the Koran teaches more than obedience to the will of God. It teaches not only submission to what may at first appear as an infinitely distant God, or sheerly overwhelming Power, but also commitment to the goodness of God and a return for refuge to "God within us, at the deepest level of our heart," one who is "infinitely near."[8]

It is important to realize that the previous is not representative merely of a small elite in the course of the history of Islam. As Bishop Kenneth Cragg, the noted British specialist in Islamic studies, reminds us, "Sufism . . . has often been the major element in the religious history and the popular experience of Islam. It served over long centuries to interiorize the terms of Islamic dogma."[9] And Louis Massignon, the distinguished Roman Catholic scholar who devoted 55 years to the study of Muslim spirituality, said that "Muslim theology was essentially a mystical structure deriving from the Koran itself as the primary source of its development."[10] Influences from pre-Islamic Persian Zoroastrianism and Eastern Christian monasticism probably played significant roles in the development of historic Sufism, but powerful elements of religious interiority lie within the Koran itself—and in the life of Muhammad.

This also means that the more obvious aspects of the Koran and of the Prophet's public ministry, especially in his last ten years in Medina—aspects that Kenneth Cragg denotes as "dogmatism, autocracy, power"—are by no means the whole story of either the Book or the career. It is indeed remarkable and historically very significant that what Cragg calls "a system so instinctively authoritarian and absolutist as Islam, and so essentially confident about political sanctions in religion," should bear within it this stream of religious interiority and vitality that seems to give inner—and at times also outer—freedom for believers to find their own way in human life, against theologians, however dogmatic, and against rulers, however autocratic. The ultimate quest of Islamic faith and piety may well be to "seek the face of God," a quest wherein relationship with God is properly, indeed inseparably, associated with compassionate conduct toward and sharing materially with fellow humans (K 2:272; 13:22; 92:20).

We see, therefore, that Leighton Ford, who wants to be fair and to build bridges, is only partly right. He is also partly wrong. For today, and over long centuries, the spiritual way (*tariqah*) of innumerable Muslims has taught that God is very near, and in close communion with his "friends" (*wali*), as indeed the Sufi like to characterize themselves.[11]

Some Muslim representatives contend that many Westerners are trying to demonize Islam. Westerners, of course, recall the late Iranian Ayatollah Ruhollah Khomeini's description of the United States as "the Great Satan," a term evidently intended to convey a critique with religious, cultural, and political overtones. On our side, former Vice President Dan Quayle is alleged to have said that the three greatest evils of the twentieth century are Communism, Fascism, and Islam. Quayle of course is admittedly not the most knowledgeable or perceptive among our political leaders, but his statement may represent wide ranges of public opinion in the United States and beyond. With deeper insight, conservative journalist George Will, after the suicide bombing of the USS *Cole* on October 18, 2000, and in the context of the Israel-Palestinian crisis, asserted that we are witnessing not adjustments over small pieces of land but the clash of two civilizations.

We talk of Islam and the Judeo-Christian West, but these terms do not have the geographical significance they once did. In Egypt, Lebanon, Syria, Iraq, Iran, and even more in lands of larger Islamic population to the East, such as Pakistan, India, Malaysia, and Indonesia, there has continued to be an institutional Christian presence (in the form of churches claiming apostolic origin) and, far less, a Jewish one. And the West has seen a large growth of Muslim populations in Europe and North America since the end of the Second World War. Continental

Europe saw the influx of North African and Turkish workers and their families. The United Kingdom saw the coming of relatively large numbers of persons of Islamic faith from British Commonwealth lands. The result is an apparently abiding presence of perhaps 25 million Muslims in Europe. The number of Muslims in France, mainly of North African origin, is between three and four times the number of French Christians adhering to the *Reformed* tradition, a church reaching back to the period of the Reformation and making historically notable contributions to every aspect of French political, cultural, and religious life. In the United States, Islam is said to have overtaken Judaism in numbers of adherents, to become the second largest religious community in the land.

These large-scale movements of populations and consequent shifts in the internal makeup of contemporary nations and cultures make clear that the issue of "bad feeling" needs to be addressed for the sake of domestic peace and cooperation and for international harmony. That bad feeling is held and directed toward the historic West by not a few Muslims, especially in the Middle East, has been graphically portrayed in television shots of angry crowds denouncing the United States in the Ayatollah Khomeini's Iran, in Jordan, or more recently in Palestinian territory, Yemen, or even Egypt. Admittedly, these demonstrations have more often than not been "staged" by government policy and arrangement (and sometimes by nongovernmental groups) in Iraq and elsewhere, but the sights and sounds of the demonstrations have created powerful images and abiding impressions in the psyches of millions of viewers around the world in this day of "instant and universal" communication.

That bad feeling is held in the West toward historic Islam and Muslims in particular is clearly evidenced by widespread revulsion revealed in the media against Muslim holding of Western hostages and, even more, against the acts of self-styled Muslim terrorist groups in recent decades. But the activities of these terrorist groups must not be seen as representative of all Muslims, nor of Islam itself. Anwar Sadat, the late president of Egypt, did not hesitate to say in public that the Iranian Ayatollah Khomeini was not a good example of Muslim faith or character. He clearly regarded the support of terrorist activities by the Iranian government under Khomeini's leadership as abhorrent to the Muslim moral sense.

In our contemporary world, one-third of the world's governments use torture "as a routine method of suppressing political dissent." The twentieth century saw a series of genocides that began with the Turkish massacres of Armenian subjects in 1896 and continued beyond the ending of the First World War. It resurfaced most virulently in the Stalinist policies that led to the death of 13 or more millions of Russian citizens in the 1920s and '30s, and in the German National Socialist elimination, under Adolf Hitler, of over six million Jews and other "minority groups." The list continued with the post World War II bloodbaths of millions of their fellow Cambodians by the Communist Khmer Rouge, the bloody Chinese military invasion and ongoing occupation and subjection of Tibet from the early 1950s, and the brutal Indonesian invasion and illegal annexation of East Timor in 1975—after which at least one-third of the population was wiped out. No continent is exempt, as evidenced by events in Idi Amin's Uganda, Rwanda, and Burundi, or in the Americas, north, south, and central.

Events in the Middle East, and especially Iraq, force us to a deeper level of evaluation, however. John Healey, executive director of Amnesty International, in a letter written to members of the organization in the early 1990s, pointed out that there is a "human rights crisis of massive dimensions not just in Iraq, but in most countries throughout the Middle East and the rest of the world." Healey's letter went on to report that, for years, Amnesty had "publicized well-documented evidence of gross violations [of human rights] by the governments of Iran, Syria, Turkey, Egypt, Libya, Morocco, Saudi Arabia, Israel, and even Kuwait."

Healey lamented the relative indifference of the government of the United States to these human rights abuses, and identified examples "almost too numerous to list," including routine incommunicado detention and torture in Morocco, tens of thousands of political prisoners held and tortured in Turkish jails, thousands of detentions without charge or trial in Egypt, a constant pattern of Israeli abuses of Palestinians, and 10,000 to 25,000 Syrians killed under Hafez Al-Assad.[12] These alleged violations of human rights are largely, although not exclusively, perpetrated by Muslims against fellow Muslims. Is there some kind of ineluctable connection between Islam, defined by Kenneth Cragg as "a system so instinctively authoritarian and absolute," and this multitudinous and geographically widespread pattern of human rights violations?

Muslims may take umbrage at the idea.

Some, perhaps many, will at once remind us of Western colonialism in historic Muslim lands in the past three centuries. Some will certainly want to go back to the six Crusades.[13] I myself—at this point making a countercharge—am forced to remind readers both Muslim and non-Muslim that the major expansions of Islamic faith, especially in its earliest centuries, were made in the context of prior military conquest. Remembering this massively significant historical fact is important not only to inform Western peoples, but to help Muslims engage in the kind of severe historical, cultural, and religious self-criticism that Western civilization has engaged in, however imperfectly, with increasing momentum since the time of the Crusades. Beginning as a small trickle with the criticism of the religious motivation and the military methodology of the Crusades by persons like Roger Bacon, Raymond Lull, and Francis of Assisi, this broadly cultural self-criticism from the West has not yet found a comparable public parallel in historic Muslim lands.[14]

Islam arose in Arabia in the early seventh century of our common era as a religious movement with a distinct, although not totally exclusive, self-identity and a "definite thought and behavior pattern" relatively well established by the time of the death of Muhammad on June 8, 632 C.E. The Arabian peninsula, however, was a largely barren land of rocky desert and sand. Compared to other parts of the Middle East and the Mediterranean littoral, it was culturally backward. Muhammad himself may or may not have been illiterate in the strict sense of the term, but he and the other Arabic-speaking inhabitants of even the towns of the Arabian peninsula south of the Fertile Crescent could not begin to compare in formal education or cultural sophistication with the educated classes of the citizens of the Greek-speaking Byzantine Empire to the north, the Persian-speaking Sassanid Empire to the east, or the Latin-speaking peoples to the west.

No one could therefore have foreseen what has been called the "lightning-like" appearance of Islam in the years immediately after the death of Muhammad. This emergence of Islam, first on the edges, then in the very heartlands, of these ancient and highly developed civilizations, primarily through military operation, impelled by the force of a political religion and lust for booty, has been called one of the most astonishing events in world history.[15] Within 20 years, the victorious Muslim armies were able to conquer and, by the most skillful methods of military occupation, to rule permanently the greater part of the Middle East and North Africa. This almost unimpeded series of military marches resulted in the destruction of the Zoroastrian Empire of the Persians and the reduction to half its former size of the Christian Byzantine Empire. Within two to three generations, the momentum of this extraordinary outburst of physical and psychic energy, which also included elements of more authentic spiritual dynamism, expanded into a vast area extending from the borders of India and Western China across the whole of North Africa and Spain to the Pyrenees Mountains, with incursions into southern and central France. And unlike the periodic explosions of the later "Mongol hordes" from the steppes of Asia, Islam was there to stay.

It would be out of place for us to enter into an in-depth inquiry into possible reasons for this extraordinary series of events. But a few observations are in order to account for this expansion of Islam, by means of relatively small military forces, to rule peoples largely of higher culture and monotheistic faith, whether Christian, Zoroastrian, or Sabaean (Yemenite). Indeed, the whole series of events outside Arabia proper seems almost "just to have happened," without prior purpose or plan. The Muslim conquest of pagan Arabia was evidently by religious principle and developing plan, but there is no clear evidence that Muhammad himself envisaged any further geographical expansion of the structures of his faith community, military or religious. His brushes with the Byzantine Empire seem to have been motivated primarily by fear of invasion by them.

These "brushes" with the Byzantine Empire, which we shall consider again in connection with the life of Muhammad, occurred only toward the end of the Prophet's life. But however brief and limited the experiences of his generals and troops had been with the larger world of the Middle East up to this time, they may have been sufficient for them to gain a sense of some of the possibilities that lay before them. Their appearance on the borders of the Byzantine Empire and then of the Persian occurred at a time when both these great civilizations had exhausted much of their energy and resources in a long series of wars against each other. North Africa had been under the political and military control of either Byzantium or Rome for centuries, but was no longer.

Furthermore, the Semitic and Coptic-speaking Christian subjects of the Byzantine Empire were becoming increasingly restive under the cultural discrimination, oppressive taxation, and specifically religious persecution of Monophysite and Nestorian Christian churches by their Greek-speaking Christian rulers of Eastern Orthodox persuasion. Resentment of Sassanid imperial rule and Zoroastrian state-church alliance and clerical dominance seems to have been comparably strong in the Persian Empire. In this context, the Muslim forces were apparently viewed by many in these lands as representing a new monotheistic movement no more alien to Semitic and Coptic-speaking Christians than was the Greek Orthodoxy of their Byzantine masters. The result was that, in many instances, Muslim troops were welcomed as liberators from hated oppressors. It seems highly unlikely that at least the initial stages of Muslim expansion outside the Arabian peninsula could have been achieved so easily and quickly without these favorable circumstances.

Yet circumstances alone cannot account for the extraordinary energy and staying power of the outward movement of Islam as military empire or as religion. Muslims tend to regard it as the result of divine guidance and help; Christians look at it as the product of forces of imperial and colonial expansion. What we in the West cannot deny is that, beyond the motives outlined here, there was indeed a spiritual dynamism at the core of the entire activity that derived from authentic religious faith. Certainly, many Muslims see it that way.

The point of the present discussion, however, is to identify the fact that the expansion itself was first and foremost a military expansion. The winning of converts to Islamic faith was a long process, taking many centuries, and was much more peaceful and gradual. This point of military expansion, however, has been highlighted by a witness perhaps more impartial than most in Christian-Muslim interrelationships, the distinguished English-speaking novelist and historian V. S. Naipaul. Born in 1932 in Trinidad, where his grandfather had emigrated from India, Naipaul received his higher education in England (at Oxford); indeed, he has lived most of his life in London. But his Indian ethnic background and his relative religio-cultural independence from both Christianity and Islam give his experiences and observations unusual credibility in the contemporary world.[16]

Beginning in August 1979, V. S. Naipaul made a six-month live-in investigative tour of four Muslim countries then in the process of a heady Islamicization: Iran, Pakistan, Malaysia, and Indonesia. He concluded that in these countries where Islam is proclaimed to be "a complete way of life," the past is being selectively forgotten and history has come to serve the needs of theology (a development admittedly not without precedent in other societies). Somewhat earlier, Naipaul had written comparably about the land of his ancestors, after a year spent in India. He writes: "When men cannot observe, they don't have ideas; they have obsessions. When people lead instinctive lives, something like a collective amnesia steadily blurs the past."[17]

Regarding the early thrust of the Muslim armies to the east, Naipaul quotes from an English translation of the *Chachnama,* a Persian writing from the twelfth century that, in turn, depended on a much earlier Arabic manuscript preserved by the family of the Muslim conqueror of Sind, Bin Qasim. The Hindu-Buddhist territory of Sind was roughly the equivalent of present-day southern Pakistan and southern Afghanistan. The Arabic conquest of Sind began some time between 634 and 644. This means that provisional planning for movement that far eastward may have begun within two years of Muhammad's death. The Arabs had to fight hard, making ten attempts over 60 or 70 years before final conquest was achieved.

Naipaul summarizes the motivation for this activity as follows: "The aim of the final invasion, as the *Chachnama* makes clear, was not the propagation of the faith. The invasion was a commercial-imperial enterprise; it had to show a profit. Revenge was a subsidiary motive, but what was required from the conquered people was not conversion to Islam, but tribute and taxes, treasure, slaves, and women." It is not necessary to give details of the frightful final slaughter of the warrior class of Sind "and the enslaving of their dependents," with killings of wider ranges of both military and civilian populations in earlier invasions. Naipaul would, however, inform us that "there are resemblances to the Spanish conquest of Mexico and Peru, and they are not accidental. The Arab conquest of Spain, occurring at the same time as the conquest of Sind, marked [the whole history of] Spain. Eight hundred years later, in the New World, the Spanish conquistadors were like Arabs in their faith, fanaticism, toughness, poverty, and greed."[18]

The main purpose in Naipaul's treatment of this segment of Islamic and Asian history is not to dwell on the gruesome details of ancient genocide. His primary goal is to set forth what he clearly considers a widespread flaw in contemporary Islamic thinking. Naipaul writes that the *Chachnama,* with its frank and full depiction of a series of Arab military invasions, "might be said to be an account of the Islamic beginnings of the state [of Pakistan]. But it is a bloody story, and the parts that get into the schoolbooks are the fairy tales." Naipaul goes on to delineate a number of instances in which Pakistani schoolbooks and other official or government-sponsored publications falsify history, ancient and later, to an egregious degree.

Naipaul is, of course, aware that the distortion of national or ethnic history in favor of groups currently in control of a nation is widespread in human history, East and West, North and South. But he evidently believes that, in historic Islam, the development of a process—whereby "history has to serve theology"—has gone well beyond the usual. Naipaul sees the Arabs of the seventh century, for all their cupidity and cruelty, "as a people stimulated and enlightened and disciplined by Islam, developing fast, picking up learning and new ways and new weapons (catapults, Greek fire) from the people they conquer, intelligently curious about the people they intend to conquer." But as a result of a centuries-long process of ever less ability to engage in self-criticism, Naipaul contends that "Islam, which made the seventh-century Arabs world conquerors, now clouds the minds of their successors or pretended successors." He holds that "history as selective as this leads quickly to unreality . . . the faith begins to nullify or overlay the real world."[19]

Two wrongs do not make a right. Nevertheless, the contemporary widespread Muslim self-image of the Islamic world as primarily historical victim of Western imperial expansion and colonialism needs considerable qualification.[20] Between historic Islam and historic Christendom, over long centuries, the latter has been more often the victim than the victor. The Middle Eastern lands of predominantly Christian faith—Palestine, Syria, the heartland of Eastern Orthodox Christianity, Asia Minor (modern Turkey)—Egypt, and the littoral of North Africa were conquered by Muslim armies and most inhabitants gradually became Muslim believers. They remain such to the present day. We must also remember that Spain remained totally and then partially under Muslim rule for nearly eight centuries. The Mediterranean Sea was, for about seven centuries, a "Muslim lake," whereon European Christians could venture only on Muslim sufferance.

Again, two or more wrongs do not make a right. But contemporary Christian-Muslim relations can be brought to new levels of reconciliation and cooperation only as both sides back off from shrill denunciations based on either ignorance of history or deliberate falsification. A fresh mutual religious and cultural modesty, even repentance, will be the key to bringing down walls of separation and opening doors to authentic interpersonal relationships.

Another perspective, as realistic as focus on military invasions and brutal greed, enables us to see another side. There is a great deal of quiet goodness in the world, among all peoples in all periods of history. This conviction is born partly of faith, partly of long observation and experience. This quiet goodness works in the midst of, and in spite of, the horrors of human mistreatment of others. It acts in slow but healing contravention of these horrors and puts the lie to theological doctrines of "total depravity." If such were not the case, I believe that our societies would explode en masse. I believe, in particular, that there is very much "quiet goodness" in the world of Islam, past and present, even as I make my appeals to both "them" and "us" for more honest and rigorous corporate and individual self-criticism.[21]

My concern in this study of Islam is not denunciation but reconciliation, with as much mutual forgiveness and mutual respect as is humanly possible, even to the end of possible cooperation in the higher goals, both human and divine, that include and transcend political, social, and cultural activities.

This task is not easy, at least in part because I want to be utterly honest in this inquiry and neither gloss over nor overstate the difficulties involved. I began this discussion with a brief quotation from Leighton Ford that highlights the common origin in the historical Abraham of the three great monotheistic faiths of Judaism, Christianity, and Islam. A French scholar, however, made the same point in the context of what he calls "one preliminary fact: although the three great religions of the monotheist faith came from the same roots, they developed separately from each other. They have not supplemented but rather opposed each other in a perpetual conflict."[22]

I shall return to these issues of interrelationship in a later chapter. For now, it is necessary to lay the groundwork by considering the primarily significant facts of the life and public career of the Prophet Muhammad and the theological and ethical content of the Holy Book of Islam, the Koran. Without knowledge and sensitive evaluation of these basic data, no intelligent dialogue with Islam, or with individual Muslims, is possible.

II

The Life of Muhammad, a Sketch

The first matter to be clarified is the authenticity of sources. The primary source for the emergence of Islam is the Koran, and here we are on relatively sure ground. A large part of the Koran had already been written down before the death of Muhammad in 632 C.E. The Prophet himself apparently did not write any-thing,[1] but surahs (chapters) or parts thereof are said to have been written by the believers on palm leaves, white stones, the breast-bones of humans or animals, leather, and some bits of papyrus: that is, on any material available where paper was not known until the eighth century (K 80:13). New surahs were continually added to the corpus as long as Muhammad was alive. It is said that he employed secretaries for the writing, but in the early or Meccan period of his prophethood the ordinary believers must have done this writing themselves, for we read in the Koran that the Book is read or recited to the Meccans (K 29:51). Much, too, was evidently committed to memory in those days when most lit-erature was transmitted by word of mouth.

According to the traditional Muslim view, the first caliph (*khalifah*) or successor, Abu Bakr, in the year after Muhammad's death ordered the scattered portions of the Koran to be collected. The immediate occasion was the death in battle of a large number of those who knew much or all of it by heart. Modern scholars, however, doubt whether this work was completed under either Abu Bakr or his successor, Umar. Variations of readings were found in the copies in use, perhaps largely due to the inadequate Kufic script. We are also told that some collections contained more and some less than what came to be the authorized version.[2] The third caliph Uthman (644–656 C.E.) was responsible for establishing this authorized text and he apparently ordered the destruction of the rival copies. Only the Muslims of Kufa (north and east of Medina) refused to accept Uthman's version, and their text is reported to have been extant as late as 1000 C.E. Muhammad's secretary, Zayd ibn-Thabit of Medina (Madinah), had evidently been active in preliminary work under Abu Bakr and Umar, and he took a prominent part in the work of the commission to which Uthman entrusted the task of establishing the authorized version.

This work was probably completed within 20 or 25 years of the Prophet's death, with the consequence that the Koran constitutes source material possessing a degree of textual purity rare in the history of religious literature. It furnishes us, therefore, with singularly reliable material regarding Muhammad's life and person and the content of his proclamation teaching. But what it tells us of his life is relatively meager, and Islam has from the beginning drawn on other sources for details. In these other sources, or traditions, we meet with formidable problems of authenticity.

During his life, not only did Muhammad communicate to the believers what he believed to be the Word of God, but the Prophet also gave authoritative direction for the ordering of the community's practical (personal, social, economic, political) and more specifically religious duties. As we shall see, the genius of Islam from the beginning of the Medinan period was that it made no distinction between religious and secular realms, between what we choose to call church and state. With the death of Muhammad, this authoritative direction came to an end. He was so esteemed that no caliph could ever be regarded as possessing authority in the same way as the Prophet.

The Koran was, of course, the final authority, but it was not possible to derive from it specific direction for all of life's particular contingencies and it, too, required authoritative explanation. The first generation of Muslims accordingly used as their authoritative guide, apart from and subsidiary to the Koran, their memory of what Muhammad had said and done. In the first generation, especially among the community at Medina, where large numbers possessed personal memory, it evidently worked effectively and possessed a high degree of authenticity. But very soon it became clear that what the Prophet was reported to have said and done was not always the same as what in fact he had said and done. Differing reports and many obvious forgeries emerged to confound the community.[3]

Several relatively small collections of these traditions (*hadith*) were made during the Umayyad dynasty (661–750 C.E.).[4] In time, the collections greatly increased in size, partly in response to the changing conditions and needs of the vastly expanded Arab Empire, and large numbers of the items were recognized by Muslim scholars as spurious. No collection of the *hadith* has ever been recognized as canonical, although many, like Ahmad ibn Hanbal, the founder of the conservative Hanbali school of Islamic law, have attempted to create dependable and authoritative collections.

One principle emerged by which authentic *hadith* were to be distinguished from spurious, the principle whereby authenticity is constituted by the proper backing or support (*isnad*) of a chain (*sanad*) of narrators. "Proper" backing is established by the inclusion of the name of each person in a chain of witnesses that must extend from an eyewitness or companion of the Prophet to the scholar who writes down the *hadith*. Investigating the authenticity of *hadith* by ascertaining whether the chain of witnesses was historically valid and by questioning the veracity of each link in the chain became one of the chief religious sciences of Islam.[5]

The weaknesses of this procedure are obvious. If it is possible to create spurious *hadith*, it is also possible to forge the names of witnesses. Both devices were frequently employed to establish rival claims to the caliphate, to condemn the positions of opposing theological schools—in short, for selfish and partisan purposes. Furthermore, investigation of the moral character and truthfulness of the witnesses is necessarily highly subjective. Also the *isnad* technique was developed only in the third and fourth generations, after many altered or spurious *hadith* had already come into general circulation. Worse, this methodology generally took precedence over consideration of the intrinsic probability of tradition in terms of its contextual fitness to the best authenticated facts of the Prophet's life and teaching, especially as these are known from the Koran.

The result is that while the *hadith* constitute our primary source for almost all the early history of Islam and give much detail regarding Muhammad's life and ethical directions, it is as yet exceedingly difficult to determine the historical authenticity of much of this material. Muslim scholars have generally not employed the kind of historical/critical criteria that Western scholars deem necessary, and the latter have not sufficiently examined the vast amount of material that must be considered. Even by the procedure of Muslim scholars, relatively few of the *hadith* could be authenticated as genuine and, in consequence, many Western scholars are inclined to admit even fewer.[6] Nevertheless, we should not reject the *hadith* in toto, as some Western critics have wished to do. Even spurious material may be useful in reflecting developments in the Islamic community.[7] In consideration of Muhammad's life and activity, however, we need to remember that we must exercise great caution in accepting that which does not come from the Koran itself.[8]

Mention may be made of the life of the Prophet compiled by Muhammad ibn Ishaq of Medina (died ca. 768 C.E.). This work is not extant in its original form, although much of it has been reconstructed from quotations in later authors. Ibn Ishaq was accused by at least one of his prominent contemporaries of transmitting false material, but his work seems to have been the most authentic and the earliest biography of the Prophet.

The Time and the Place

The man who became the Arab Prophet par excellence and the greatest statesman of his time was born in Mecca around the year 570–571 C.E. The first entirely certain date in his life is that of the *Hijrah*, or migration of the small Muslim community from Mecca to Medina in 622. His prophetic activity at Mecca is known to have lasted at least ten years, but the accounts of his age at the time of his call vary from 40 to 43. His name is regularly cited in the Koran as Muhammad, except that once it appears as Ahmad (K 61:6).[9] He was born of a clan of minor importance in the Quraysh tribe, the Hashim.

Both the time and the place of Muhammad's career are of great importance in understanding the emergence of Islam as the latest of historic worldwide religions. The time of Muhammad's prophetic activity coincided with the decline in political and cultural power of the great empires to the north, east, and west of the Arabian peninsula.

From at least six thousand years before the time of the Christ, perhaps even from ten thousand years before, all the advanced civilizations of humanity—except the Yangtze River civilization of China and the Indus Valley civilization of northern India—developed close to the borders of Arabia. Pharaonic Egypt, the Hittite, Assyrian, and Babylonian empires, and the empire of the Medes and the Persians were all off the northern or western borders of the main body of the Arabian peninsula. They were followed by the empires of Alexander the Great and his successors from 334 B.C.E. and the Roman Empire from 64 B.C.E., all of which encompassed the eastern Mediterranean littoral and much of the Middle East. The peoples of the dry hinterland of Arabia, largely of Semitic ethnic and linguistic stock, seem not to have shared in the cultural life and activity of these great empires, but they were, of course, aware of them and not untouched by their influence.

For a concatenation of circumstances and events, comparable to the time of Muhammad, we may properly look a thousand years before to Alexander the Great. Following the death of his father, Philip, in 336 B.C.E., Alexander quickly reestablished Macedonian hegemony over Greece and beyond it to the north and west. His famous march to the east began evidently with a plan to conquer the kingdom of Persia in retaliation for Persian efforts to conquer Greece from the times of the earlier Persian kings Darius I and Xerxes I more than a hundred years earlier.

Alexander's astonishing career led him to the borders of India and beyond, and brought about an empire of vast geographical scope and cultural impact that changed history for the next thousand years. Alexander's motives were no doubt mixed, but, steeped as he was in Greek literature and its traditions of heroic and libertarian ideals, he clearly desired to promote the diffusion of this culture and its spirit as widely as he could. It was Alexander's policy to treat native religions and customs with respect, a spirit of tolerance that increasingly aimed at breaking down cultural and ethnic barriers between the European West and the Asian East. As Alexander advanced eastward and made increasing political and military use of national peoples, his respect for them evidently developed to a remarkable degree, even to the extent of creating some resentment and resistance among the Macedonian soldiers who had followed him faithfully from the beginning.

Upon Alexander's death on June 13, 323 B.C.E., this vast new empire was divided among his chief generals, each of whom became the founder of a dynasty that was to last for several generations. Ptolemy secured control of Egypt and Palestine. Seleucus gained control of Babylonia and later of Syria. Neither general had the commanding boldness of Alexander's cultural vision, nor his spiritual energy, but both, and with their successors, continued to promote the process of Hellenization.

The coming of Roman rule did not significantly alter this process of Hellenization, for the Romans conducted their imperial rule in the eastern Mediterranean and Middle East through the medium of the Greek language and under the aegis of the broader Hellenistic culture. For seven hundred years, the lands bordering the eastern Mediterranean Sea remained under Roman rule, with the eastern borders of the empire varying with the military fortunes of Rome and Parthia (the revitalized and increasingly powerful new form of the ancient Persian Empire).

More than two generations ago, the distinguished British historian of Greece, J. B. Bury, wrote that in some deep sense "the world was waiting to be transformed" by Alexander's activity.[10] I should like to suggest that a similar statement might well be made of the world just before the prophetic career of Muhammad. A similar concatenation of developments and events seems to show a world historical readiness for the acceptance of new influences and consequent political, cultural, and religious changes. The culturally creative power of Christian faith in the Roman Empire both east and west seems to have considerably played itself out with its ever-greater emphasis on minute credal uniformity and religious political unity in place of the vitalities of character-transforming power that characterized the faith in its earlier centuries.

The internal life and activity of the Roman Empire were in significant decline. Areas that had previously known populous cities, thriving industries, and international trade, where sophisticated forms of literary and other cultural life had flourished for centuries, had slipped into depopulation and dilapidation. The internal factors that led to these results were greatly augmented by external forces. Increasing inability to recruit and pay the soldiers needed to maintain the boundaries opened them to invasion in the north and east by wandering tribes of Germanic and Slavic origin. Some of these tribes had already become Christian (albeit Arian), but their cultural level made it no longer possible to maintain the former cohesive unity of the Roman Empire. Substantial areas of Britain, Gaul (France), Spain, Italy, and North Africa came under the political rule and increasing cultural dominance of these largely illiterate tribes.[11]

The eastern portion of the Roman Empire, with its capital in

Constantinople, or Byzantium, in northern Greece (now western Turkey), was able to retain a far larger measure of its politico-military power, its cultural and specifically religions institutions. It was able to maintain its northern borders mostly if not always intact against pressures from Germanic-Gothic or Slavic tribes. The empire in the East, however, was afflicted by the almost constant warfare—for some centuries before Muhammad's life-time—with the Persian Empire of the Sassanid dynasty. Trade with India and Asia farther to the east had become an important part of the economic life of the Byzantine Empire, and the revitalized Persian Empire had the power to block overland trade routes. The armed conflict that resulted seems to have been an important factor in the internal weakening of both empires. In fact, a climax in intensity of this rivalry occurred during the very period of Muhammad's public prophethood. The Persians defeated the Byzantines in battle, conquered Syria and Egypt, and entered Jerusalem in 614. But soon the situation was reversed and the Persians eventually sued for peace, leaving the Byzantine provinces they had occupied. In 630, only two years before the death of Muhammad, a symbolic conclusion to the hostility was effected by the restoration to Jerusalem of the alleged True Cross of Christ, taken by the Persians in 614.

Another factor in the weakening of the Byzantine Empire was religious. Emperor Constantine I was determined to obtain religious unity as an instrument for achieving political and social unity. An imperial church and a policy of imperial government interference in ecclesiastical affairs became the accepted norm. Deviation from official orthodoxy became civil crime and religious heresy.

Unity or conformity in human life, whether religious or political, is far more often desired than achieved, and all the forces of imperial authority were not able to prevent the development of variations in the forms and practices of Christian faith. Disputes between the theological schools of Antioch in Syria and Alexandria in Egypt in the first half of the fifth century led to the emergence of two so-called heresies, the Nestorian and the

Monophysite. Nestorius, patriarch of Constantinople during the years 428 to 432, was actually closer to the position of the church of Rome than his victorious rival, Cyril of Alexandria (patriarch 412–444). Similarly, the proponents of the position known as Monophysitism followed the views of Cyril with little variation. What ensued, however, was that many of the Semitic and Coptic subjects of the Byzantine Empire combined their grievances against the cultural and political dominance of the Greek-speaking Byzantines into a heady blend of ethnic disaffection and religious resentment. Following the Council of Chalcedon in 451, Palestine, Egypt, and then Syria experienced almost revolutionary turmoil, and much of Byzantine imperial policy over the following two centuries consisted of attempts, generally unsuccessful, to lessen or modify these tensions. The later "success" of Muslim arms in these areas is owed in no small measure to this history of tensions wherein ethnicity and politics long carried as much—or more—weight as the niceties of theological doctrine. And, as we shall see, a major thrust of Muhammad's prophetic teaching was to brush aside fine theological distinctions or theological speculation that seemed to divert believers from their primary responsibility to believe and to surrender (*Islam* means "surrender," or "full commitment") to the Lord of the Worlds.

Muhammad's Early Life and Call to Prophethood

Muhammad's father, Abdullah, is said by some sources to have died before the child was born; others record that he lived until the boy was 28 months old. His mother, Aminah, died when he was about six years of age, and he was reared by his grandfather, Abd al-Muttalib and, after the latter's death, by his paternal uncle Abu Talib.

We know very little of Muhammad's early years. Tradition relates that when he was 12, he accompanied his uncle on a caravan journey to Syria, on which trip he met a Christian monk named Bahira who hailed him as God's messenger.[12] More reliable is the account contained in a manuscript of Muhammad's earliest biographer Ibn Ishaq. According to this, Zayd ibn Amr ibn Nufayl, who was very likely a Hanif, one of the group of emerging monotheists in Mecca at the time of Muhammad's youth, was remembered by the Prophet himself as reproving him for his worship of idols. "He was the first to blame me for worshipping idols and forbade me to do so." The incident is described in some detail with the Apostle's conclusion: "After that with that knowledge I never stroked an idol of theirs nor did I sacrifice to them until God honored me with His apostleship."[13]

This account requires elaboration. At the time of Muhammad's youth, a majority of the people of the Arabian peninsula south of Palestine and Syria were what we may perhaps best designate as polytheistic. There seems to have been some sense of a high God called Allah (*the* God in Arabic), but this awareness was apparently overshadowed by closer and more vivid relationships with "lesser" spirits associated with particular places, such as springs, wells, and trees. Before the emergence of Islam, many persons also evidently had small stone images of religious significance in their homes. Both Judaism and Christianity conceived of the Creator God of their faith as indeed Creator also of a heavenly host of archangels, angels, and other spirits. They were, however, generally more insistent on the supreme authority and supervising control of the Creator over all things created, whether material or spiritual. This decisive aspect of authentically monotheistic faith, a cosmically ordered worldview, seems to have been lacking in much of Arabia, but various influences emanating from the historic monotheistic faiths were strongly at work and evidently growing in force.[14]

As we have noted, there was no organized community of Christian or Jewish faith in Mecca at the time of Muhammad's youth. The towns of Najran, Sana, and others to the south and east of Mecca seem to have been the only places with a substantial number of Christian believers. Some of the oases, however, in the western portion of the Arabian peninsula had groups within them who were Jewish in faith and practice. We shall see that the city of Medina, the birthplace of Muhammad's mother, which was three hundred miles to the north of Mecca and the place where Islam was to find its first public recognition, had a culturally and economically significant minority community of Jewish believers. These were evidently in most cases ethnic Arabs, converts or the descendants of converts to Jewish faith. There must also, however, have been communication with Jewish Palestine and some passage of personnel.

In Mecca, again, the polytheistic tradition was still strong, in large part because its sanctuary of the Ka'bah was the object of religious pilgrimage for persons from all over the Arabian peninsula. Hubal, the chief deity associated with this shrine, was represented there by an image in human form. The Ka'bah itself, now famous across the world as the central focus of Muslim pilgrimage to Mecca, was a simple cube-like (hence the name) structure that served to house a black meteorite long venerated as a fetish giving spiritual power, which seems, furthermore, to have been connected with Abraham by a tradition existing from before the time of Muhammad.[15]

But in spite of the continuance of polytheistic faith and practices in Mecca—the pilgrimages also contributed substantially to the financial prosperity of the city—it seems clear that Allah was regarded by many in Mecca as the supreme Creator, Provider, and Helper in peril (K 6:10–23). If this were not the case, it is hard to see how the early Meccan surahs recorded in the Koran would have been intelligible to the hearers of Muhammad. Terms like prophet, scripture, revelation, prayer, and praise were used in his messages without explanation and imply a background of corresponding knowledge in the community. The name of Muhammad's father was Abdullah (*Abd Allah*, the slave of Allah). We may perhaps conclude that a kind of incipient monotheism was emerging widely in the Arabian peninsula, of which in Mecca the Hanifs were particular examples.

The word *hanif* originally meant "those who turn away" (from idol worship) but later came to have the more general puritan sense of "upright" because persons of this group considered the right way to be that of right conduct and right belief.[16] They apparently did not form an organized community but were clearly dissatisfied with the common beliefs and practices of the polytheism of the day. From the Koran, it is reasonable to infer that this group, however loosely related, believed itself to be followers of the religion of Abraham and to worship the same God as Jews and Christians. Muhammad ibn Ishaq, an early biographer of the Prophet, identifies the group with a collective noun, *Hanifiya*, and affirms their spiritual lineage as deriving from Abraham. The elderly Waraqa ibn Naufal, however, of whom we shall take note later in connection with the prophetic call of Muhammad, seems to have been known specifically as a Christian.[17]

Polytheistic Arabs evidently developed no cosmogony or mythology of a complexity to compare with that of the Babylonians. They appear to have had no faith concept of a resurrection, for instance, beyond perhaps, like the early Hebrews and Greeks, some vague notion of continued existence in an underworld after physical death. It was of another order of perception in comparison with the clarity and power of Muhammad's early preaching.[18] Increasing numbers of Arabs, however, especially among the townspeople, many of whom through their trading activities had come to acquire considerable knowledge of other peoples and cultures, came to be dissatisfied with the prevailing religious situation. There was, furthermore, a notable lack of specifically religious commitment of any force or consistency, a lack quite out of keeping with the ethical ideals of Arabic pre-Islamic poetry, denoted especially by the word *muruah*, a term indicative of courage, loyalty, generosity, and "protection of the weak in peace."[19] It has been said that the mercantile leaders of Mecca of the time of Muhammad had developed "intellectual faculties and moral qualities of prudence and self-restraint" of a high order for the Arabia of their time.[20] There seem, therefore, to have been forces at work at deeper levels of Arab life of which prevailing religious concepts and practices were quite unable to take account of or deal with adequately.

The Hanifs in Mecca, then, seem to have been a specific religio-ethical expression of this dissatisfaction, a dissatisfaction that coexisted with aspiration for a better order of things in both individual and corporate life among those who were unaligned with Judaism or Christianity. The British translator of the Koran Mohammed M. Pickthall describes the Hanifs in Mecca as more individual seekers than persons forming a community, "each seeking truth by the light of his own inner consciousness."[21] It is, however, of the highest significance for a proper understanding of the person and the prophetic career of Muhammad to note that he was evidently one of these Hanifs.

Tradition is unanimous in affirming that Muhammad came to be employed by a wealthy widow of the Quraysh tribe, Khadijah, who was independently carrying on the trading activity of her husband after his death.[22] Although she is said to have been 15 years his senior, this noble-minded lady was evidently so impressed with Muhammad's person and competence that she proposed marriage. Muhammad was then perhaps 25 and, from this point, his life emerges into the relatively clear light of recorded history. Their married life of 26 years was evidently happy and Muhammad took no other wife until after her death. There were two sons and four daughters born of this marriage, both sons dying in infancy.[23]

We find in one of the early Meccan surahs unmistakable evidence of the transformation in life wrought by this marriage, which Muhammad evidently believed to be according to the will and guidance of Allah. The Lord of the Worlds tells him that his latter portion will be better than his former and reminds him that He (Allah) found him a wandering and destitute orphan. Therefore, Muhammad (and the Muslims) are not to oppress the orphan or drive the beggar away. His discourse is to be of the bounty of his Lord (K 93:4–10). This passage, reminiscent of the highest levels of Hebrew prophecy,[24] also reveals that, by his marriage to Khadijah, Muhammad came to possess a new position of means and rank within the Meccan community. Tradition records that for his conduct in these years he was called *al-Amin*, "the trustworthy."[25] He also made use of his relative leisure to withdraw for meditation and prayer to a little cave on the hill of Hira outside Mecca.[26]

In this place in the month of Ramadan (610 C.E.), on what later came to be named "the Night of Power," Muhammad received his call to prophethood. He heard a voice, which three times commanded him to recite:

> Recite: In the Name of thy Lord who
> created Man of a blood-clot.
> Recite: And thy Lord is the Most Generous,
> who taught by the Pen,
> taught Man that he knew not (K 96:1–5).

This was evidently his first revelation, the first of many that were to come to him throughout his subsequent life.

From the Koran itself, it is clear that Muhammad experienced other modes of revelation, specifically visions or vivid dreams that he considered revelations from the Lord Most High, "terrible in power, very strong," revelations sharply distinguished from "the word of an accursed Satan" (K 53:1–18; 81:15–25; cf. 8:45–46). It is not clear whether the two visions here referred to occurred before or after his call to prophethood; some scholars think that these visions, and possibly others, may have occurred before the experience of call to prophethood.[27] Another mode of perception may have been simply awareness of divine meaning that Muhammad naturally and easily turned into his native Arabic. One passage in the Koran refers to God's speaking to mortals as "from behind a veil," a mode of divine communication seen as alternative to "revelation" or the sending of a messenger (K 42:50). Muhammad held firmly throughout his subsequent life to a conviction that he was the receiver of authentic and true revelations from the Lord of the Worlds.

Analysis of the content of the revelation involved in the call of Muhammad indicates three themes: that the Revealer is the Creator of all humanity; that the nature or character of this

Creator, who is also Sovereign Lord, is generous and gracious (all surahs of the Koran but one begin with the phrase, "In the name of God, the Merciful, the Compassionate"); and that the Lord of all Being reveals to humans that which "he knew not," through the instrumentation of the human word.

Muhammad is called both *nabi*, "prophet," and *rasul*, or "messenger, apostle, one who is sent," terms that are to be understood primarily in the significance given them in the Judeo-Christian Scriptures. Among the pre-Islamic Arabs, there existed a class of shamans called *shairs* (knowers) who received special knowledge from a familiar spirit (*jinn* or *shaytan*). This term later came to have the meaning of "poet" because these shamans uttered their predictions or communications in a rhymed prose with a rough rhythm.[28] Muhammad, however, strongly dissociated himself from the shamans, even though he was called a mad poet by some of his fellow Meccans (K 36:69; cf. 69:41–42; 37:35).[29] He was the receiver of revelations from the Lord of the Worlds, although he was evidently in a kind of trance, an altered state of consciousness, when he received them. Muhammad was, it seems, able to remember with considerable precision what he heard or saw in this altered state. He apparently became chilled in this condition and regularly wrapped himself in a cloak (K 73:1; 74:1). He may also have had what we now call "out of body" experiences (K 17:1). Both Muhammad and his followers came to believe that the inspired words he received while in trance or in vision had primary revelatory significance, and his followers evidently did not confuse them with his directions, however wise and intrinsically worthy of respect, given as a consequence of normal processes of thought.

Unlike the "poets," Muhammad emphasized the clarity of the revelations he received (K 2:93). He made a plain communication of the message given him (K 5:92).[30] He was given divine revelation, he believed, as the Lord had revealed to "Noah, and the Prophets after him, and We revealed to Abraham, Ishmael, Isaac, Jacob and the Tribes, Jesus and Job, Jonah and Aaron and Solomon, and as We gave to David Psalms, and Messengers We have already told thee of before and Messengers We have not told thee of; and unto Moses God spoke directly" (K 4:162). Muhammad insisted that he was not motivated by unwholesome curiosity toward the invisible realms; he did not claim to possess the (hidden) treasures of Allah nor to have personal knowledge of the unseen. He was no angel, he asserted, and followed only that which was revealed to him (K 81:24; 6:50, 107).[31] The unseen belongs to Allah (K 10:21). Furthermore, nowhere in the Koran, to my knowledge, does Muhammad say that his reception of divine revelation was perfect or his verbal expression thereof inerrant. Like Hebrew prophecy before him, however eloquent or heart-searching, the style was rough-hewn. The process as a whole seemed also to involve the travail of the human heart in understanding, appropriating, and communicating what was perceived as divine message (K 2:92–93).

At first, however, Muhammad was evidently not at all sure that his experience was not of the same kind as that of the "poets." According to tradition, on the same "Night of Power" after being awakened from the trance and remembering the words "as if inscribed on his heart," he went out of the cave and heard the same terrifying voice say to him, "O Muhammad! Thou art Allah's messenger and I am Gabriel (*Jibril*)." He looked up and saw the angel standing in the sky in the likeness of a man, and the voice spoke the same words again to him. He remained where he was for a long while until the vision vanished. He then returned in great disturbance of mind to his wife. It is not entirely certain that the voice was identified on this first occasion as that of Gabriel, for we read that the voices of the early revelations varied and sometimes sounded like the "reverberating of bells."[32] Khadijah, however, comforted him with her assurance that, because of his conduct, Allah would not let an evil spirit harm him or lead him astray.

On their return to Mecca, it is recorded that Khadijah took Muhammad to her cousin Waraqa ibn Naufal, a very old man "who knew the Scriptures of the Jews and Christians," evidently another Hanif, and who gave his view that the heavenly messenger who had appeared to Muhammad was the same as the one who had long before come to Moses.[33] The early biographers of the Prophet relate how it was supremely his wife who "tested the spirit" of the early revelations he received and persuaded him that they were good in content and therefore of Allah.[34] Gradually, as the revelations continued, the conviction grew and was strengthened that he had indeed been chosen as the slave of Allah and the Prophet of his people.[35]

It is important to realize that the goodness and the power of God were prominent in what seem to be among the earliest of Muhammad's messages to his fellow Meccans. In the context of the incipient, if vague, monotheism slowly emerging among thoughtful Arabs in and outside Mecca, Muhammad's focus was to call the attention of hearers to the evidence for providential goodness to be seen in the processes of nature and events of human history. If the power of God is to be seen in the works of nature, his goodness may equally be seen in the generous provision he makes for the support and growth of all that lives (K 88:17–20; 80:24–32; 106:1–2). A central element of Muhammad's message from the earliest period to the latest was the call to praise the Creator; he considered ingratitude among the most heinous of sins (K 87:1–4; 17:45–46; 80:16). Like Hebrew Prophets before him, Muhammad coupled his own experience of the goodness of God with its proper human ethical responses. And he saw the social and economic injustice perpetrated by the powerful merchant families of Mecca against the background of the goodness and the unity of God (K 89:18–21). In an early Meccan surah, we read that the Creator has made available two ways for humanity. One is the "steep," the upward path, and this is defined as:

> The freeing of a slave,
> or giving food upon a day of hunger
> to an orphan near of kin
> or a needy man in misery;
> then that he become of those who believe

and counsel each other to be steadfast,
and counsel each other to be merciful.
(K 90:10–17; cf. Deut. 30:15–20; Mic. 6:8).

These early messages in Mecca show that, in basic outline, Muhammad stood within the structures of Judeo-Christian monotheism. He followed that tradition with its concept of God as Creator and Sovereign Lord, with its belief in a final resurrection and judgment. And, as we have seen, he most assuredly believed in divine revelation. The very earliest messages manifest a belief in the Last Day, or Day of Doom, but it is clear that Muhammad also believed in a moral order operative in human history wherein human conduct—faith and works together—is rewarded or punished according to its quality of religious commitment and ethical nature (K 89:11; 91:15). Muhammad saw this moral order operative in the rise and fall of empires and in individual human experience, but he expressed this faith in proclamation rather than in niceties of quantitative assignment (K 22:44–47). The Last Day will demonstrate the perfection of divine judgment (K 99:6–8). For now, let all persons return to their Lord (K 96:8).

For perhaps the first three years after his call, Muhammad proclaimed his faith and message only to his family and close friends. Conversions were at first secretly made, but the small group's practice of daily prayer made their new commitment known. The response of the larger community was to mock Muhammad as mad. The statements in the Koran that refer to public opinion of him in the Meccan period probably all derive from the time of his public preaching, but they reveal the intensity of hostility and contempt in the general reaction. He was called a man possessed (K 15:6; 68:2), bewitched (K 17:51), treated as a jest (K 25:43), lying sorcerer (K 38:3). Muhammad, for his part, came to realize that no messenger was sent by God but that people said he was a sorcerer or a man possessed (K 51:52). And there are indeed statements in the Koran that indicate this "acrimonious obduracy" on the part of the Meccans at times caused deep anguish and even physical wasting in Muhammad personally (K 26:3; 18:5; cf. Jer. 20:7–18).

Muhammad's first convert was his wife, whose decision was evidently made in no small part as a result of the influence of her Hanif cousin Waraqa. His cousin Ali was perhaps second and then his servant Zayd, formerly a slave.[36] His father-in-law, Abu Bakr, followed, together with some of his slaves and dependents. However, the leader of the most powerful and aristocratic Umayyad branch of the Quraysh, Abu Sufyan, remained resolutely apart.

At the end of the third year of this kind of private witness, the Prophet received what he believed to be the command to proclaim his message in public (K 74:2). From this time, converts were gradually added, although never in large numbers and mainly among the lower classes and slaves. Hostility from the leading personages of the Quraysh grew correspondingly (K 43:31).[37] This hostility evidently did not derive primarily from their opposition to the content of Muhammad's faith and proclamation per se, but from concern lest they lose their profitable position as custodians of the Ka'bah, in which was placed the black stone of Mecca that had long been the center of pilgrimage for pagan Arabs from the entire peninsula. They consequently turned from verbal ridicule to active persecution short of physical violence, measures that were in various ways particularly felt by the poorer and socially defenseless members. The nature and extent of this persecution were such that Muhammad advised those Muslims who could do so to emigrate to the Christian land of Ethiopia.[38] First 11 and then 83 families emigrated to Ethiopia in 615 C.E. The Negus of that country protected the emigrants and refused to deliver them into the hands of their enemies. The Muslims were also given complete freedom to practice their religion in their own manner.[39]

The presence of Abu Bakr as a respected and well-to-do merchant gave the small Muslim community some substance in Mecca, and the sturdy protection of Muhammad by his uncle Abu Talib compelled the Quraysh to caution, as they did not dare to provoke an Arab blood feud. The accession of Umar ibn al-Khattab, who as the second caliph was to be a leading figure in the establishment of the Islamic state, gave even further substance to the community.[40] The Quraysh became alarmed and tried to arrange a compromise, offering to make Muhammad their ruler if he would give up his attacks on idolatry and allow some qualified status for their gods. Muhammad was at first apparently willing to make some adjustment,[41] but it was found impossible for both sides to be satisfied and the negotiations failed. The Quraysh tried other measures, with the result that Muhammad and his kinsmen were forced to live separately in one of the gorges leading to Mecca.[42]

In the midst of this highly unfavorable environment, Muhammad committed his cause to Allah (K 40:44), and revelations continued to come to him. These he faithfully proclaimed to the believers. It should be noted that he was apparently not able to control the coming of revelations, for there was a period when they ceased, a fact of no small embarrassment (K 93:3). From a reference in the Koran, we may infer that his manner of teaching was to use both public proclamation and private appeal (K 71:8).

Something of the nature and habits of Muhammad's religious life at this time may be inferred from statements in the Koran that, sometimes alone and sometimes with a group of believers, he spent "nearly two-thirds of the night, or a half of it or a third of it," in prayer (K 72:2–4, 20). The depth and fervency of his worship are also suggested by the lines that "those who are with Him wax not too proud to do Him service neither grow weary, glorifying Him by night and in the daytime and never failing" (K 21:19–20). His relations to the believers is revealed by a surah, which, although belonging to the late Medinan period, describes with at least equal truth the situation of the more intimate Meccan days. The messenger who had come to them, Muhammad declares, is one of them,[43] full of concern and pity, gentle toward the believers, a man deeply pained when in any way they suffer (K 9:129). He is closer to the believers than their very selves (K 33:6). The nature of this relationship is also revealed by the oft reiterated statement that no fee is ever requested by Muhammad for his prophetic role, a role which clearly also comprised pastoral dimensions (K 6:92; 36:20; cf. 1 Cor. 9:12–18).

Muhammad's language of self-designation included that of the slave of Allah. He was the messenger of God, but only a messenger, mortal, like those who had gone before (K 2:21; 3:73, 144; 17:95; 48:28–29). He was only a hearer (of God's revelation), but a hearer of good, a man who trusts others and a mercy to believers (K 9:61). He was a messenger of the truth, the bringer of good tidings and warning, a summoner to God by His permission, and a lamp that gives light (K 2:113; 33:44–45). In the Meccan days, he was frequently asked for a portent from God to confirm his mission; he could only point to the wonders of the created world (K 6:37–38; cf. Mark 8:11–12), and to the unique wonder of his "recitation" (Koran), which was such, he contended, as could never be invented by humans unaided (K 10:38–39; 2:21). Muhammad could never "guide"; this is the prerogative of Allah (K 28:56). He was not a guardian of persons; God alone is their Protector (K 17:50–51; 42:7). Muhammad was told that he was not to be held responsible for the response of others, only for his own (K 4:83; cf. Ezek. 3:16–21).

Yet Muhammad clearly had a high view of his role as God's messenger, as high in his mind as any of those who had come before him. Men and women should come, he declared, to that which God has revealed *and* to the messenger; they should ask forgiveness of God and the messenger; they should obey God and the messenger, although such is the prerogative of every messenger (by Allah's leave) (K 4:61–64, 83).[44] These concepts came to be formulated most clearly and forcefully in the Medinan period, after the "preaching became a polity"; the admonition to the believers to refer any dispute to Allah *and* the messenger occurs in a Medinan surah and may have been conceived first in that period (K 4:62; cf. 1 Cor. 11:1). Of the same period is the teaching that it is no more proper to question Muhammad than for the

Jews to have questioned Moses (K 2:103), and that whoever opposes God and his Messenger, his punishment is the fire of Gehenna (K 9:61–64).

It should not be thought that Muhammad was an unrelieved autocrat. He was instructed not only to be lenient and to pardon, but also to consult with others in the conduct of affairs (K 3:153). His conception of prophethood was that the messenger of God, however he may be (initially) scorned and rejected, ultimately receives victory both in this world and in the hereafter (K 22:15). Yet Muhammad's assumption of political authority was primarily for religious purposes, a fact consistently demonstrated by his manner of life at Medina. He saw his function as that of the messenger who will recite Allah's revelations, instruct men and women in this Scripture and in wisdom, and purify their lifestyle (K 2:123). He believed himself to be a bringer of good tidings, that men and women may have a sure footing with their Lord (K 10:2). He was concerned to break down the old barriers of clan and social rank.[45] It is clear that he was neither implacable nor vindictive (K 63:5; 60:7; 33:24). Muhammad's call was to penitence before God, penitence leading to submission and obedience to the divine will, a religious posture evidently little practiced in Arabia at that time but now offered as a saving, transforming option for all persons (K 50:8, 30, 31–34). The gracious protection and guidance of Allah had been ever great toward him (K 4:113); Allah and his angels bless the Prophet (K 33:56). But he was ready to admit his own faults and proclaim publicly Allah's corrections of his words and deeds, at Medina and at Mecca (K 33:37; 66:1; 80:1–10). Throughout the Koran, there are countless references to Muhammad's role as a messenger and Prophet. Only once, however, does the phrase occur that has been made so much of in subsequent Muslim thought, that Muhammad is the Seal of the Prophets (K 33:40).[46]

The situation in Mecca did not improve. Muhammad's loyal wife died, as did his uncle Abu Talib, his chief protector against the Quraysh.[47] Muhammad tried to find support and protection from nomadic tribes that attended mercantile fairs held in Mecca.

Even though there were Christian believers among them, his efforts brought no substantial results. These events, coupled with strong opposition from Abu Lahab, the new leader of the Hashim clan, evidently led Muhammad to feel that the future of the movement lay elsewhere. He then made an exploratory trip to the upland town of Sana, 40 miles to the east of Mecca. He tried negotiations with some leading men there and also proclaimed his message for several days, but met not only abuse and insult, he was so pelted with stones that he was compelled to flee, cut and bleeding. On returning to Mecca, moreover, he was not permitted to enter the city until he secured the protection of a distinguished citizen, al-Mut'im ibn Adi. This was the lowest point in the worldly fortunes of the Prophet.

At about this time (ca. 620 C.E.), six pilgrims came to Mecca from the city of Medina, as yet called Yathrib, the birthplace of Muhammad's mother. They had come to worship at the Ka'bah, but listened to the Prophet's message, believed it and the man, and returned to Medina, in effect, as convinced Muslims. Conditions at Medina were such as to provide fertile ground for the growth of this tiny seed. The city had been long disturbed by violence issuing from the feuds of two Arab tribes, the Aus and Khazraj, each of which was supported by different Jewish tribes. All were evidently weary of the strife and looked for a leader to mediate.

The enthusiastic commendations of the six pilgrims were successful in making possible a meeting the next year between Muhammad and a delegation of a dozen men from Medina at the neutral spot of Mina. These, too, apparently accepted the faith of Islam. The presence of strong Jewish communities in their midst had evidently predisposed the Medinans to a monotheistic faith, but not to becoming Jews.[48] Then in 622 C.E., a deputation of about 75 men and women came to Mecca as pilgrims and invited Muhammad to Medina, pledging him their full physical and spiritual support.

The Meccans became aware of what was happening and pursued the returning pilgrims, of whom, however, all but one or two were able to return safely to their city. In anger, the Meccans renewed their persecution of the Muslims with such severity that Muhammad decided to order the entire community of believers to migrate to Medina, an action that had evidently been contemplated for the previous two years. More than a hundred men were able to slip away safely, with only the Prophet, Abu Bakr, and Ali remaining. Leaving the last to look after the women and children, who were able to follow later, Muhammad and Abu Bakr also eluded the Meccans and reached Medina, where on September 24, 622 C.E., they received an enthusiastic welcome. Thus was completed the *Hijrah* (Latin: *Hegira*), the formal beginning of the Muslim era and of the Muslim state.

The Preaching Becomes Polity

How was it possible for successive groups of people from a distant city to invite a man to become their religious and civil leader, when he was rejected and of so little account in his own city? The answer lies not only in the desperate state of Medina's need, but also in the quality of the man and his message. Muhammad evoked respect and confidence from those who knew him best.

We have already noted that, in the Meccan days, Muhammad had come to be called *al-Amin*, the "trustworthy." In his youth, his character and abilities were such as to make possible the unusual fact of his employer, a wealthy widow, proposing marriage. Tradition relates that Khadijah was particularly impressed by a highly favorable report given of him by an old servant who had accompanied him on a caravan trip.[49] Ibn Ishaq's account of Muhammad's first vision and call contains the words of the latter's wife given to comfort him after what was an emotionally shattering experience. Khadijah assured Muhammad that Allah would not deceive him for "He knows your truthfulness, your great trustworthiness, your fine character, and your kindness to your family."[50] These words hardly constitute a verbatim report, but they are evidently in harmony with authentic tradition. From the various statements in the Koran that Allah loves just dealers and from similar injunctions to fair dealing in business, it is clear that Muhammad placed a high value on economic justice and social responsibility (K 60:8). He was a keeper of agreements and a payer of obligations.[51] More than this, a forgiving spirit and an element of generosity kept him open-ended in human relation-ships (K 60:7). He could laugh heartily.[52]

Muhammad was also a man of eminent common sense. He was able to make shrewd appraisals of people, and he evidently understood the significance of what was happening in the larger world of his time. He has been called the greatest statesman of the age. Not all of this was immediately known to the deputations from Medina, but enough was discernible to give them full confidence. The tact that characterized his relations with others is revealed by an incident recorded of his arrival in Medina. With no house of his own to live in, he was besieged with appeals from all sides to dwell with this family or that, each belonging to one of the factions rending the city. Muhammad refrained from making a decision by leaving it to his camel. The camel finally knelt at a home belonging to two orphans of the clan of Banu Malik ibn al-Najjar and here Muhammad stayed.[53]

Muhammad was now the head of a religious community that was dominant in the city and increasingly the determining element in civil and religious life. The nature of government at Mecca and Medina left considerable autonomy to the individual tribes and clans, and most community decisions were made as a result of consultation and compromise with the tribal leaders. The system had evidently worked much better at Mecca than at Medina, where the intertribal and clan feuds, exacerbated by religious differences between Jews and pagans, had been so acute as to compel calling in an outsider as mediator and leader.

Muslim tradition is clear that, in the Meccan period, the Prophet had not been given permission by Allah to fight or to shed blood; "he had simply been ordered to call men to God, endure insult, and forgive the ignorant."[54] Muhammad had followed this way with remarkable faithfulness, enduring both insult and physical abuse. From the beginning of the Medinan period, however, he had evidently come to the conviction that since no compromise with idolatry could be allowed, it would be necessary to destroy it by force. "Idolaters whose very existence was an insult to the one true God would have to accept Islam or the sword."[55] This is the principle that gave rise to the widespread notion that the later Muslim armies ruthlessly and indiscriminately compelled conversion wherever they went. The notion, however, is incorrect. With Muhammad, the principle applied only to idolaters, that is, polytheistic pagans. Monotheists, including Jews, Christians, and Sabaeans, were to be allowed to retain their own faith and religious practices; they were later compelled to pay a special tax, however, which came to denote social and religious inferiority.[56] A point of great significance in this discussion is that in the expansion of the Islamic empire in the generations following Muhammad's death, the large majority of the populations "conquered" were already of monotheistic faith and generally welcomed the Muslim troops as liberators from hated Persian, Byzantine, or Roman rule. Conversions of Christians and Jews were almost all voluntary, at least formally, and took place gradually in succeeding generations. Polytheists or pagans were few outside Arabia proper. In Muhammad's own lifetime, Muslim activity did not go beyond the Arabian peninsula, and we shall see that, in this time and place, relatively little blood was shed. Muhammad consistently preferred negotiation to violence.

The consequence of this policy at Medina was that the whole of the pagan community became Muslim within a short time. It was puzzling and frustrating to Muhammad that the Jews did not welcome him as a brother in the faith. The Jewish tribes had once been dominant in Medina (then Yathrib), but not long before the coming of Muhammad they had been reduced to a subordinate position by the leading pagan Arab tribes of Aus and Khazraj, each Jewish tribe becoming a dependent of one of these two. They maintained, however, a unique religio-cultural ascendancy as a result of their possessing Scripture and practicing "occult" science. Pagan Arabs evidently consulted Jewish rabbis on occasion.[57] The Jewish tribes of the area insisted on remaining religiously separate and, after the arrival of Muhammad and the other Muslims from Mecca, were at first allowed to retain their traditional faith and practices. In the charter for the entire community drawn up within a year or two of Muhammad's arrival in Medina, Jews are mentioned as "a community along with the Muslims."[58] This charter, of which an abstract is extant, established the bond of faith, the brotherhood of Islam, as taking precedence over all other ties, including blood relationships.[59] Muhammad now had the legal and religious basis not only for exterminating idolatry, but also for welding the feud-rent community into a harmonious unit. The position of the Jews in the charter, however, was ambiguous. They were allowed to maintain their own existence as a separate religious community, but the charter was an edict of Muhammad the Prophet, and while all disputes must be referred to Allah and to Muhammad in his capacity as political leader, for the Muslims his political authority unquestionably rested on his status as a prophet and it was so promulgated. The Jews thus had to serve a political leader who conceived of his political role as primarily subservient to religious goals that they did not fully accept.[60]

The Prophet's task called for tact, firmness, and farsighted planning. The long tradition of pagan life and customs, of unhappy feuds and rivalries, was compounded by the problem of the need for peaceful integration of the Emigrants (*Muhajirun*) from Mecca into the community of Medinan Muslims (*Ansar,* "Supporters"). The former in particular suffered considerable economic distress. Muhammad also evidently believed from the beginning of his public mission that his message was at least for all Arabic-speaking peoples. Mecca, as his native city and the place of origin of the faith, remained for him the special object of concern. With the intent to compel the adherence of this important city, he began a series of moves designed to achieve this goal and to give both occupation and economic sustenance to the needy groups in Medina.

These moves were small raids, the first of which was the interception of a summer caravan returning from Syria to Mecca. The small scope of these early actions is revealed by the fact that in the first instance only six Muslims and four Quraysh guards of the caravan were involved in the fray. The scope, however, gradually developed into the later battle at Badr in 624, where three hundred Muslims under the leadership of Muhammad himself attacked and put to flight over one thousand Meccans. This victory was made possible in part, it would seem, by the faith of the Muslims in God's assistance and their consequent fervor, in part by the military skill of the Prophet. The Muslims, both of Medinan and Meccan origin, had initially been very hesitant to move against the Meccans, perhaps largely as a result of traditional Arab fear of the consequences of blood feuds. The Medinans had ties of marriage and blood with Mecca, and trade and participation in the ancient pilgrim rites. Muhammad, however, proclaimed the principle of war against idolatry as a sacred duty (*jihad*), and in this way he felt able to excuse the fact that the initial attack against the Meccan caravan occurred during the month of Ramadan when, by universal Arab agreement, war was banned.[61]

In the following year (625 C.E.) at Uhud, the Meccans under Abu Sufyan avenged their defeat,[62] largely as the result of a contingent of Muslims deserting their post to seek booty, and Muhammad himself was wounded (K 3:150–153). But defeat proved to be no more than a setback. In the year 627, a force of some ten thousand men, including Bedouin and Ethiopian mercenaries, marched against Medina. Muhammad showed his customary wisdom by taking the advice of a Persian convert, Salman, and had a deep ditch dug about the town where it was open to attack. The trench rendered the enemy's cavalry useless, and their daily showers of arrows were no more effective. The situation, however, was exceedingly serious for the Muslims, since a Jewish tribe of Medina, the Bani Qurayzah, had evidently conspired with the enemy, and their own forces were greatly outnumbered. Distrust developed between the Quraysh and their

Jewish allies, but, according to Muslim tradition, the culminating factor on behalf of the Muslims was a wind that blew in from the sea for three days and nights so strongly that "not a tent could be kept standing, not a fire lighted, not a pot boiled."[63]

Whether this description of the fierceness of the wind be hyperbole or not, the besieging forces felt compelled to withdraw at the end of a month, with the total loss of men on both sides, according to different estimates, no more than eight to 20. The nature of the climate and terrain of Arabia does not permit sustained sieges without the kind of logistical support of food and water that was hardly possible at that time. The Jewish tribe failed to make its promised diversionary attack, and the assembled forces returned dispirited to their several homes.

Muhammad then turned to deal with the Jews who had allegedly betrayed Medina in its time of need and had broken the terms of the charter. As noted previously, Muhammad had been singularly disappointed by the refusal of the Jews of Medina to recognize him as an authentic prophet of the God of Israel.[64] There had evidently been discussions, perhaps both public and private, in which they showed no sign of openness, and they added ridicule to this spiritual injury. Ibn Ishaq states that when Muhammad proclaimed to the Jews his belief in God and "that which has been sent down on us, and sent down on Abraham and Ishmael, Isaac and Jacob, and the tribes, and in that which was given to Moses and Jesus, and the Prophets, of their Lord," and added, "We make no division between any of them, and to Him we surrender" (K 3:78; 2:130), the leading Jews answered that "they had no belief in Jesus nor in anyone who believed in him."[65]

The relative economic supremacy of the Jewish tribes of Medina must have been an additional irritant, especially to the poor *Muhajirun* who had emigrated from Mecca. Medina was not only on the west Arabian trade route between Syria and Yemen, it was, unlike Mecca, a well-watered oasis especially suited to the cultivation of date palms. The two main Jewish tribes, the Bani Nadir and the Bani Qurayzah, had been the principal elements in developing this agriculture and profited accordingly. From some-what later tradition, there is reason to believe that among the Jews there were also physicians, musicians, and merchants.[66] They were evidently the cultural elite of Medina. The Jews were not, however, the only opponents of the Prophet. There was also a substantial Arab element in Medina that had become formally Muslim, but resisted in various ways the leadership of Muhammad. In the Koran, these are called the Hypocrites, and allusion is frequently made to them. They evidently sympa-thized with the Jews and encouraged them (K 59:11).

Relations with the Jews had deteriorated after Badr (624) to the point that Muhammad felt compelled to take measures. The smaller Jewish tribe of Qaynuqah[67] was besieged in its fortified towers, subdued, and forced to emigrate to Syria. After Uhud (625), the Jewish tribe of Bani Nadir received the same treat-ment. The Muslim Hypocrites, contrary to their promise, neither aided the Jews nor went with them into exile. The property of the exiled Jews was divided largely among the poor Muslims, especially the *Muhajirun* (K 59:5–9). It was about this time that Muhammad, who in prayer had hitherto turned his face toward Jerusalem in the manner of the Jews, directed his followers to pray facing Mecca. He claimed Abraham and Ishmael to have been the founders of the shrine of the Ka'bah in Mecca and thereby established Islam as the independent, although related, Arabic form of faith in the one, true God. Friday was substituted as the special day of worship in place of the Sabbath, Ramadan was made the month of fasting, the call from the minaret (*adhan*) was established in place of the use of trumpets and gongs.

The measures taken against the Jewish tribe of Bani Qurayzah, after the siege of Medina had been lifted, constitute what some non-Muslims have thought to be the most serious blot on Muhammad's entire public career. The Qurayzah were attacked and forced to surrender. Their old Arab allies, the Aus, pleaded on their behalf, and Muhammad asked if they, the Aus, would accept the judgment of one of their own leaders. They agreed, and Muhammad then appointed as a judge a man who was suffering from a fatal wound received in the recent fighting with the Meccans, a person hardly in a mental condition conducive to compassion.[68] The verdict was that the adult males of the Bani Qurayzah should be killed and the women and children sold as slaves. The sentence was carried out, and the Meccan Emigrants were given possession of the now ownerless date plantations of the Qurayzah. Of about eight hundred male Jews, only one renounced his religion to save his life. Muhammad's action, to be sure, has been equaled or outdone by nominal Christians and Jews, but as Alfred Guillaume has written, it is hardly to be expected from "one who comes with a message from the Compassionate and Merciful."[69]

From the spring of 628, Muhammad began a series of actions designed to encircle and subdue Mecca. After the failure of the Meccan siege of Medina, it became clear in what direction events were moving, and Bedouin tribes from the interior increasingly came on their own initiative to attach themselves to the new movement. The first action against Mecca in 628 may have been intended to be an attack, but when it became obvious en route that military action was premature, the expedition of about 1,400 men was transformed into a religious pilgrimage. The Muslims met with Meccan negotiators at a place outside Mecca, called Hudaibiya, with the result that a ten-year truce was effected, which permitted the Muslims to perform the pilgrimage to Mecca on the following year and to remain there for three days. Muslims were also given the formal right to proselytize freely within Mecca without hindrance from the Quraysh.

The truce made it possible for increasing numbers of the Bedouin and Meccans to become Muslim, but its military inconclusiveness evidently disappointed some of the most ardent Muslims. Perhaps to divert their complaints, Muhammad ordered an attack on the Jewish oasis of Khaybar, north of Medina. The Jews of Khaybar are said to have contributed to the Meccan campaign against Medina in 627. This action, which ended in swift victory, although the inhabitants evidently fought with remarkable bravery, was the first instance of Muslim dealings with a conquered non-Muslim people outside Medina. The Jews were forced to give up much of their personal possessions, but were spared their lives and lands. They were also compelled to pay an annual tribute of 50 percent of their produce. This principle, with some modifications, would be adopted for the vast territories that the Muslim armies were to occupy in the succeeding century. Jewish colonies in other places surrendered on the same terms and, in consequence, the Muslim conquerors, including the formerly indigent Emigrants from Mecca, came to be wealthy owners of lands, camels, horses, and weapons (K 33:26–27).

In the following year (629), Muhammad and about two hundred Medinans went on a pilgrimage to Mecca. As a consequence of the truce and the growing power and prestige of the movement, converts had been won in Mecca itself, including some men of position and substance.[70] In January of 630, however, the Meccans attacked a tribe that was in alliance with the Muslims[71] and, in retaliation for this violation of the truce, Muhammad marched against Mecca with a large-scale expedition of some ten thousand men. The city was taken almost without bloodshed. Muhammad entered the sanctuary of the Ka'bah and with his troops smashed its 360 idols, allegedly declaring, "The truth has come, and falsehood has vanished away" (K 17:83). The inhabitants of Mecca, however, he treated with special magnanimity, although we learn from tradition that the "house" of Abu Sufyan was proscribed—perhaps temporarily. The result was that the whole city accepted him as the Prophet of God and, within a few weeks, a large number of Meccans were fighting in the "cause of Allah" alongside the Medinans.

Islam, which had begun as the movement of a despised minority, had now come into possession of the major centers of the Arabian peninsula. It was in the interests of everyone to conform to it (K 49:17).[72] The year 630–631 is called the Year of Deputations (*Sanat al-Wufud*) because during it delegations flocked from all parts of Arabia to offer allegiance to the Prophet.

The allegiance offered was primarily political and was evidently so understood by Muhammad. The relationships thus created, however, offered opportunity for religious teaching, and Muhammad sent missionaries and political agents to all these places during the last two years of his life.[73] Muhammad's final goal of authentic religious conversion was by no means altogether achieved throughout Arabia, but at least in a formal way idolatry was largely brought to an end in the peninsula. The so-called Declaration of Immunity of 630, which limited pilgrimage to Mecca to Muslims, with the exception of pagans with whom there were treaties in force—and these were not to be renewed— marks a decisive point in the process.

There is no need to consider the minor military campaigns of Muhammad during the Medinan period; in all there were 27, in nine of which there was serious fighting. Brief mention, however, should be made of the military movements against Byzantium. In 629, on hearing that the Byzantine emperor was mustering a force to attack the new Islamic power, the Prophet sent a force of three thousand men to Syria. Tradition records that the Muslims encountered a Byzantine force of 100,000 and, in spite of their reckless courage, were worsted and compelled to retreat, their three chief leaders killed.[74] The next year saw a similar Muslim mobilization and march to Syria on the assumption that the Byzantines were again gathering an army for action. On arriving at Tabuk, on the borders of Syria, the Muslims learned that no such army had gathered, and they returned without engaging the enemy in battle.

The British historian H. A. R. Gibb suggests that Muhammad was contemplating further action against the Byzantine empire before his death. The sending of the expeditions against Syria by the caliph Abu Bakr almost immediately after the Prophet's death can hardly be explained otherwise.[75] About this time, Muhammad came to modify his hitherto relatively friendly and appreciative attitude toward Christianity (K 9:29–34). This change may possibly be, at least in considerable part, the consequence of fear of military action from the Greeks and their Christian Arab allies. A very unfortunate result of the change was that the term *mushrik* came to be applied for the first time to Jews, Christians, and pagans.[76]

Muhammad was frequently absent from Medina because of these campaigns, but strong evidence shows that religious goals remained his primary concern. "The center of all his preoccupations was the training, educating and disciplining of his community,"[77] first at Medina and, as he was able, in ever-widening circles. After the conquest of Mecca he gave particular attention to sharing with his former opponents something of his own exalted faith and moral seriousness to equip Medina for becoming a responsible center of Muslim influence after his death. He preached frequently at the mosque in Medina and continued to give religious teaching and instructions on the moral and civic issues that increasingly came to occupy his attention as civic ruler. Central to the new codes being developed was the institution of fixed hours of prayer, an alms tax, and fasting.[78]

As noted, the community at Medina was primarily religious in its formal orientation. Indeed, it was the first instance in Arabian history of the establishment of a social organization that had religion, rather than blood, as its basis. The new community was the *Ummah* or "People of Allah." The organization of this community, out of which the later Islamic state developed, showed the cautious, diplomatic character of the Prophet. It retained many tribal structures and customs, especially those pertaining to outsiders, but within the *Ummah* full brotherhood and equality were to prevail. By the primacy of the bond of faith, blood feuds were eliminated, at least in principle, and replaced by the methodology of arbitration. A new basis of ruling authority was also created, out of which, under less charismatic leaders, later Islamic autocracy developed. Instead of the provisional authority by consensus, "grudgingly granted and always revocable," that the Arab tribes had known, Muhammad as the Messenger of Allah became *Shaikh* of the *Ummah* with the full authority of God's vice-regent on earth.[79] The government was, therefore, a form of theocracy.

Unlike later Islamic rulers, Muhammad exercised this authority, even in his highest years of pan-Arabian power and glory, with remarkable restraint and simplicity of life. He lived in a modest clay house of a few rooms that opened on an inner courtyard. He was often seen mending his own garments. The small property he left at his death he regarded as belonging to the state. He was apparently always accessible to the community for advice and the arbitration of disputes (K 4:68, 106).[80] In fact, rules had to be formulated to protect the private life of the Prophet, as that believers should not enter his house for a meal without permission being granted beforehand nor call to him when he was in his private rooms (K 33:53; 49:4). He had to ask them not to shout above his own voice (K 49:2). Al-Bukhari, a later biographer, records an incident when Muhammad's wife, A'isha, marveled at his cheerful and kindly reception of a man of whom he disapproved. He answered her, "Why, A'isha, when have you ever seen me act grossly with people? Verily, the worst place on the resurrection day in the sight of God will be that of the man whom people avoided fearing his mischief."[81]

The Muslim community, with its focus on the Prophet, had "no priesthood, no hierarchy, no central see. Its mosque was its public forum and military drill ground and its place of common worship."[82] The leader of the community in prayer, the imam, was properly the one to command its armies.[83] Under the moral leadership of Muhammad, an earnest, almost puritanical atmosphere came to prevail. Wine, which was at first permitted in moderation, was abolished, as was gambling (K 5:92). Singing came to be frowned upon; the call to prayer and the recitation of Scripture were preferred. Truthfulness and purity of speech were enjoined. Pagan practices such as the burying alive of female babies were abolished, and certain legal rights of women were established.[84] Even more strongly than the Koran, tradition records the Prophet as being exceedingly severe in his condemnation of adultery, fornication, and homosexuality (K 7:78–79).[85]

The intense seriousness of this moral tone, however, was not to remain at the same level after the Prophet's death; with the rise of the Umayyad dynasty, it largely ceased among Islamic political rulers. But what Muhammad initiated greatly elevated the level of moral life throughout the Arabian peninsula. And under his personal leadership, this moral seriousness on the whole was not harsh; it was profoundly qualified by the Prophet's kindliness and generally compassionate character. He was apparently somewhat shy (K 33:53).[86]

Muhammad had lived for 26 years with Khadijah as his sole wife. After her death toward the end of the Meccan period, he married a widow called Sauda and was betrothed to and later married A'isha, the daughter of Abu Bakr, his oldest friend, at the latter's request. In all, he took about a dozen wives, all of whom, except A'isha, were widows. Western writers have frequently commented acidly on the many wives of the Prophet. A Muslim apologist like M. M. Pickthall, however, stresses the fact that, with one exception, all Muhammad's later marriages were with widows whose husbands had been killed in war or for other reasons were in some condition of physical need.[87] Two marriages, perhaps three, were primarily political. Muslims were limited to four wives, although they were permitted sexual access to their female slaves (K 70:29–30).[88] Muhammad alone was allowed a larger number of legitimate wives presumably because as head of state he was in a position to be responsible for a larger number of those in need. This practice could perhaps be justified in the context of contemporary Arab customs, but it left a most unfortunate legacy, which developed into the harems of later Islamic caliphs and sultans, where the personal needs of women were hardly of primary concern. But Muhammad himself never ordained the veiling or segregation of all women. He segregated his own wives because of his special status as the Messenger of God. It was unfortunate—and not his intent—that Muslims came to take his practice in this matter as precedent for their own.[89]

It must be emphasized that the teaching and practice of Muhammad himself represented a notable advance over that of pagan Arabia.[90] He was "extremely kind" to his wives.[91] They enjoyed considerable personal freedom, even to the extent of presumption. He was keenly sensitive to the outward proprieties and strongly forbade any lewdness of conduct (K 24:30–31; 4:23). His concept of the sexual relationship between men and women was that it is a gift of God, to whom glory should be ascribed therefore (K 36:36). According to tradition, he asserted that each time one performs the conjugal act it is an alms before God.[92] He considered the married state the normal one and refused to allow one of his followers to take a vow of chastity.[93] His view was clearly that of sexual relationships within the strictest limits of social and economic responsibility, as he understood such responsibility. He considered love and mercy between husbands and wives to be the ordinance of God (K 30:20); indeed, he is reported to have said that no one has tasted the sweetness of faith who does not love fellow humans for no advantage other than God's sake.[94]

In the last year of his life, Muhammad entered Mecca again at the head of the annual pilgrimage. After his return to Medina, he was busy with arrangements apparently for another expedition to the borders of Syria. He suddenly became ill and lay sick with a fever for several days. He rose from bed to attend prayers at the mosque and, possibly as a result of this overexertion, died the same day, June 8, 632. Thus passed from the scene of human history the greatest man Arabia has produced.

III

THE TEACHING OF THE KORAN

The text of the Koran is considered by Western scholars to be one of the most reliable of sacred texts in the entire history of religions. The present text, the so-called authorized version, was brought into its present form in the 20 years after the Prophet's death, and the content had been in the process of collection throughout Muhammad's prophetic ministry and over the following 20 years.

The order of surahs in the present version is not primarily temporal. Apart from the very first surah, the longer chapters are placed first, and the chapters that are believed by both Muslim and Western scholars to be the earliest in origin tend to be the shortest and are placed toward the end of the book. In general, we are able to distinguish between the materials given in the ministry at Mecca and those given at Medina.

This writer, as a Western scholar, considers himself under obligation to employ the historical-critical methodology common among Western scholars in the history of religions, including the comparison of religions. This procedure brings us, of course, to considerations of interpretation of content, as distinguished from the issue of textual reliability. Western scholars believe themselves obligated to use a wide array of rational critical tools in the investigation of religious data, including, of course, the sacred texts of religious traditions. The methodology implies an impartial, fair-minded approach to source materials, as if the subject matter were not as emotion-laden as religious studies can become. It does not mean, of course, absence of a particular personal focus of faith on the part of the critical scholar.

The application of this kind of historical-critical methodology to religious texts emerged at least in part as a result of the work of seventeenth-century rational philosophers in Europe from René Descartes (1596–1650) to Thomas Hobbes, Baruch Spinoza, and John Locke. The procedure was applied and developed by a succession of German scholars, especially Johann Gottfried von Herder (1744–1803) and Friedrich Ernst Schleiermacher (1768–1834), who were significantly influenced by the philosophical currents of their day. The nineteenth and twentieth centuries witnessed an ever wider use of these critical methods, albeit with extremes of rationalistic skepticism in some cases, into Great Britain, North America, and the rest of the world. Probably a substantial majority of the scholars using this methodology have done so responsibly and with due moderation.

I apply this historical-critical methodology to the data of historic Islam, as I do to the data of my own faith, its Sacred Scriptures, its tradition(s), quite without apology. I do so because, as a Christian believer, I am quite as open as the most devout of Muslim believers—I so affirm!—to the fact of God and the possibility of revelation (self-communication) from God to humans on this earth. In the application of historical-critical methodology, however, I believe that I—in collaboration with and under correction from my peers of both faith and scholarship—am doing no more than using my freedom and right as a human being to "think about" the matters under consideration. This I propose to do responsibly, with due modesty and caution, and, above all, respectfully. For I recognize that the ground on which I walk is holy ground. And, as I am accustomed to do, I have already taken off my shoes!

Evaluating religious texts with historical-critical methods presents a major problem for some because the process, when honestly and fairly used, seems almost always to issue in some discrimination of the moral and spiritual quality of materials. Historically, the Christian Church has generally distinguished between inspiration, which is individual (yet respected), and revelation, which is corporate, because tested by time and the approval of the community of faith. Both the Bible and the Koran as Sacred Scriptures have become canons of faith for their respective religious communities. But when the Christian Church employs historical-critical methodology, it finds reason, at times, in some tension with revelation. It finds also that the selective process that it is called upon to make at a deeper spiritual level the "discernment of spirits" (1 Cor. 12:10) combines with reason to make certain distinctions as it works with the materials alleged to be revelatory. These are not only distinctions between truth and falsehood—as of historical truth or the facts of natural science—but also, and more significantly, between data that are more or less clearly of higher spiritual and moral value and those that are lower.

Such distinctions cannot properly be made merely on the basis of criteria that can appear extraneous to the material, such as the reasoning process of interpreters. They may well be made on the basis of criteria that emerge clearly from the sacred texts being investigated, such as the person, words, and deeds of a "supreme" personality. Such a person may be regarded by his followers in a tradition of faith as the One Focus of divine revelation they have come to accept as uniquely true, authoritative, and therefore normative as a channel of divine revelation for them. They may accept and warmly appreciate other foci of divine revelation as authentic, such as the Old Testament for Christians or the Judeo-Christian prophetic stream for Muslims. But their One Focus alone is supreme and normative, the set of criteria by which all else in human life is evaluated, whether true or false, whether good or bad, or somewhere in between in truth and value.

For Protestant Christians, Jesus Christ is their one supreme and normative Focus of divine revelation. For Roman Catholic Christians, the normative Focus is the evangelical truth of Jesus Christ and Scripture and Tradition as mediated and interpreted by the magisterium (the bishops of the Roman Catholic Church, in council with and subject to the approval of the bishop of Rome, the pope). For Eastern Orthodox Christians, the normative Focus is the totality of the ecumenical creeds of the first six centuries of the history of the Church, the first seven ecumenical creeds, in working or reciprocal relationship with the Sacred Scriptures as these were accepted by the early Church.

Some Protestants, from the very beginnings of the Reformation, have accepted the Bible as a whole as their normative Focus, their criterion of all truth and value. But from John Calvin on, an important segment of Protestant theological thought has seen Jesus Christ as indeed the supreme Focus on earth, but one mediated to humans in a reciprocal process—both revelatory and corrective—through the Bible (objective), the guidance of the Holy Spirit (subjective), and the tradition(s) of the fellowship of the people of God (social). Martin Luther's more existential approach to and acceptance of the normative centrality of Jesus Christ were essentially no different.

For Muslims historically, the one supreme Focus of divine revelation is not Muhammad, most revered though he is as the Messenger of God and the Seal of the Prophets (K 33:40), but the Koran itself, *the* Book, "the finality of prophecy per se." Muhammad and all Muslims have acknowledged with appreciation and gratitude the fact of previous prophethood, especially the Prophets of the Judeo-Christian Scriptures, culminating in Jesus the Messiah, son of Mary, referred to also as the Word of God and one strengthened by the Spirit of God. They acknowledge the authenticity of other Prophets; indeed, Prophets are sent to every people (K 10:48; 116:38). "Every age (*ajal*) has its book" (K 13:38).[1] It should be added, however, that while not a few learned Muslims read the canonical Scriptures of other religions, the great majority of Muslims derive their knowledge of the roles and messages of other prophets from the Koran alone. I should also note in this context that the great literary Prophets of the Old Testament—Amos, Hosea, Isaiah, Jeremiah, Ezekiel—are not mentioned in the Koran.

God's relevance to humanity, British Islamic scholar Bishop Kenneth Cragg reminds us, consists in prophecy. It is a relevance that is essentially educational and religious in the broadest sense of those terms. At its deepest level, prophecy establishes or restores personal relationships—between humanity and its Maker, among humans, between humans and the whole of creation. But it foretells the Word of God, even as it may say something of the future or the past. In so doing, it tells us much about the nature of God, of his mercy as of his will. His will is that which sets the structures and, in some measure, directs the course of human history. As Kenneth Cragg puts it—with Islamic faith-understanding particularly in mind—"prophecy is an education which enlightens, informs, guides, exhorts, warns, disciplines, prohibits, enjoins. Its gist is law, its pattern habituation, its goal obedience. All the world's a school."[2]

Islam has historically understood the prophecy that comes to climax and focus in the Koran as the perfection and possible correction of all that has gone before. There is therefore nothing more to be looked for in the sense of further Prophets or ongoing revelation. In historic Islam, there is no doctrine of the Holy Spirit in the sense of personal divine guidance and continuing divine revelation to be expected apart from the one Book. In this time frame of the education of humanity, the one supreme Guidance is the Koran. It is possible, however, that in much of his prophetic ministry Muhammad thought of divine guidance of believers as extending beyond what he was able to tell them.

This all means that to apply historical-critical methodology to the understanding and interpretation of the Koran is for most Muslims past or present tantamount to blasphemy. Scholars and laypersons in the West have normally found sacred texts to be something other than a "seamless robe" of unvarying truth and quality in terms of either historical fact or religious and moral value. Indeed, they have found—not necessarily to a profoundly disturbing degree—varying levels of truth and quality in the sacred texts, and have often not hesitated to make their conclusions publicly known. Most Muslims, however, find it impossible to employ a process that may result in distinguishing among parts of the Koran and assigning a "lower" value, in truth and authority, to some parts than to others.

This posture toward the Koran on the part of Muslims, reminiscent of some communities of faith within the Judeo-Christian tradition, is often called "fundamentalist," a term that came to be used in theological controversies within North American Protestantism in the early part of the twentieth century. In contemporary Christian-Muslim discussion, however, the term has tended to denote Muslim calls to return to and restore in large measure the practice of the *Shariah*, or the Koranic and extra-Koranic forms of Islamic law as they developed in the early centuries after the death of the Prophet. Hence we can largely dispense with the use of the term "fundamentalist" in our present discussion. There are similarities, however, between modes of understanding among these "restorative" Muslims and those of Christians who view the Bible as inerrant.

As a Western Christian scholar, thinking from a background of many years' study of Judeo-Christian prophetic figures and of the Koran, I respectfully suggest that Muhammad as Prophet was in fact a more open-ended and pragmatic religious figure than later Islam has generally been willing to admit. Indeed, in my judgment, Muhammad was primarily a charismatic leader, not a theologian, and the Koran primarily a religious book, not a theological treatise. As we have seen, Muhammad came to believe that he was indeed an authentic Prophet, a Messenger of God in the historic mold of the Judeo-Christian scriptural tradition. He believed that he was truly receiving authentic revelation from the Lord of the Worlds, from God Most High, the Creator of all, the Merciful, the Compassionate, even as that Supreme Object of faith is portrayed in the Judeo-Christian Bible.

But the issue for Muhammad was primarily, it would seem,

one of religious authenticity and essential truth rather than inerrancy or literal infallibility. William Ralph Inge, dean of Saint Paul's Cathedral in London from 1911 to 1934, made a significant observation with regard to this kind of evaluative issue. Christians in the early Church spoke often of inspiration, never of inerrancy, often of authority, never of infallibility. The church fathers often quoted the Bible in a somewhat free fashion, even as they revered it. As I have written elsewhere, "Muhammad was a religious figure remarkably free from fanaticism or institutionalism," and "the Koran is not merely a book which reveals law; it also reveals God, whose hands are spread wide in bounty [K 5:59]. Islam, at its best, is not a bargaining religion; it creates free and responsible men [and women] who love God and want to do his will. The ethics of the Koran is at bottom an ethics of the heart."[3] My intent with historical-critical methodology is therefore not to "nitpick" but to focus on the "heart" of the matter.

To be sure, Islamic orthodoxy came to believe that the whole of the Koran, totally and without qualification, is the literal Word of God. Indeed, a view that later prevailed widely was that the Koran is uncreated, coexistent with God from all eternity. Kenneth Cragg has asked us to try to understand this attitude "with a lively sympathy. It has parallels in other faiths." This we shall try to do. But Cragg also contends that "revealed solutions are of necessity entrusted to cooperative minds . . . For the Eternal relates to our temporal allegiance not in a passive acceptance but in an active obedience."[4] I am convinced that Muhammad himself manifested precisely this kind of "active obedience." Both he and the Book affirm human freedom and human responsibility, even though some verses in the Koran, like some verses in the Bible (e.g., Exod. 7:3 ff.), seem to ascribe some or even all activity in human history to God as determinative cause. But then, again, very many verses clearly assume both human freedom and responsibility, and call for willing, active human response.

This latter dilemma of "inconsistency" in textual content, as distinguished from issues of textual reliability, is one with which historical-critical methodology is accustomed to dealing. As we come now to consideration of the teaching of the Koran, I wish readers to note again that this is the way I also interpret and evaluate the Scriptures of my own faith. May we all be responsible and fair, honest in our quest for the truth—and the goodness—of the God whom we worship in common.

A final brief word in this context may be that, here and now, historical-critical methodology is appropriate with reference to the Koran only in a limited way. That is, the niceties of this discipline, especially as they have been developed in the West over the twentieth century, are neither fully applicable nor feasible. I refer to methods such as form criticism, literary criticism, structural analysis, and the like. In the case of the Koran, we have only one textual tradition and only limited materials from tradition as to the time and place of the chapters or the parts thereof. The longer chapters clearly contain materials delivered on more than one occasion. It is possible to discern some development in the content of faith and thought of Muhammad over the years of his public ministry, especially in comparing the years in Mecca and those in Medina. But on the whole, the most that can be said is that there are some changes in emphasis and then, more especially, focus on the new and different needs of the communities addressed in the two cities.

We have a collection of materials that a prophetic, charismatic person believed had been communicated to him interiorly by the Creator and Lord of the Worlds, either directly or through the mediation of an angel of this God, most particularly the angel Gabriel. As we have seen, the bulk, indeed the great majority, of the inhabitants of Mecca during Muhammad's public ministry were not willing to accept him as an authentic Prophet nor receive his message as true and authoritative. Not a few may have wondered whether he was "for real," but with the opposition of the leaders of the community almost entirely unyielding, it was not possible for any but the bravest to come forward in approval. We may say therefore that public evaluation of the man and his message was—either in Mecca or in Medina—colored from beginning to end by the political, economic, and social contingencies of the situation. It was not conducted in the context of free, calm, and rational inquiry. Quite to the contrary, commitment to the cause in Mecca was a matter of life and death. In Medina, however, failure or hesitancy to believe and commit oneself fully was in the context of strong and ever-increasing sociopolitical pressures to believe and follow.

This leads me to say that I focus in this chapter on communicating the content of the message of the Koran in its main lines and emphases. Of necessity, this leaves the fine points of historical criticism as a later task. I should say, however, that—from my point of view—it is possible and legitimate to use the Judeo-Christian Scriptures as criteria for the analysis and evaluation of the content of the Koran. Muhammad himself accepted the essential authenticity of these Scriptures, even as he ventured to criticize the faithfulness of their transmission and offered some corrections of their content.

God (Allah)

God is One.[5] Surah 112, named "The Unity" (Al-Tauhid), often cited as giving the essence of the message of the Koran, says "He is God, One, God, the Everlasting Refuge, who has not begotten, and has not been begotten, and equal to Him is not anyone" (cf. Mark 12:29).[6] The unqualified unity of God is central to Muhammad's perception, and the point that he "has not begotten" is made to emphasize that any notion of his having a child or a consort is an abridgement of his unity and is derogatory of his character and of his transcendent majesty (K 4:168–170; 5:77; 6:100–102). In the Medinan period especially, Muhammad denies that God has a son. Whatever is in the heavens and on earth is his, including the Messiah, Mary's son. All are subservient to him (K 19:31–36, 91–94). (I discuss later the larger range of the Koranic views of the person and role of Jesus, the Messiah, but note at this point that the Koran has a high theological view of Jesus the son of Mary, as Messiah, as the Word of God.)

As the Koran itself reveals, central to Islamic faith is the word *Islam*, which denotes the condition by which good is opened to humans—and other beings. *Islam* means "surrender," with commitment implied, and those who have surrendered are termed *Muslim* (plural *Muslimun*), regardless of their external or institutional religious affiliation. The surrender is to God, the Lord of the Worlds. Whoever submits his will to God, his reward is with his Lord (K 2:106). The issue is primarily between true worship and idolatry, between surrender and commitment to the Creator of all (who is ultimately "Other" and independent of all his creation) and worship of what is ultimately dependent (K 3:92; 29:5). A practical and a theological distinction is made between the permanency of "what is with God," and the transitoriness of what humans believe they have (K 16:98; 17:19; cf. Matt. 6:19–21).

It is said that God does not forgive the sin of ascribing associates to God. This is "a mighty sin" (K 4:52). This language, we should note, is to be taken seriously but, as with many Koranic statements, we must place it in its larger context; in this case the larger context is the mercy and compassion of God, who does forgive the sins of all who seek his forgiveness (K 110:3; 4:110).

God is affirmed again and again as the Creator (K 2:26–27; 55:3,13). He says "'Be,' and it is"; his sovereign will and word are sufficient to create (K 16:42; 2:111). God created neither the heaven and the earth in play, nor aught between them (K 21:16); nothing was created in vain (K 38:27), but all purposefully, to establish truth, unto a structured end (K 30:7). He created humans that he might have mercy on them (K 11:121).[7] There is no imperfection in the creation of the All-merciful (K 67:3) and the creation of all that is, is said to be for the sake of humans (K 2:27).

The Koran proclaims the sovereignty of God in many ways and with wondrously eloquent language. To him belongs the kingly rule of the heavens and the earth, "whithersoever you turn, there is the Face of God" (K 2:101, 109; 3:186). God is "the Living, the Everlasting;" he is the Eternal, overcome by neither slumber nor sleep, the true King (K 2:256; 20:110,113; cf. Ps.

121:3–4). He only is the Hearer, the Knower of all things, the All-wise, the All-aware (K 2:123, 30; 6:18). God knows what is hidden, the secrets of human hearts (K 2:72, 236; 3:4; 4:66). "With Him are the keys of the Unseen . . . not a leaf falls, but He knows it" (K 6:58–59; 4:88; cf. Matt. 10:29).

The power of God is frequently stressed in the Koran. He is the Giver of all (K 3:7), the All-mighty (K 69:34; 2:18), particularly over his servants who believe (K 6:18). This power of God is often set in the context of Muhammad's proclamation of the final Day of Judgment, a theme that played an important role in his early preaching in Mecca and continued to be expressed in the Medinan years (K 1:4; 2:6). Muhammad's language is strong and graphic; he does not hesitate to describe in some detail what could be called primitive aspects of disbelievers' experience of Gehenna. God is said to be "vengeful" and All-mighty (in A. J. Arberry's translation; M. M. Pickthall prefers to speak of Allah's being able to exact a "heavy doom"). This is in the context of God's ability to requite the wrong that individuals have done (K 3:3). As Master of the "Day of Doom," God will raise up the dead; they will be returned to him for judgment (K 6:36). God is severe in punishment (Arberry—"terrible in chastisement" [K 2:161]), but fair. Each person shall be paid in full only what he or she has earned (K 3:155; cf. Luke 12:5).

Equal to God's creative and majestic sovereignty, however, is his mercy. When we consider the sovereignty of God in the Koran in more detail, we shall note some problems that arise as a result of apparent logical inconsistencies between Koranic affirmations of God's sovereignty and his mercy. Whatever the problems of formal logic, however, both aspects of the divine were equally affirmed. Surah 1, sometimes called the Lord's Prayer of Muslims, without whose recitation no serious transaction in Muslim society is complete, begins "In the name of God, the Merciful, the Compassionate." He responds to those who seek his forgiveness (K 110:3). Muhammad rejects the claim that "none shall enter Paradise except they be Jews or Christians," and insists that whoever in the world submits his will to God and does good shall receive proper reward. "No fear shall be on them, neither shall they sorrow" (K 2:105–106, 129; cf. Acts 10:34–35).

The Koran frequently states that God will forgive whom he will, statements intended perhaps as much to check human presumption as to affirm the sovereignty of God (K 2:284; 3:124). The Koran frequently affirms that those who do wrong, but then "remember God and pray forgiveness for their sins" will receive forgiveness—provided they do not continue in their wrongdoing (K 3:129–130). God's generosity to all peoples is stressed, even though most are not thankful (K 2:244). (To Muhammad, ingratitude was one of the most detestable of human sins.)

The passage just quoted (K 3:129–130) promises forgiveness even to those who commit sin knowingly. Another passage states that God shall turn in mercy only toward those who do evil in ignorance, but the context reproves those who postpone change of lifestyle until their deathbed. Muhammad affirms chastisement for them, even as for those who die disbelieving (K 4:21–22).[8] But far more frequent are the promises that whoever does evil—or wrongs himself—shall find God responsive to his prayer for forgiveness (K 4:110). God pardons evil deeds, but expects repentance in believing, with amends, and a life of righteous deeds (K 42:24–25; 4:145).

For Muhammad, God's nature is thoroughly and clearly good. The call of God is to good (K 3:100; cf. Mark 10:18, Matt. 19:19). Whatever blessings humans enjoy come from God (K 16:55). God tells the truth (K 6:57; 4:89); he is the manifest Truth (K 24:25), although he may also speak to humanity through similitudes (K 24:36). The call of God is to receive pardon, guidance along a straight path, and a glorious end in Paradise (K 2:221; 24:45). A repeated Koranic affirmation is that Prophets have been sent to every people in history (K 10:48; 16:38; cf. Acts 14:17). In particular, Muhammad's own experience has been of the ever great and generous bounty of God. He speaks of receiving the Book [Koran] and the Wisdom [of God], of being taught that which he had not known. He speaks of this bounty of God in providential terms, reaching into the ordinary needs and troubles of daily life (K 4:112–113).

God's summons is to a final Abode of Peace, but in the present he gives warning and guidance along a straight path, which is the service of God, and mercy and healing of the inner pain of those who believe (K 10:26, 58; 36:60). His word of welcome to believers is peace (K 36:58). Even as there is no God but he, he upholds justice on earth; his prophets call, and have always called, humans to justice (K 3:16, 20). Indeed, God does not desire injustice to be experienced by any being (K 3:104; cf. Gen. 9:8 ff). God does not wrong humans in any way; they wrong themselves (K 10:45; 11:119). God himself does not wrong his creation "so much as the weight of ant"; his way is rather to be generous in his repayment of all human good (K 4:44). Muhammad clearly expected all humans to understand the ways of God in the world in this manner. In the Koran is no such thing as "original sin," no statement of any genetic transmission of evil in human life. "Whosoever earns a sin, earns it against himself alone." He does not receive it from God nor inherit it from ancestors (K 4:110; cf. Jer. 2:9; 31:29–30; Ezek. 18:1–32). In the context, however, of discussion of divine prescriptions for marriage and the right ordering of human sexuality, the Koran states that humans were created "weak" (K 4:32). This seems to be the one area of human being and activity wherein some natural inadequacy is acknowledged. At the same time, stress is laid on God's compassion. He desires to turn toward humans in mercy, even "to lighten things for you" (K 4:25–33; cf. Matt. 11:29–30).

The Koranic view of God emerges clearly in the affirmation that God always warns before he punishes. He has never destroyed a city unless its inhabitants were evildoers and Messengers of warning had been sent to them (K 26:209; 6:42). And the Lord God would never destroy cities if their people were in the process of "putting things right" (K 11:119). The Koran combines the perception of divine punishment within history with an emphasis on the Last Day's far weightier chastisement of evildoers and disbelievers (two aspects of rebellious humans that are distinguished but never separated in the Koran).

Muhammad could point to specific instances of divine punitive action, all evidently known to his hearers in Mecca (K 69:1–10). At

65

the same time, he affirmed a divine self-restraint, in that divine punishment within history is not yet proportioned to the enormity of human deserts. A respite, even an "enjoyment of days for many years," is given persons as a time to heed the warnings. But Muhammad's style affirms this fact of respite with language surprisingly slighting in tone. It is as if, for example, the time of freedom were given only that unbelievers "may increase in sin," or even that God is intentionally deceiving them as to the truth of his ways (K 3:172; 7:181; 13:32; 26:205).

A central theme of Muhammad's preaching in his Meccan ministry was God's favor to the oppressed. We read in the context of the experiences of the people of Israel in Egypt that God desired to be gracious to those who "were abased in the land," even to make them leaders among humanity and the heirs of great good. He answers the cry of those who are wronged and takes away the evil that they have experienced (K 28:4–5; 27:63). Muhammad is told to proclaim good news to the humble, whose hearts tremble when the name of God is mentioned. They endure patiently, whatever their experience in life, are faithful in prayer, and give of their means for others (K 22:36). Muhammad does not work these affirmations into a carefully crafted doctrine of divine providence at work in the world. His primary concern is to proclaim the availability of divine help in every situation of human need and to point to the victory, or "success," that lies ahead in this world, and the next, for those who believe and do good. In the meantime, the community of faith must "feed the beggar and the suppliant" (K 22:37).

A certain polarity-in-tension appears in Muhammad's teaching that is more than mere paradox. On the one hand, the blessing and mercy of God were given to the children of Israel; they were even—for a time and for covenantal purposes in which others might share—preferred "above all beings." In a lengthy passage in the longest chapter of the Koran, we read of God's repeated pardonings of the Israelites, to the end that they should be thankful. We may note that in the Koran a thankful person or people is one of the clearest signs of God's saving power at work.

But God's mercy is also as unlimited as it is particularized. In Medina, Muhammad proclaimed that Jews, Christians, and Sabaeans, whoever "believes in God and the Last Day, and works righteousness," will receive God's reward. For now they shall experience neither fear nor sorrow (K 2:38ff.). The intent appears to include as fully acceptable to God every form of monotheistic faith—if it is accompanied by right living.

Muhammad came to stress the particularities of divine mercy and blessing experienced by those who have surrendered and believe and do good. This teaching was focused on the emerging and growing community of Muslims in Medina. God is their protector and helper, the best of helpers (K 2:101; 3:61, 144). He is their guide and refuge (K 39:37; 41:36). But these assurances of divine favor, mercy, and compassion are almost invariably given with various warnings to believers not to presume or to separate belief from practice. In language reminiscent of the Apostle Paul, but perhaps more frequently than he, Muhammad sets his assurances of divine mercy and aid alongside words of warning (cf. 1 Cor. 10:12; Gal. 6:7). God is gentle toward his servants; indeed, if they "slip" in their obedience after entering the peace of faith, they may know that the power and wisdom of God are manifest in his mercy. Yet God is "terrible in retribution" (K 2:204–207). The tension, even the uncertainty, of this polarity that was designed to create a God-fearing community of faith and obedience permeates every part of the Koran and was clearly a central element of Muhammad's preaching from the beginning of his prophetic ministry to the end. His preaching never loses sight of this theme.

Then, again, we note the appeal to believers not to despair of God's mercy, "surely God forgives sins altogether." But such words are applicable only until "the chastisement comes upon you, then you will not be helped" (K 39:54–55). Thus, once again, there is warning and consequent tension. God helps and defends believers, but in a covenantal relationship of mutual responsibility. God helps those who help Him (K 22:39–42). This last statement, we may note, was evidently made in the context of

Muhammad's appeal to the Muslims in Medina to give of their substance and to fight for the cause of Allah. Sanction to fight is now given to those believers who have been wronged. We find the statement elsewhere, however, that the goal of such activity is that disbelievers become believers and that there be love between the Muslims and those with whom they are at enmity (K 60:7). The believers are reminded that their present community of cooperative faith is the result of God's blessing on them when they were still enemies, one to the other. His blessing was to the end that their hearts be brought together and they become brothers (and sisters). Muslims are reminded that they themselves had been "on the brink of a pit of fire" and that God had delivered them from their peril. Hence all are to hold fast to God's binding rope that binds believers to God and to one another (K 3:96–99). God works to perfect his light among all humanity (K 61:8).

The relationship between God and believers is intended to be open and unreserved, even intimate. The awesome solemnity and sublime majesty of the Koranic portrait of God are often spoken of, but the dimension of intimacy is never lacking. God in his awareness is near to all (K 4:134; 50:15; 34:49). The statement that "God stands between a man and his own heart" follows an appeal to believers to respond to God and his Messenger when God calls them into what will give them life. It immediately precedes a warning that, ultimately, all persons will be "mustered" to give final account before God. Again it is said that "God is terrible in retribution" (K 8:24–25).

It is generally recognized that the longer chapters of the Koran are collections of preaching or teaching given on more than one occasion. We are not certain therefore that one passage that immediately follows another in our present text necessarily comes from the same original context. Yet it is not without meaning that, following the promise and warning, a number of statements are made reminding believers of the concrete help, generous bounty, and forgiving mercy of God (K 8:26–29; cf. 8:33). It would seem that the words at the end of the seventh surah, which Muhammad believed were given by God with special significance for himself, show us the kind of believer that Muhammad envisaged for the community of the committed (Muslims):

> Remember thy Lord
> in thy soul, humbly and fearfully,
> not loud of voice,
> at morn and eventide. Be thou not
> among the heedless.
> Surely those who are with thy Lord
> wax not too proud
> to serve Him; they chant His praise,
> and to Him they bow (K 7:204–205).

God is indeed God, but concretely this means that he is sufficient for all human need, most generous in his bounty (K 4:83; 3:146, 167–168). And in his providence, God will provide a "way out" of dilemmas for every person who fears God. There is the further suggestion that God is able to "bring something new to pass" in the course of human events (K 65:2–4; cf. 1 Cor. 10:13). We are hereby given insight into a distinct open-endedness in Muhammad's view of God, the world, and human life. Thus Muhammad affirms that God does not compel faith, although no one can believe except by his permission (K 10:99–100). Indeed, in the second surah, the longest of all, the statement is flatly made that there is no compulsion in religion (K 2:258). The implication is that such is Muhammad's intent even as it is God's way. We have seen, however, that in Medina, Muhammad came to believe that he had divine authorization to create a favorable climate for authentic monotheistic faith by eliminating the outer forms and practices of Arabic polytheism, even if necessary by military force.

In this context, we may properly consider the meaning of the Arabic term *hubb* in the Koran, usually translated in English as the word "love." The Arabic word does not mean precisely what is commonly intended by the English term. Christian understanding of the mind of God, influenced by biblical teaching of the unconditioned love of God for all creation, has tended toward an all-inclusive, even undiscriminating, prior favor toward all (cf. John 3:16; 17:23; Rom. 8:32; 1 John 4:10). The Koran, as we have seen, says that God is good and guides persons to their gain (K 10:108); he has concern for the welfare of all; he sends his Messengers to every people. But in the Koran, the term *hubb* is not used to express this inclusive concern, but instead denotes God's approval of those who do his will.[9] Thus God cannot be described as "loving" evildoers, however much he and his Messengers strive to call them to their eternal—and temporal—welfare.

Thus we read that God loves those who put their trust in him (K 3:153). God loves those who do good (K 5:17, 94), the just (K 5:46; 60:8). He loves those who fight in his cause in (military) ranks (K 61:4). He loves the god-fearing (K 3:70). In another passage, Muhammad is told to proclaim to believers: "If you love God, follow me, and God will love you, and forgive your sins" (K 3:29). The primary meaning of human love of God would seem to be their recognition that he is good and worthy of all worship, while God's love (*hubb*) of persons is conditioned upon their response of obedient faith. This same verse, we may note, repeats the admonition to obey God *and* the Messenger, and the verse concludes with the warning that "God loves not the unbelievers."

Therefore we read, after some strong injunctions against the practice of usury, that God does not love any "guilty ingrate" (K 2:277). God does not love the doers of evil. (Muhammad seems to consider evildoers synonymous with unbelievers.) He does not guide them (in their wrongdoing [K 3:50; 2:255, 260]). God does not love the guilty traitor, nor the workers of corruption nor boasters (K 4:108; 5:69; 28:76). There are statements that God does not love transgressors of his commandments, specifically in the context of repeated warnings against corruption, primarily political and economic injustice (K 7:53–57). Muhammad insists that it is not right for a Prophet of God to be fraudulent in any of his dealings (K 3:155). Nor again does God love the wasteful (K 6:143).

Therefore the term *hubb* expresses ethical evaluation and, accordingly, we note that there are degrees of approbation and reprobation before God. This perception seems to emerge particularly as Muhammad had to deal with those believers in Medina who gave lip service to the faith but found excuses not to follow Muhammad on his military forays. Believers who sit at home are not to be considered equal to those who fight in the way of God with their persons and their possessions (K 3:156–162; 4:97–98). At this time and place, those who went out to fight generally provided their own weapons, food—very simple and light, perhaps only dates—and means of transportation, that is, horses or camels.

No passage in the Koran reveals more clearly Muhammad's concept of God and the nature of his relationship with God than the words recited as if spoken by Abraham:

> They are an enemy to me, except the
> Lord of all Being,
> who created me, and Himself guides me,
> and Himself gives me to eat and drink,
> and, whenever I am sick, He heals me,
> who makes me to die, then gives me life,
> and who, I am eager, shall forgive me
> my offence on the Day of Doom (K 26:76–83).

Muhammad concludes that whatever is in the heavens and the earth praises God, who is the Light of the heavens and the earth. The birds who spread their wings in flight do so in praise of God—and God knows the prayer and praise of each (K 24:35, 41–42).[10] (Any others who may be called in prayer possess "not so much as the skin of a date-stone" [K 35:14].)

A brief word to conclude this section. What was the personal and larger effect of this faith-understanding?

We must recall that we are dealing with a background series

of events that Muhammad believed to be divine-human encounters, encounters that were allegedly not only personal encounters between a human being and his Maker, but also the means by which an increasingly large body of specific theological and ethical instruction; practical guidance; and ordinances for the ordering of ordinary life, public and private, came to be given. One is reminded of the visionary experiences of the Roman Catholic nuns Anna Katerina Emmerich (1774–1824) and Therese Neumann (1898–1962), of the British poet Thomas Traherne (1636–1674), or of the American clairvoyant Edgar Cayce (1887–1945). Especially in the cases of Sr. Emmerich and Edgar Cayce we have instances of relatively large quantities of material of religio-ethical content reaching into the widest ranges of theological, even cosmic, thought.

The effect of these experiences on Muhammad's religious faith and worldview was formidable. The effect was also formidable in the experience of others, beginning with his wife Khadijah, who came to believe that Muhammad was indeed an authentic Prophet and Messenger of God. Muhammad's religious associations and practices in youth and early adult life made more or less comprehensible to him the revelatory experiences that began with the "Night of Power" when he was about 40 years of age. But clearly a central effect of these latter experiences was to create a profound sense of awe before the reality of God, the Creator of all, who had deigned to call him to be his Messenger to the Arabic-speaking people of his time. This awe issued from a heightened sense of the ethical judgments of God at work in the world and supremely on the day of final judgment. This sense of impending doom cannot be accounted for on the basis of Muhammad's experiences with the content of Jewish or Christian faiths. It must have been significantly rooted in his own visionary experiences. But this profound awe was completely impregnated with an equally profound gratitude for the mercy and compassion that this same God wished to manifest, Muhammad believed, to the whole of his creation.

This mercy and compassion of God were for the good of all.

But God's call, especially to his human creatures, was to return to their Maker, to repent and change their lifestyle into one of faith and obedience. This involved changes in every segment of human life, public and private, personal and corporate. It was intended to create new and better interhuman relationships, in political and economic life and in family and personal living.

God's call, however, was supremely to worship. And this, according to the ordinances developed by Muhammad, first meant worship three times a day and later five times a day. The mode of worship included prostration of the forehead to the ground, a symbolism denoting the awe and submission proper before the sovereign majesty of God. It meant a new and all-encompassing role for religion in the lives of believers. It meant that religion came to have a supremely forceful, dominating role in the lives of believers that the Arabic-speaking peoples (except those who had directly participated in the Judeo-Christian tradition) had never known.

The Sovereignty and Providence of God

Graphic portrayals abound in the Koran of God as Creator of all, Maker of the heavens and the earth and of all within them, Lord of the Worlds. God is cited as all-hearing, all-seeing, all-knowing, all-powerful, all-encompassing. God provides to all beings their life and physical sustenance. To humans, he provides their spiritual opportunities—in varying degrees, as he wills. The all-encompassing nature of this divine power and provision looms large in these portrayals. Indeed, it often appears from the descriptions of this boundless activity of God as if there were no space left for free human action. And not a few Muslims, perhaps the majority over the centuries, have taken their theological tradition to mean that everything that happens in the world, especially as external events, happens according to God's will and specific ordering. This is *kismet*, the Turkish word from the original Arabic *qismah*, a word often heard in the Western world a generation or two ago, the belief that all events are completely fated.

We must remind ourselves, however, that the Koran is a collection of oracular, charismatic statements made at different
times and places in the public career of the Prophet Muhammad.
It is not a carefully reasoned, logically sustained theological treatise. To be sure, not a few statements in the Koran in their ejac-
ulatory form suggest a totally determinist worldview. But their
larger context almost always makes it clear that Muhammad himself consistently implied the presence of human freedom—and
responsibility—under the overarching sovereignty of God. As
noted, there was a kind of open-ended and pragmatic element in
Muhammad's style. He was a religious reformer, calling for radical changes in religious faith and in personal and corporate, private and public, inner self and outer lifestyle.

In a Meccan surah, Muhammad proclaims that God chooses
for relationship with himself whomever he wills. Immediately
following this, however, we read that God guides to himself whoever turns to him in penitence—which is clearly a free human act.
Humans are given knowledge from on high and opportunities for
inner response and outer turning (K 42:6–12; 2:165). In affliction,
believers are to think first that such may issue from their own
doing, then remember that "surely God is powerful over everything" (K 3:159).

All power originates with God, and to him belongs the rule of
the heavens and the earth. Thus Muhammad affirmed that physical phenomena are of God's ordering: clouds, rain, hail, lightning,
the revolutions of day and night and of the seasons (K 24:43–44).
Many of these passages, often reminiscent of kindred verses in the
biblical book of Job, are powerfully evocative, drawing the imagi-
nation of hearers to soar upward, compelling awe (K 25:47–51;
35:13–14; 2:157–159; cf. Job 38–41). But Muhammad proclaims
also that these physical phenomena are expressions of divine
favor; made serviceable to human needs. As things external, they
are linked with blessings internal and—since the term "sub-
jected" is used—are subject to a certain measure of human control (K 22:63; 31:18; cf. Gen. 1:28). The worldview sees an
ordered structure in the cosmos, within which humans are

granted a certain measure of interior and exterior freedom of action. This combination of gracious divine giving and human reception, with human accountability for use of the gifts, we may call "stewardship." The context is affirmation of the goodness of God, of his creation, of his favor toward humans (K 2:19–20; cf. Acts 14:17). There is no metaphysical dualism of matter and the spirit in the Koran. God does not scorn matter and assign higher value to spirit. To the contrary, the throne of God includes the heavens and the earth; it is no burden to God's spirit to preserve them, both the seen and the unseen (K 2:256–257; 22:60–64).

But we note that the Koran states that the true destiny of humans is in the Hereafter, particularly after "the Day of Doom." The context is often the preaching given to persons in Medina who were afraid to fight and possibly die in the cause of God. Muhammad insists that the enjoyment of the things of this world is slight. "The world to come is better for him who fears God" (K 4:76, 79). In this context of faith and thought, the life of this world is nothing but fleeting vanity, as N. J. Dawood has translated the verse (K 3:182). To Meccan disbelievers who contended that there is nothing more than our present life in this world, Muhammad proclaimed that, in comparison, life here is nothing but "a sport and a diversion." The Last Abode is better for those who fear God (K 6:29–32; 47:38).

We read that all events happen only by God's permission. But, as we have seen, God also grants to humans some freedom of movement, and all is ethically purposeful. Thus, on the one hand, no affliction occurs except by divine permission; indeed, it is "in a Book" before God brings it into being (K 64:11; 57:22). Some statements indeed move beyond affirmation of divine *permission* into positive divine *decrees*. Believers are to say that nothing, untoward or not, will happen to them unless God has prescribed it (K 9:51). No one shares in his divine government; God gives royal power on earth to whom he wishes, as to Saul and David (K 18:26; 2:247, 253). No human being may die but by God's permission, and that is at a time appointed (K 3:139, 150). Every nation has its term in human history, and none can alter its timing "by a single hour" (K 7:33). We read frequently in the Koran that God leads astray whomever he wills and sets on a straight path whom he will; he will forgive whom he will, and punish whom he will (K 6:39; 2:284).

These statements are properly understood, however, as proclamations of religious *potentiality* rather than descriptions of literal *fact*. Once again, the Koran is not a collection of theological affirmations that can be analyzed as if they were literally and totally true in themselves apart from context and emotive intent. *Especially*, one needs to try to perceive the emotive intent. If the language itself at particular points is "logic-abusive," one needs to read on. Almost invariably, Muhammad himself comes to modify or qualify extremities of speech that appear, by themselves, to take the hearers or readers beyond what Muhammad intended. Something of this mode of speech, with its attendant problems, can be found in the literary Prophets recorded in the Hebrew Bible. But this style is "dangerous," and difficult, both for religious understanding and for application in life. At bottom, the Koran reveals a God who is not arbitrary, but of ethical responsibility, supremely of constructively purposeful action.[11]

A few specific references make this conclusion clearer. The Koran frequently admonishes hearers to travel in the land (Arabia) and see the workings of God's judgments on towns and peoples. The destruction of towns was not only because the people rejected God's Messengers, but because they "cried lies" and did evil and wrought injustice (K 3:131; 6:11; 21:11; 27:71). God never punishes unless he has sent a Messenger to each particular societal group, for—Muhammad insists—God has never done wrong (K 17:16–17; 26:209; 28:59). Every arrogant tyrant will ultimately fail of his goal (K 14:19; cf. Luke 1:51–52). This process, this testing of nations and persons with good and evil things is to the end that they may return to their God, that they may be humble (K 7:167; 6:42). The sending of Messengers, such as the Hebrew patriarchs Abraham, Isaac, or Jacob, such as the kings David and Solomon, is that humans may rightly worship and do good deeds—with especial concern for the poor (K 21:71). And we find repeated assurance that God never lays responsibility on any individual except according to his or her capacity (K 2:286; 7:40; 23:63; cf. 1 Cor. 10:13). If, for example, "the peoples of the cities" had believed and become god-fearing, God would have poured out upon them blessings from heaven and earth (K 7:93). But even in the case of those who disbelieve, if they cease from their disbelief and persecution of believers, that which is past will be forgiven them (K 8:38). Thus, at the heart of Muhammad's perception of the nature and workings of God is a distinct open-endedness in the mind and will of God, one which, as we shall see, extends to (and possibly beyond) the Day of Judgment.

The problem of justifying the ways of God in the world evidently gave Muhammad much concern. In the materials that we have in the Koran, he approaches the problem from several different aspects and, like other religious teachers, never reaches a logically satisfactory conclusion. He works at it, however, by continuing to affirm both the sovereignty and the goodness of God. Thus, in the same passage, Muhammad affirms that everything is from God and yet that whatever good humans experience is of God, whatever evil is of themselves, not of God (K 4:81–82). One verse in the Koran seems to say specifically that humans are given a measure of free rein to sin (K 3:172); another, as we have seen, proclaims that whoever sins reaps its consequences "against himself only." If in the process such a person hurts the innocent, the consequences on self are heightened (K 4:110–111).

Throughout the Koran, Muhammad emphasizes the visitation of divine judgments on human wrongdoing. There will be a like recompense for each evil deed (K 10:27). Yet the process is not merely a rigorous karmic law of consequences. There is an unexpected generosity in God's dealings with humanity. Those who do evil will be requited only for what they did. Those who believe and do good will be forgiven their evil deeds and then be recompensed according to "the best of what they were doing" (K 29:6). It would seem that God looks upon the intent of the human heart and judges accordingly, but acts generously. If the recompense of goodness is goodness, God will repay it double, even tenfold (K 55:60; 6:161; 4:44). As with other state-ments, Muhammad's arithmetic is more poetic than literal.

Another dimension of the problem of human evil, divine for-giveness, and generous treatment of the repentant is that of the "cosmic disposal" of evil. As in the Buddhist classic the *Dhamma-pada* (173), Muhammad affirms that, with prayer, the good deeds people do will surely "drive away the evil deeds" (K 11:116). Secret giving of alms for the poor is said to acquit people of their evil deeds (K 2:273). But Muhammad nowhere claims that such human doing takes care of everything. There is in the Koran as a whole a certain doubt or ambiguity about the completion of the process of disposal of human wrongdoing. But the possibility that the consequences of such wrongdoing are not yet completely dis-posed of does not lead Muhammad to conclude that God is not merciful or does not fully forgive. The mystery of some ambigu-ity is perhaps intended to teach believers that they should not presume. Before such ambiguity and awareness that each human soul "earns" specific consequences for what it does, the final prayer of Muhammad is:

> Our Lord
> take us not to task
> if we forget, or make mistake . . .
> pardon us,
> and forgive us
> and have mercy on us (K 2:287; cf. 1 Cor. 10:12).

There is in the Koran no doctrine of atonement, no specific concept of theologically significant vicarious suffering. No soul can bear the load of another, only what it earns on its own account (K 6:164; 17:16; 35:18; cf. Jer. 31:29–30; Ezek. 18:20; Gal. 6:2). Muhammad rejected the enticements of unbelievers (Christians?—the surah is allegedly of the late Meccan period) when they say, "Follow our path, and let us carry your offenses." His answer was that these persons "carry" their own offenses, but will be respon-sible on the Day of Resurrection for their own loads—"and other loads" (K 29:11–12). The teaching of the Koran is that only God can forgive; he loves those who when they do wrong pray for forgiveness—and "do not persevere in the things they did" (K 3:129). God is sufficient for whoever puts his trust in him, and he will provide a way out of all dilemmas, provision from a source humanly unexpected, for those who fear him (K 3:167; 65:3; cf. 1 Cor. 10:13). And yet intercessory prayer may avail as God permits; he graciously hears prayer (K 34:22; 21:84). How this is all cosmically possible lies for Muhammad in the mystery of God's sovereign will and work.

We have noted the Koranic emphasis on the blessings promised, especially in the Hereafter, to those who believe and obey their Maker. An additional emphasis in the Koran points to victory and prosperity in this world and forgiveness and an immense reward in the Hereafter (K 5:61; 48:29). One aspect of this assertion is the statement that Muhammad had been sent as the Messenger of God with the guidance of God "and the religion of truth, that He may uplift it above every religion" (K 48:28). This, to my knowledge, is the only statement in the entire Koran that seems to promise the historical success of Islam in this world, vis-à-vis other religions, whatever their measure of truth.[12] But there are frequent promises of worldly success—victory in battle, prosperity in material things—to those who repent, believe, and do good. Likewise, disbelievers do not prosper (K 28:67, 82; 3:140–144). Yet both these affirmations are qualified.

Just as the word "haply" (i.e., possibly) is deftly but frequently inserted into promises of prosperity to believers, so disbelievers may be permitted to enjoy for a time, even for a long time, the pleasures of this world. They will, however, be appropriately charged on the Day of Resurrection (K 28:66, 62). Especially in the context of affirmation of the need to fight in the cause of God, Muslims are told to expect affliction and hardship before they enter Paradise. Indeed, this has been God's way with believers from ancient times. But God's help is always near

(K 2:208–212). And it is a mistake, Muhammad insists, to consider persecution received from fellow humans as chastisement from God (K 29:9). Both believers and disbelievers experience hurts in this world; these serve to prove the believers and blight the others (K 3:140–144). God is the protector of believers, the best of helpers, an affirmation never to be forgotten when trials are experienced that do not fall exclusively upon those who are evildoers (K 8:25; cf. Luke 13:1–5). This warning against assigning guilt precisely according to the degree of external misfortune led Muhammad also to insist that there is "no fault in the blind, and there is no fault in the lame, and there is no fault in the sick" (K 48:17; cf. John 9:1–3).

The reward of God, which (to anticipate) is an integral part of true faith, is thus not to be fully evaluated on the basis of present experiences or appearances in this world. The Last Abode is the final goal, the ultimate reward. In this world, the bounty of God may be thankfully received, but believers should not presume or exult therein. It is God's prerogative to give them more or less here on earth (K 28:76–84). Yet in the midst of whatever fear or hunger or loss of goods the committed ones experience, the final Koranic word is "good news." Even those who were slain in pursuit of God's way are not to be called dead; "rather they are living," even though that fact be beyond the awareness of those left on earth. They are living with their Lord, "joyful . . . because no fear shall be on them, neither shall they sorrow" (K 2:149; 3:164; cf. Rev. 21:1–4). We are told that God does not allow the work of any person, male or female, who labors in the cause of God to be wasted (K 3:165, 193). We note also that in this specific inclusion of women as equally recipient of God's just, nay generous, providence, Muhammad adds, "the one of you is as the other." These workers shall never be (cosmically) wronged, even to the extent of the hair upon a date (K 4:79).

The concept of election in the Koran is also qualified. If a people called do not "go forth" (with military service possibly included) in the cause of God, he will choose another people in their place (K 9:39). Similarly, in the case of individuals, if any Muslim turns from his religion, God will bring others in their place, persons whom he loves and who love him. The ideal Muslims are humble toward fellow believers, stern toward unbelievers (M. M. Pickthall's translation), persons "who struggle in the path of God, not fearing the reproach of any reproacher" (K 5:59; 4:132; back again to A. J. Arberry's translation). The Koran teaches the original solidarity of all humanity. They were in the beginning "only one nation" (K 10:20). The implication is that subsequent divisions are the result of human sin and caprice. The Koran aims at the creation of a new community of faith that transcends all human divisions, but nowhere do we find assertion that this community will encompass all humanity before the Last Day.

The promise of divine protection of believers is an important theme in the Koran. God is often proclaimed as the protector of believers, but such affirmation is qualified by various other statements. To God belong all things on earth and above, his is dominion over all, "protecting and Himself unprotected" (K 9:51; 23:86, 90). But security in life is assured specifically to believers who do not distort their belief with wrongdoing (K 6:82). Satan has no authority over, and therefore no authority to harm in any integral way, those who believe and trust in their Lord (K 16:100). The overall worldview recognizes the existence of evil and, at the same time, proclaims the all-encompassing sovereignty of the Creator. That is, whatever happens, happens only by God's decree, or by his permission within the limits of freedom allowed humans— and Satan. Yet Muhammad insists that God's servants experience liberation "from the shadows of land and sea"; God delivers his servants (slaves) "from every distress" (K 6:63–64). The promise is sure that believers who are faithful to their commitment and do good will somehow make it to the end with faith and inner self essentially unscathed. (This promise is never made in the Koran, however, apart from admonitions that believers are to remain alert, never to presume.)

It is important to recall that Muhammad includes within the

category of "believers" those who are true and consistent believers in the Torah and/or the Gospel. Indeed, included also are all those who have responded with faith and obedience to the Messengers whom God has sent to every people over the course of human history. Thus, if Muhammad states that "those who are with him are hard against the unbelievers, merciful one to another" (a verse of ominous portent if taken out of context!), the statement must be seen as more open-ended than it may sound at first hearing (K 48:29).

The same principle of interpretation needs to be applied, we may briefly repeat, to those relatively numerous passages in the Koran that, taken in isolation, seem to imply an absolute divine determinism in human life and affairs (K 2:6, 9, 137; 6:25, 39; 4:90, 142; cf. Isa. 6:9–10; Matt. 13:14–15). If one hears or reads on, we find that statements that "God leads astray whom he wills" are because of what such persons have earned. It was never God's way to lead a people astray unless he makes clear to them his faith and ethical demands and gives them his guidance. "He leads none astray save the ungodly" (K 9:116; 2:24). Those who do evil are not guided by God in their wrongdoing, nor are disbelievers in their disbelief (K 2:260, 266). If it is said that "God singles out for His mercy whom He will," the statement is immediately followed by assurance that "God is of bounty abounding" (K 2:99). The sovereignty of God is affirmed in principle in the statement that God could have brought all humans into submission to his guidance if he had willed (K 6:35). But he did not, for, Muhammad proclaims, there is no compulsion in religion (K 2:257). (Muhammad, however, did not follow this principle himself in his policy toward fellow Arabs of polytheistic faith, nor did his successors in leadership in satisfactory measure over wider areas and many peoples. Like the history of Christian practices, the Muslim story is mixed.)

But Muhammad seems to see a continuing open-ended possibility for humans to return to their Maker with a decision for submission in faith and obedience. Whether in the context of the people of Israel vis-à-vis their Prophets in ancient times or in the situation of contemporary Arabia, the warnings of God's Messengers are to the end that hearers may respond and escape their due chastisement (K 7:164). Nothing prevents humans from believing—or disbelieving— when the guidance of God comes to them (K 18:53, 28). We have opportunity to repent, believe, and do good perhaps to the very Day of Resurrection— though the price of sin must be paid in the meantime, and doubled on that Day. If people repent, God will change their evil deeds into good deeds—a Koranic mode of divine rectification of human sin and evil in the world! "God is ever All-forgiving, All-compassionate" (K 25:69–71). Specifically, Muhammad does not allow notions of divine determinism to excuse humans from their responsibility to spend of the means that God has given them to feed the poor. Unbelievers are in error to ask why they should feed those whom God, if he willed, would feed (K 36:47). For Muhammad, human choplogic that is but an excuse for moral irresponsibility does not deserve the dignity of a reasoned reply.

The Koranic conception of the sovereignty of God is therefore one of sovereignty sole in principle, open-ended and flexible in practice. The sole sovereignty of God does not constitute a sole working of the divine will, but allows human freedom—with responsibility. Regardless of what later Muslim theology and practice did with the concept, the Koran itself proclaims an openhearted God and an open-ended universe.

The Last Day

Central to the teaching of the Koran, as evidently to the faith experience of Muhammad himself, is a vivid and powerfully expressed concept of the Last Day, one of the terms used in the Koran for its vision of the end of human history and of the present forms of the earth. It is also the Day of Resurrection, a dreadful day for those who disbelieve and do evil, a day of entrance into the joy of their reward for those who believe in God and the Last Day, and do right. Indeed, for Muhammad one definition of authentic religious faith—whether Muslim, Jewish, Christian, or Sabaean—is to believe in God and the Last Day, and to do right (K 2:59).

The awe that so distinctly characterizes Muhammad's sense of God would seem to derive in considerable part from his convictions regarding the judgments of God to be manifested on that Day. And the existential force and clarity of the language with which these convictions are expressed suggest that the origin of these convictions lies, at least in part, in Muhammad's personal inner experiences. This is not the mode of speech of a reflective scholar or rationalistic philosopher.

We may note again that, in the Koran, the judgments of God are seen as working in the personal lives of humans as in the larger corporate forms of society. This process, while ever at work, may be in part deferred—by the permission of God—until the Last Day. In other words, we do not now see the whole picture. This process may appear awesome as it is manifested in human history, but, for Muhammad, the Last Day is supremely "aweful."[13] Statements are repeated of Muhammad's fear of "the chastisement of a dreadful day" if he should rebel against his Lord (K 6:15; 39:15). Indeed, we read that a primary characteristic of all Muslims, as of all who fulfill God's covenant, is to "fear their Lord and dread the evil reckoning" (K 13:19–21; 14:18–20; 39:40; 79:34–40).

This eschatological aspect of religious faith is a central element in Muhammad's preaching, and the fire of his certainty is most graphically seen in his earliest proclamations in Mecca (K 96:7–8, 15–18; 101:1–8; 104:1–4). The fearful aspects of the Last Day loom large in these depictions: painful will be the chastisement of those who disbelieve and scorn the needs of others (K 107:1–6; 101:1–8; 84:20–24). Yet one must not lose sight of the balance that the Koran consistently maintains. Against the horror of the retribution to be visited upon those who have rejected the Almighty and his Messengers is set the bliss of those who have believed and obeyed: "Gardens of Eden, underneath which rivers flow"; God "has procured them radiance and gladness" (K 98:8; 76:11).

And if the goal of the divine purpose toward humanity is to bring them all together on the Day of Resurrection, this proclamation is prefaced by the statement that God has prescribed mercy as his preferred way of dealing with humans (K 6:12). No one is among the "inhabitants of the Blaze" unless a Warner has come to them (K 67:6–9). The very surah that begins with reference to Muhammad's vision of a "Night Journey" (out-of-body experience?) to the temple in Jerusalem—denoted in the text as "the Further Mosque"—emphasizes that God never punishes, in this world or the next, unless a Messenger has been sent beforehand to those he then punishes (K 17:16–17).

The primary orientation of faith in the Koran is therefore eschatological. One central aspect of disbelief is to prefer "the present life over the world to come" (K 16:109). It is the essence of true belief to desire the world to come and to strive for it with all the effort necessary (K 17:20). The Last Abode is truly Life, if persons did but know it (K 29:64).

On that Day, the Lord will come with angels, rank upon rank (K 89:21). There are two references in the Koran to Gog and Magog, the mysterious figures who appear in the Revelation of John, in the New Testament, as personifications of the armies of Satan gathered together to make final assault upon the powers of God and his Christ before their total defeat (Rev. 20:8; cf. Ezek. 38–39). In the Koran, the naming of Gog and Magog similarly seems to suggest a period of heightened evil on earth shortly before the End. There is also reference to God bringing forth a beast of the earth to tell humanity of their failure to believe the divine revelations or signs given them (K 21:96–97; 18:92–99; 27:84–85; cf. Rev. 17:1–14). Otherwise, the emphasis in the Koran is entirely upon the Day itself. The Lord God alone knows the Hour (K 7:187; 33:63; 79:43–44), but it will come upon humanity suddenly, "when they are not aware" (K 7:187; 29:53). It would seem that the time is appointed, and Muhammad evidently believed the time to be near (K 29:4; 53:58). In an early Meccan surah, he proclaimed that "Nearer to thee and nearer" is the Day of Reckoning (K 75:34–35). But then in a later surah from the Medinan period, we note that the qualifying word "haply" (possibly) is attached to a statement that "the Hour is nigh" (K 33:63).

Especially in early Meccan surahs, we find highly metaphorical depictions of large-scale cosmic cataclysms that will occur on the Last Day. On that Day, when "the Terror shall come to pass, and heaven shall be split," we read that the Trumpet is blown with a single blast "and the earth and the mountains are lifted up with a single blow" (K 69:14–15; cf. 1 Thess. 4:16). Heaven will be as molten copper, and the mountains as mobile as tufts of plucked wool (K 70:8–9). The earth and the mountains will quake and the latter become "a slipping heap of sand," a day that will turn grey even children's hair (K 73:14, 17). The moon will be eclipsed and the sun and moon brought together (K 75:8–9).

This is not to be understood as a picture of total destruction, however. The heavens and the earth are seen as abiding, as the Lord wills (K 11:108, 111). Even now God "revives the earth after it was dead" (K 57:17). But the earth and the heavens will be changed into a new relationship with "God, the One, the Omnipotent" (K 14:48–49). On that Day, God is said to roll up heaven as a scroll of writings is rolled up. Just as he made the first creation, he will restore it. At this point, Muhammad quotes the Hebrew Psalms in Arabic form to say that "The earth shall be the inheritance of My righteous servants" (K 21:104–105; cf. Ps. 37:9, 11, 22).

On the Day of Resurrection, God will raise up the dead, they will be returned unto him (K 6:36). In the Koran, the term "life" is used in at least two senses. God first gives life to humans at their birth, but special emphasis is given to the affirmation that God gives (spiritual) life on earth to those who are spiritually dead. He will make people die a physical death and then will give life again, on the Last Day (K 2:26; 6:122). Muhammad emphasizes that "every soul shall taste of [physical] death," even as everyone shall be paid their wages in full on that Day (K 3:182; 39:32; 50:20). We may note that prior to the Last Day, Muhammad imagines that a person at death's door may ask God to return him to this earth that he may right his wrongs, but this is impossible

(K 23:101–102). Likewise, on the Last Day, every nation will be summoned to answer for what is written of its conduct in "its Book" (K 45:28). It would seem that detailed cosmic records are kept of the conduct and being of every person and of every nation (K 10:62–63; 17:14; 83:7–8). The actions of creatures on earth or of birds in the sky are similarly known and recorded (K 6:38; 11:58–59). There is not a thing in heaven and earth but what is known and recorded—even what human hearts would conceal (K 27:76–77; 69:18–29; cf. Matt. 6:6, 10:26; 1 Cor. 4:5).

On the Day of Resurrection—a "hard day" for those who have cried lies to the Messengers of God and followed their own willful ways—all who have died will come forth from their graves, "running with outstretched necks to the Caller." They have been called forth from their state of sleep (K 54:1–9; 36:51–52). We have already noted that God takes into his keeping the souls of humans at the time of their (physical) death during the present order of cosmic time. They are said to be sleeping. But Muhammad seems to suggest that human souls return to God in some mode during their hours of normal sleep even before their physical death (K 39:43). Another passage states that the angels of God receive human souls into their care at the time of physical death, to restore them to God "their Protector, the True" for judgment on that Day (K 6:60–62). We have also noted that believers who were slain while fighting in the cause of God are not to be counted dead but as "rather living with their Lord," well provided for, apparently sufficiently aware to rejoice "in the bounty that God has given them" (K 3:163–165).

Muhammad, however, was not a theological prisoner of his practical or partisan needs. On the Day of Judgment, God will "pluck forth from every party" (or sect) those most hardened in rejection to the All-merciful (K 19:70). In an early Meccan surah, "alive with the confrontation between Muhammad and the lords of the city," as Kenneth Cragg puts it,[14] the primary issue of human life is depicted as a choice between two highways. One is the path of steep ascent, the path of belief that humans have been created by One over them in power, the path of ethical responsibility and strenuous effort thereon. This path leads to acceptance as companions of the Right Hand of God. It involves moral specifics, such as the "freeing of a slave, or giving food upon a day of hunger to an orphan near of kin or a needy man in misery." It is the path of mutual help and moral encouragement. The path that ends in placement as companions of the Left Hand of God, covered by fire, is the way of both disbelief and failure to show mercy (K 90:1–20; cf. Deut. 30:15–20; Matt. 25:31–46). All are given opportunities to choose.

In the longest surah of the Koran, the second in order, we find repeated twice in identical language the statement that on that Day "no soul for another shall give satisfaction, and no intercession shall be accepted from it, nor any counterpoise be taken, neither shall they be helped" (K 2:45, 116).[15] Humans will be judged individually, separately. Neither kindred nor children shall avail on that Day; God shall distinguish one from another (K 60:3). Appeals to God will not help any on that Day (K 23:67, 110). The tidings of God's Messengers formerly heard will be dimmed for the guilty on that Day (K 28:65). No confession of sin will then avail, no friend will help, no intercessor will be heeded (K 40:11–12, 19; 39:55). Upon those who disbelieve and die disbelieving "shall rest the curse of God and the angels" and of other humans. "Never shall they issue from the Fire" (K 2:156, 161–163).

But the dominant flavor of the Koran is adequately savored only if one notes that, immediately following the strong language just cited, Muhammad again proclaims that "Your God is One God; there is no god but He, the All-merciful, the All-Compassionate" (K 2:157). Mercy is God's preferred way of dealing with humans. Muhammad would warn his fellow Arabs of the consequences of human perversity in disbelief and evil conduct, insisting in language that we could call excessive—"God is terrible in chastisement" (K 2:161). He warns repeatedly against following the steps of Satan, who commands persons only toward evil and indecency (K 2:164).

It is of historical and theological significance that Muhammad understood Christian (and Jewish?) teaching to affirm that for some persons there may be only a limited period of stay in the Fire. We do not know the extent of Muhammad's knowledge of this element of Judeo-Christian faith; to my knowledge, nowhere in the Koran does he identify or distinguish by name between Gehenna and Purgatory. But Muhammad's response was clearly and repeatedly that the "inhabitants of the Fire" shall dwell there forever (K 2:73–75; 2:37). And those who believe, and do deeds of righteousness, the inhabitants of Paradise, shall dwell there forever (K 2:76). In Gehenna, persons will neither die nor live (K 20:77).

One passage of the Koran suggests, however, that the period of abiding in Gehenna has a possible termination, as the Lord wills (K 11:109–111). Non-Koranic tradition records that the Prophet once said that "a time will come when hell will be empty, and the cool breezes of God's mercy will blow through it."[16] A contemporary Muslim religious liberal, Zafrulla Khan, derives from Koranic statements of the divine purpose—that God created humans to have mercy on them, to the end that they might serve him (K 11:120–121; 51:56)—the conclusion that all humanity will ultimately accept and participate in the gracious mercy of God, for the divine purpose cannot but be fulfilled in respect of all.[17] The Koran itself, however, is by no means so explicitly hopeful (cf. K 39:55, 59; 42:44–46).

The Koran is graphic, as we have noted, in its descriptions of the Hereafter, of the evil homecoming of the Fire and of the bliss of a great Kingdom (K 2:121; 76:20). The fire is the recompense of God's enemies, who denied the signs that God sent them (K 41:28). Garments of fire shall be cut out for them "and there shall be poured over their heads boiling water whereby whatsoever is in their bellies and their skins shall be melted" (K 22:20–21). They shall be given boiling water to drink such as "tears their bowels asunder" (K 47:17). As often as their skins are consumed in the fire, God will give them fresh skins so that they may continue to experience their chastisement (K 4:59). Angels will take the unbelievers and beat their faces and backs, telling them all the while that the burning is only the consequence of their own doing and that God is never unjust (K 8:53). (Students of the history of religions know of course that language of this kind is to be found among popular evangelists of all the major religions of the world.)

Koranic language concerning Paradise is similarly graphic in its depictions of peace, bliss, and delight. Much is said about the gardens under which rivers flow—language particularly appealing to desert peoples. Believers will be provided with fruits in perfect condition from the gardens, and "purified spouses" (K 2:23). Believers and their wives will in joy be served from platters and cups of gold whatever their souls desire and their eyes delight in (K 43:70–71). Muhammad acknowledges that he is using the language of similitude when he describes the eternal Paradise promised believers. He speaks of gardens abundant with waters that go not stale, rivers of milk, whose flavor never changes. There are also rivers of wine—"a delight to the drinkers"—and rivers of purified honey (K 47:16–17; 77:41–42).[18]

In an early Meccan surah, we read that believers are promised recompense for their patience: a garden and silk garments. They shall experience neither hot sun nor bitter cold, neither weariness nor fatigue (K 35:31). They shall recline upon couches in the shade when they wish; clusters of grapes will be in reach for their plucking. In this passage, the vessels are said to be of silver and the goblets of crystal. Believers will be served by immortal youths, in appearance like "scattered pearls." Believers will be adorned with bracelets of silver. Their silk and brocade garments will be green in color, like the green of garden and pasture, a color subsequently revered in Muslim tradition and found in many of the national flags of predominantly Muslim lands (K 76:11–23).

In the gardens of green, with green pastures and gushing fountains, with palm trees and pomegranates, there will also be *houris* available for believers. These are maidens, cloistered in cool pavilions, "untouched before them by any man or jinn." They are always spoken of as good and comely, as modestly restraining their glances (an ancient ideal, we may note, throughout Asia) (K 55:56, 64–76). And God will wed these "wide-eyed *houris*" to believers (K 52:20; 2:23). It would seem that polygamy will prevail in Paradise as on earth, apparently without limitation to the earthly permitted number of four spouses.

One cannot deny the sensuous aspect of these images, nor that, apart from segments of the Sufi movement, they have been understood as somehow literally true by most Muslims in subsequent Islamic history. In the Koran, however, the whole complex of such imagery is carefully set in the context of ethical goodness, sexual purity, and responsibility. For Muhammad, polygamy always entailed the moral, social, and economic responsibility of husbands for their plural wives, even though divorce was a simpler procedure for males to initiate than was the case in most centuries in predominantly Christian lands. The Koranic imagery of paradisiacal sexuality is of *wedded* bliss. Not only are the *houris* themselves pure, restraining their glances "as if they were hidden pearls," and good (K 37:46–47), but believers themselves are no longer what they were. To be sure, the goodness seen as the inherent quality of Paradise is the reward of goodness (K 55:60). As we have repeatedly noted, believers are persons who do good and believe the Truth. Yet believers are never claimed to be perfect—nor did Muhammad ever claim total moral perfection for himself. Therefore when such believers are welcomed into the gardens and fountains "in peace and security," a further work of God is that God will strip away "all rancor that is in their breasts" (K 15:45–46). Such language would seem to imply a thoroughgoing divine work of interior purification of believers on the Day of Resurrection.[19]

In Paradise, believers will not hear even a whisper of the sighing in Gehenna. A wall shall be set up between the two, with a door on the inward side of which is written mercy and on the outer side chastisement (K 21:100–101; 57:13–14).[20] There is one reference, however, to a believer concerned over the fate of a disbelieving comrade being given permission to look down and see him in the midst of Hell (K 37:50–54; cf. Luke 16:19–31).

Muhammad's perception in an early Meccan surah is that of the two parties of humanity, one in Paradise, one in the Blaze. The numbers in the Gardens of Delight will contain many from ancient times, "how few of the later folk" (K 42:6; 56:14). Perhaps Muhammad changed this view somewhat, as the formal ranges of Islam expanded in the last years of his public life, but we have, to my knowledge, no specific correction thereof in the Koran.

It seems proper to append some further consideration of the teaching on God's judgments, rewards, and punishment in this world. One primary characteristic cited of disbelievers is their loss of the guidance that God would give to obedient believers. God lets them wander blindly in their insolence and error. Koranic anthropology emerges in large measure in passages like this. Humans are seen as originally or natively possessing light, but God takes away their light as the consequence of their purchase of error. Yet, again, we read that fitful flashes of light are given them; they still retain their hearing and sight (K 2:12–18; 28:60–61). They may even be given enjoyment for a while (K 2:121).

In his strenuous efforts to find and hold together the emerging community of faith in Medina, Muhammad emphasizes that those who break covenant with God "after its solemn binding" shall be called losers. He notes also that such persons are those who work corruptly in the land (K 2:24–25). Muhammad draws on his knowledge of Old Testament accounts of how the Hebrew people experienced the burden of God's anger because they did not believe the revealing signs of God and wrongfully slew his Prophets. They experienced both social abasement and material poverty. But Muhammad immediately follows these words with strong affirmation that those who believe in God and the Last Day and do right—whether Jews, Christians, or Sabaeans—shall receive their appropriate reward. "No fear shall be on them, neither shall they sorrow" (K 2:57–59).

In this second surah, the longest in the Koran, we note again and again statements of Muhammad's perception of the tension in the history of Israel between the faithful and the unfaithful, the obedient and the disobedient. Muhammad recognizes unhesitatingly the full religious authenticity of Israel's historic experience of God's "signs," including specifically its Prophets and their messages, most notably Jesus, son of Mary, to whom God gave "the clear signs"—God "confirmed him with the Holy Spirit" (K 2:45, 81, 116). At the same time Muhammad speaks sharply of what he perceives as contemporary Jewish and Christian narrowness, their grudging attitudes toward the possibility that God would share his generosity beyond the boundaries of their own communities of faith (K 2:84, 114).

Indeed, throughout the Koran, Muhammad's faith vision consistently includes a larger range of concern. God never does wrong (K 26:209). His concern, like his judgments, ranges across the whole of humankind (K 17:57, 62).

God's intent was that all whom he created should be god-fearing and serve their Lord with deeds good, just, and merciful. For them, the earth was meant to be a resting place, the sky a canopy, with water and fruits abundant for their sustenance and enjoyment (K 2:19–20). Believers thus already have their reward in significant measure. They—we read in one passage—received life from God when they were dead (K 2:26; cf. Eph. 2:1–2). They may expect security even if they be slain in God's cause. That is, they may expect "the reward of this world and the fairest reward of the world to come" (K 2:120; 3:142; 10:65; cf. Mark 10:29–30). Muhammad repeatedly affirms that the reward of the world to come is the greater reward, but at the same time he deftly works in assurances that God protects and provides for believers, including believing communities, in this world as well (K 16:43). Believers may have to experience various afflictions in life like disbelievers, but throughout the Koran the dominant note is believers' victory in history and in the cosmos. The prevailing pattern is that of divine providence and just judgments at work in this world aimed at the worldly blessing and eternal reward of those who respond with true faith, surrender their self-will, and give obedience to the good will of God. Most significant, amid the working of processes of divine judgment and just judgments, the mercy and forgiveness of God—the generous provision to humanity of opportunities to repent—are seen as making God's universe open-ended. Human history is replete with fresh opportunities (K 3:130–135). The early centuries of Muslim cultural openness were clearly in accord with this spirit of their Prophet.

To return finally to the theme of this section, the Last Day, we may say that, apart from the brief mention of Gog, Magog, and the beast, with possible indication of a period of heightened evil shortly before the end, and the suggestion that the time is near, the Koran does not teach a "salvation history." The Day will come when no one knows, and before it all human distinctions or concepts of history pale. The awesomeness of that Day is in keeping with the awesome majesty of God.

Revelation and Prophecy

This section considers the teaching of the Koran concerning what may be called "salvation history," the whole range of the work of God to reveal himself to humans and to bring them to their appointed destiny, as Muhammad phrases it. Related to this concern is the role of human Prophets or Messengers of God in this work. It has been said that the two central presuppositions of the Judeo-Christian Bible, which are assumed as needing no justification, are the existence of God and the fact of revelation.[21] Precisely the same can be said of the Koran. And central to the methodology of divine revelation to humanity is the use of Messengers or Prophets chosen to communicate his message. The focus of the content of the message in the Koran is more the will of God than his person or nature—although, as we have seen, Muhammad is insistent that God is good and his will is good for all his creation.[22]

An noted previously, in the Koran, two words are used to denote these chosen ones: *nabi*, Prophet, and *rasul* (one who is sent), Apostle or Messenger. Basic to Muhammad's understanding of his own prophethood is his conviction that he is but one of many Messengers whom God has chosen, all worthy of respect and reverence. Muhammad is the Messenger of God to the Arabic-speaking people of his own generation. It is not clear whether he thought of his religious role as extending beyond this people. Muhammad's rigorous opposition to idolatry must not be understood to obscure his frequently repeated affirmations of the authenticity and validity of the many Prophets and Messengers whom God has sent in other times and to other peoples. In a notable passage, Muhammad informed both Christians and Jews (People of the Book) that "We believe in what has been sent down to us, and what has been sent down to you; our God and your God is One, and to Him we have surrendered" (K 29:45). As we shall note, while each people had Messengers sent to them over the course of their history, the term "Prophet" is used in the Koran only for those sent to the "People of the Book" (*Ahl al-Kitab*), that is, Jews, Christians, and Muslims.[23] Jesus is called Prophet once in the Koran apart from reference to others in this tradition, but he is frequently mentioned as Prophet in connection with these others (K 19:30–31). Muhammad also identifies himself as Prophet of his people, but more often his self-designation is as Messenger, even as Jesus is frequently so named (K 7:156, 158).

Humans are said to be originally one nation, one community, and God sent to them his Messengers with both good tidings and warning. God sent down with these Prophets "the Book with the Truth," the Book that gives his criterion of judgment and is intended to be the means for the healing of differences among persons (K 2:209; 4:106). Muhammad evidently thought of Scripture as in some mode preexistent in heaven and perfect "in truthfulness and justice" (K 6:115). Differences in human perception thereof he tended to ascribe to human perversity and insolence. But God guides, and has guided, those who believe to the truth, which is also a straight path of right conduct. All is to the end that humans may "uphold justice" on earth. Significantly, this mode of revelation is linked in one passage with God's revelation of the uses of iron for the welfare of humanity (K 57:25). The reverent possession of Scripture was clearly for Muhammad one essential mark distinguishing authentic monotheistic religion from the polytheism of the recent past of his people. This perception accounts in part for Muhammad's concern to establish his reception of revelation as true Scripture, and to distinguish sharply, at least in theory, between the Koran as Scripture and all else in the Islamic tradition.

In the Koran, the process of divine revelation begins with Adam, who is identified as the Viceroy (*khalifah*) of God on earth. God teaches Adam the names of his creatures, and Adam in turn teaches the names to the angels of God, who, we learn, had demurred at the placement on earth of such a Viceroy. We are told that they were precognitively aware of the corruption and bloodshed that Adam and his descendants would bring to the world. According to the relatively long account in the second surah of the Koran, God determined to proceed with his intent. Not only does he give Adam the names first, but he requires of the angels that they bow to Adam.[24] This the angels did, all except Iblis, who is described as proud, becoming one of the unbelievers after his refusal to obey the divine command. We may note from this incident that belief, for Muhammad, is not primarily cognitive knowledge but submissive obedience. Iblis is identified as Satan and in the text is cited as "causing" Adam and his wife (Eve is not mentioned by name in the Koran) to "slip" from obeying God (K 2:28–38).

Language of this last kind has led some Western interpreters to conclude that the Koran has a relatively trivial view of sin and evil. Other passages belie such interpretation. We note elsewhere both Adam and his wife confessing their wrongdoing and Adam's role therein as specifically involving both disobedience and error (K 7:9–24; 20:114–124). Satan is said to lead the primal couple through delusion, but the wrong is done with conscious human complicity and, in consequence, enmity is set between Satan and humanity to continue until the Last Day (cf. Gen. 3:15).

A central theme, however, that runs through all the Koranic

passages that touch on the creation of humanity and describe their fall is the high dignity accorded humans in the cosmos. This dignity is particularly indicated by their being given divine revelation. And we note that God is said to choose Adam again after his disobedience and error. God "turned again unto him and He guided him" (K 20:119–120). Here is proclamation of compassionate divine initiative toward the restoration of personal relationships and the granting of practical guidance for everyday living. All the pertinent passages communicate this message of divine revelation that becomes practical divine guidance.

Muhammad identifies by name many of those of the People of the Book to whom God gave "the Book, the Judgment, the Prophethood." Abraham is cited as being given God's "argument" (God's ways of thinking, his will) over Abraham's people. Among those divinely raised up to be Prophets and rightly guided are further cited as Isaac and Jacob, Noah beforehand, then "David and Solomon, Job and Joseph, Moses and Aaron." Lest hearers tend to think that such divine election is dissociated from the response of right ethical conduct, the following are specifically cited as doers of good, as of the righteous: Zachariah and John, Jesus and Elias (Elijah), Ishmael and Elisha, Jonah and Lot, and Moses. Muhammad, as is his wont, does not go into the details of the lives of these persons as given in the Bible. His style can be called a sermonically effective broad sweep to emphasize the fact of divine election and the enablement of Prophets before him (K 6:83–93).

Muhammad also cites the names of certain Arabic Prophets who had appeared before him. Little is known of them from other sources than the Koran, but they were evidently names known to his hearers: Hood, Salih, Shuaib. They are said to have delivered their messages in a "clear, Arabic tongue"—messages, Muhammad avers, essentially one in content with that of the Prophets of the biblical tradition. He depicts this content with simple, broad strokes. Muhammad is not a theologian given to fastidious distinctions; he prefers simple, uncluttered, straightforward modes of speech. He identifies the content of the prophetic message as simply a call to turn from the many to the One, to serve the Lord of all Being—and obey his Messenger— unto purity of life, kindness to others, social and economic justice (K 7:63, 71; 11:52–70, 85–98; 26:176–198; 23:51–55; 26:105–109, 125, 131, 144, 150, 162, 179). Historic divisions of peoples into contentious religious sects Muhammad sees as the fault of the hearers of the various Messengers. Muhammad appears to see it his duty to address Arabic-speaking persons and to leave others "in their perplexity for a time" (K 23:56, 65). This last point is in accord with Muhammad's preference for avoiding religious disputes with monotheists, especially with Jews and Christians, since God is the same Lord of all. All have their origin in the creed and conduct of Abraham, a man of pure faith, no idolater (K 2:129–133; 22:66–67).

As we have noted, every nation is given its Messenger in the providence of God to the end that their peoples should serve him and give up the worship of idols (K 10:48; 16:38). Muhammad sees God as sending a succession of Messengers to humanity (K 23:46, 32; 25:40; 28:45–46) and, in every case, the people cried "lies" to the Messengers of God. The expression "cried lies" occurs frequently in this context to denote popular rejection of divinely sent Prophets both within and without the Judeo-Christian tradition and very likely reveals Muhammad's personal experience, especially at Mecca. Muhammad believed, we should note, that no other Warner had been sent in his own generation to the people of Mecca (K 32:3; 28:46).

Muhammad declares that it is God's self-imposed duty to deliver or liberate both his Messengers and believers in their situations of existential need in this world (K 10:103; 11:61, 69, 97). As we have seen, this promise is not absolute; persons may die suddenly in pursuing the cause of God, especially in battle. But Muhammad's primary religious intent, it would seem, is to direct believers toward a lively hope and expectation. This is always to look for help from God, with the sure knowledge that if all does not work out as hoped for now, there will be perfect compensation in the Hereafter. The Prophets of God experience persecution, but God again and again delivers them and fellow believers. The persecutors will meet an evil end both in this world and in the Hereafter (K 26:119, 138, 158, 170–172, 185–189). These concepts were held already in the Meccan period, but in Medina the conviction emerged with new focus that God will give Muhammad—and believers—victory in this world and in the Hereafter (K 22:15). We may note that this conviction is aligned, in the present text, with warning against those, probably in Medina, who profess to worship the one God and yet stand on the edge of full faith and commitment. When blessed with good fortune, they are content, but when trial befalls them, they turn away. They lose both "this world and the world to come" (K 22:11–13).

By far, the greater number of references in the Koran are to the Prophets who appear in the Judeo-Christian Scriptures, which, we learn, God revealed in the form of Torah (*Taurat*) and Gospel (*Injil*) as moral and spiritual guidance for the people (K 3:2–4).[25] Muhammad repeatedly states that God made a covenant with the people of Israel—and later with those who call themselves Christians. The call to covenant relationship was so that the Children of Israel should serve only the one God, they should "be good to parents, and the near kinsman, and to orphans, and to the needy; and speak good to men [the scope is universal], and perform the prayer, and pay the alms" (K 2:60, 77–78; 5:15–19). We note that continuance of covenant relationship is always conditioned; the covenant of God does not extend to evildoers (K 2:117). It is clear from these and other passages that Muhammad's perception of the content of the divine revelation given to the Children of Israel, to Noah, Abraham, Moses, and the later Prophets, is essentially the same as his own perception of divine revelation. That is to say, we find the content essentially the same as his own message, drawn with the same broad but incisive strokes. Muhammad's primary concern is not to repeat historic texts, which he probably did not know in their original form, but to affirm that he himself shares the same call, the same covenant and message. His is a theological affirmation: God is one, his character and his revelation are the same in every age, to every people. The Messengers of God are expected to proclaim essentially the same message. Muhammad was not interested in theological niceties beyond the unity of God and his call to goodness, with remembrance of the Last Day.

A few more things must be said at this point, for the references to the Children of Israel in the Koran are many and important. The affirmation is that God gave them many a clear sign; indeed, God preferred Israel above all beings (K 2:207, 44, 116; 44:30). In this preference, they were provided with many good things: "the Book, the Judgment and the Prophethood" (K 45:15). Muhammad quotes Moses as saying to his people how God had given to them "such as He had not given to any being" (K 5:24). We note several references to the liberation of the Children of Israel from the people and Pharaoh of Egypt, God's repeated pardoning and reviving of Israel under the leadership of Moses, feeding them with manna and quails (K 2:44–54). This divine preference for Israel, however, while not discussed theologically in the Koran, is clearly set in the context not only of conditioned election and covenant, but also of "preference for a time" in the economy of divine providence. As we shall see, there are also sharply critical statements made in the Koran of Jews and Christians both for their historical disobedience and present spiritual arrogance (K 5:21, 2:76).

With reference to Muhammad's self-identification with the Judeo-Christian prophetic stream, we note a significant reference to Noah in two Meccan surahs. The faith, message, and prophetic experiences of Noah are described in terms similar to Muhammad's own. Noah was among the Messengers of God, one who had put his trust in God, one of those who had surrendered to him (K 10:71–74). The political council of Noah's people complain of his pretensions to prophethood, saying that he is only a mortal like themselves, that only the most abject and unreflecting in their community follow him. Noah has therefore no right to claim superiority over them. Noah's response is that he has been given a clear sign from his Lord, and mercy. If the leaders refuse his message, he asks, how could he compel them to accept it. Noah pleads with them, saying he asks for no material compensation from them. He looks only to God for reward, and he [Noah] "will not drive away those who believe." His motivation to speak is his awareness that an ignorant people will have to meet their Lord, a motivation that is a compulsion, his responsibility before God. Noah calls on the people to "remember," language indicative of Muhammad's perceptions. Basic to authentic religious conversion is for humans to remember—reflect upon—what they are: The creation of the Lord of the Worlds, blessed in innumerable ways and in generous measure from the time of their birth. They are called to surrender, but not to Noah. For Noah disclaims unusual knowledge of the Unseen; he does not possess the treasuries of God. He is no angel. This is all in all a portrayal of Muhammad in Mecca, as of Noah in his supposed time and place (K 11:28–51).

Abraham, however, is much more a figure of primary significance for Muhammad. The religion of Abraham is portrayed in the Koran as the foundation of all subsequent monotheism, and in a special way for the People of the Book, both Jews and Christians. A straight line leads to Islam, as well. Muhammad affirms connections of Abraham and his son Ishmael by the Egyptian maid Hagar with the city of Mecca (cf. Gen. 16:1–16). Abraham and Ishmael are said to have built the Ka'bah in Mecca, which under Muhammad's leadership is to be "a place of visitation for the people, and a sanctuary." The prayer of Abraham and Ishmael to the All-hearing, the All-knowing, the All-compassionate, the All-mighty, the All-wise God is that they themselves be submissive, they and the nation of their seed (K 2:117–124). It is stated that some descendants of Abraham have lived on in Mecca to the present time. Perhaps Muhammad thought of the Hanifs as having their origins in this physical posterity of Abraham (K 14:40–41). Throughout the long surah of "The Cow," which contains all the essential elements of Koranic teaching and has been described as the Koran in miniature, assertion is frequently made that the religion of Abraham is the only true religion. This religion consists in belief that God is one—Abraham "was no idolater"—and in the surrender of human will and purpose unto obedience thereto (K 2:125–129).

To Jews and Christians, who call others to become part of their institutions as if such were a condition for receiving true divine guidance, Muhammad is instructed to say that Muslims adhere to the religion of Abraham, "a man of pure faith." This declaration of institutional and cultural—although not spiritual—independence from the historic monotheistic traditions that preceded Muhammad is immediately followed by affirmation that Muslims believe in the same God as Jews and Christians, even as they believe in what has been revealed to themselves [in the Koran]. But Muslims also believe in that which was revealed to Abraham, Ishmael, Isaac, Jacob, and the Tribes, and that which was given to Moses, Jesus, and the Prophets of their Lord; "we make no division between any of them, and to Him we surrender" (K 2:130–134; cf. 2:285–186). I note later, however, that elsewhere Muhammad does make distinctions of consequence among some of the Prophets before him, supremely in the case of Jesus the Messiah (K 2:253–254). Muhammad further asks his hearers whether the modern sectarian names of Jews or Christians with their divisive rivalries can be appropriately applied to the ancient worthies to whom all monotheists look for their human sources or intermediaries. The Muslims, Muhammad avers, are "a midmost nation," persons to serve as mediating, reconciling witnesses to their own [Arabic-speaking] people, even as he himself is the Messenger of God and a witness to them (K 2:137).

Muhammad also assigns a very high place to Moses. The word of God to him is said to be: "Moses, I have chosen thee above all men for My Messages and My Utterance." God himself is alleged to have written on the Tablets of the Law all the admonitions and distinctions of right and wrong needed by the Children of Israel, a veritable light and reminder (K 7:141–142; 2:50; 21:48–49; cf. Deut. 34:10–12). Muhammad insists that nothing has been revealed to him except what was said to the Messengers before him (K 41:41–43; cf. 28:49). They all draw from the same "Book Sublime." Hence God is alleged to appeal to the Children of Israel—whom God had preferred above all beings—to believe in that which is now being "sent down" through Muhammad, for it confirms "that which is with you." The Jews of Medina are asked to bow their heads in worship with the Muslims who bow with like faith and intent. They are asked to join in the giving of alms to the needy, and the needs of the emerging state. Indeed, there is a hint in the passage that the Jews in Medina are not as zealous in their practical piety as the Muslims (K 2:38–44, 81–83, 116; 87:17). Muhammad is evidently aware, at least in outline, of the Jewish scriptural accounts of the long history of the people's disobedience, as of the recent history of Jew fighting Jew as allies of feuding Arab tribes in Medina (K 2:85; 5:74, 82; cf. Acts 7:51–53). Such is the context for Muhammad's asking Jewish hearers how is it that they invite others to worship and right living while they do not truly practice the same (K 2:41–42; cf. Rom. 2:21–23).

In a lengthy passage in the fifth surah, entitled "The Table," Muhammad appeals to the People of the Book to perform, to practice, the Torah and the Gospel, indeed, all that has been revealed to them, or suffer untoward consequences both in this world and on the Last Day (K 5:45–90; cf. 62:5). Muhammad's teaching is consistently that there is not true religion without righteous and compassionate conduct. Those of humanity who stand closest to Abraham are those who have followed him in their conduct as in faith. Such are the ones whom God protects, and among such, Muhammad insists, are himself and his people, the Muslims (K 3:60 ff).

God sent a train of Messengers to follow Moses, persons who received revelations from God, Messengers bearing good tidings and warning (K 2:81; 4:161–163). The story of the human responses, whether Jewish or Christian, is often cited as a history of hardened hearts, rebelliousness, and disobedience. And yet Muhammad is directed to "pardon them and forgive." Both the Children of Israel and Christians are told that "they have forgotten a portion of that they were reminded of," that there are many things that they have been concealing of the Book, "and effacing many things." This is precisely the point at which Muhammad proclaims to the People of the Book that an authentic Messenger from God has come to them, as to the Arabs, now in their own time, namely in his own person. He is one who is "making clear" many things that Jews and Christians have been concealing or effacing, or have forgotten. Muhammad is bold enough to assert that he has brought a light from God (K 5:17–18; 14:1; cf. Acts 26:18; Col. 1:13).

Views of Scripture

A final word in this chapter may be in order with regard to the teaching of the Koran on the theme of Scripture. This necessarily brief account, however, may not adequately convey the frequency with which the term "Scripture" is used in the Koran nor the importance which the concept had in the faith and thought of Muhammad. Part of the profound respect that Muhammad had for Scripture may be due to the general respect for the written word in the relatively unlettered state of Arabia of his time. More significant, however, was his perception that the monotheistic religions whose origins he believed to lie in authentic Messengers of God particularly revered and boasted of their Scripture. He evidently felt that authentic religion must be primarily based on Scripture.

The perceptions that Muhammad received, in what evidently was for him a recognizably altered mode of consciousness, he came to identify—with the help, as we have seen, of the evaluations of his wife, Khadijah, and certain others of the Hanif—as authentic revelations from the One God, Creator, and Lord of the Worlds. He distinguished these revelations from thoughts or judgments that he believed to originate in his own mind, and came to consider them authentic Scripture, "a sending down from the Lord of all Being" (K 56:79). In an early Meccan surah, Muhammad speaks of God's sovereign role in putting together on the plane of human experience Scripture that is already composed in the heavens (K 75:16–19). That is, these revelations given in divinely guided process over the whole course of Muhammad's prophetic ministry are claimed to be God's recitations and explanations to Muhammad of a Book already fully written, "a hidden Book." This is evidently the noble Book hidden in the mind of God that "none but the purified may touch, a sending down from the Lord of all Being" (K 56:76–79). In one of the earliest of Meccan surahs, we read that this is a "glorious" Koran, "in a guarded tablet" (K 85:21).[26] The term *al-Koran* means recitation of the Speech of God that is already written in the heavens.

Muhammad believed that this Book had been given in an authentic way to both Jews and Christians, and to Jesus were also given "clear signs" from God. He was convinced, however, that a party of their tradition had knowingly tampered with the Scripture sent down through Moses and subsequent Messengers. Some of the common people do not know the content of Scripture and share with each other "only fancies and mere conjectures." Muhammad strongly criticized those who themselves write and sell what they call Scripture, saying, "This is from God." Not all that is purported to be Scripture is actually so. His major complaint against Jews, however, was that they did not obey the divine injunctions given them. Against both Jews and Christians, his complaint was that they do not believe the Book from God that he is sending them through Muhammad. For this Koran confirms—so Muhammad insists—what Jews and Christians already have in hand (K 2:70–86).

The Book is affirmed to be guidance for the god-fearing. Divine guidance, practical guidance in the affairs of daily life, is a major theme in the faith and teaching of Muhammad. Even the jinn say they believe in the Koran that they have heard, a wonderful Book that is a guide to right living (K 2:2; 46:28–29; 72:3). Muhammad states that God's revelations began with his words to Adam, and the language in this passage and elsewhere implies that God gives revelation and guidance in some measure to all persons (K 2:35–36). Muhammad's claim, amidst disbelief and rejections from pagans in Mecca and Jews in Medina, was that the people of Israel had rejected Moses' words as sorcery, and continue to do so (K 28:48–49). Perhaps this charge of Jewish unfaithfulness refers primarily to their rejection of Muhammad's Message, for he continues to insist that his Word confirms that which was before it, a "guiding to the truth and to a straight path" (K 46:12, 29).

I have already discussed in some detail Muhammad's initial experience of what he came to perceive as divine revelation. This is the clear Book sent down "in a blessed night" upon the heart of Muhammad by the angel Gabriel—by the leave of God. Such revelations, however, are to continue; we read in a Meccan surah that God is ever sending, ever warning, as a mercy and good tidings from the Lord (K 44:2–5; 2:92). The Koran was therefore revealed through a process of divine division, at proper intervals, that the Prophet might recite it to his fellow Arabs at intervals. Muhammad was told not to try to hasten the process until the whole had been completed (K 20:113; 17:7–8). As noted previously, the Jews in Medina evidently asked Muhammad at one time as a portent to bring down from heaven an actual Book in parchment form. His reply was that if they had been able to touch such with their hands, they would consider it no more than "manifest sorcery." When these "unbelievers" further asked why God had not sent down an angel to give authority to the person and Message of Muhammad, Muhammad's reply was that such an overwhelming presence would determine the matter, allowing no room for free human response. Such divine determinism in the cosmos would also leave no respite for humans, no freedom to believe, turn, repent, obey, and be in their Lord's care until the Day of Judgment and beyond. In short, Muhammad is saying that God's use of human Messengers, however frail or unimpressive they may appear, is the best way for the sake of humans themselves (K 4:1:152; 6:7–8).

As noted, Muhammad did not himself write down the revelations given him. Believers did this, and the final collection(s) was made after his death. He believed that writing these down himself would create occasion for doubt. For Muhammad, the process was primarily from Heart to heart, from Mind to mind (K 29:47–48; 80:11–15). Yet the writing down, the creating of Scripture, was of very great importance to him.

This interplay between personal revelation and written Scripture, whereby the first cannot but lead to the second, is one of the primary characteristics of Muhammad's prophetic ministry. All is from God, or by God's leave, but the written Scripture that is in process of emerging looms ever larger in religious importance as the years pass. Muhammad has a strong conviction—as a Word from God—of the uniqueness of the Koran. He asks his critics to bring something like it from their side. It is not something that could be created apart from God (K 2:21; 10:38–39). This is Scripture indeed, sublime, wise, a decisive word, no joke (K 43:3; 86:11–14). This Word is somehow also "Remembrance" for those who hear it; there is that in every person's soul that resonates, in some kind of recall, to the content of this Message.

Muhammad insists in the face of disbelief that this Book sublime is without falsehood, no different in content from what had been revealed to the Messengers who had preceded him, a guidance and a healing for those who believe, the fairest discourse (K 41:41–44; 39:23–24).[27] This is the blessed Book that persons who think may ponder and thus recollect their Maker and his ways (K 38:28; 39:13). It is clear testimony from the Lord, "guidance and mercy for a people of believers," healing to believers, evidently a loss to unbelievers (K 7:203; 17:84). This is Scripture "wherein is no doubt" (K 2:2). There is nothing external that prevents persons from believing when divine guidance comes to them, nothing really except that such unbelief has been common among humanity from ancient times (K 18:53).

One final point may be mentioned again in this context. The principle of the abrogation of divine revelations has been applied historically in Islam generally to the abrogation of one verse of the Koran by another, to commands rather than narratives.[28] The key passage is found in the lengthy surah of "The Cow": "And for whatever verse We [God] abrogate or cast into oblivion, we bring a better or the like of it; knowest thou not that God is powerful over everything?" (K 2:100). Another passage states, after affirmation that every period of human history has a Book from God, "God blots out, and He establishes whatsoever He will; and with Him is the Essence of the Book" (K 13:39).

This principle of the abrogation of divine revelations—seen as a revelatory procedure initiated by God himself—suggests a certain freedom on Muhammad's part from legalistic or overly rigid fixation with verbal precision or even accuracy. This is particularly the case as we note association of the principle with awareness of "the Essence" of Divine Communication, as may be distinguished from details. The presence of this principle, I believe, gives further credence to what I have contended is a characteristic of Muhammad's style in the Koran: open-endedness and flexibility.

Jesus the Messiah, the Son of Mary

I noted in the previous section that Muhammad proclaimed on one occasion that there is no distinction to be made among the many Messengers of God sent to the various peoples of the world over the course of human history (K 4:149–150). The statement would seem to refer primarily to the authenticity of their role as mediators of God's revelations and to the essential content of their messages. Elsewhere, however, we read that God has "preferred" some above others. Moses, for instance, is said to have been chosen above all humanity as the Spokesman of God's Messages and Utterance (K 17:57; 9:141). But the language of divine preference in the Koran is especially reserved for Jesus, who is most often identified as the Messiah—a term not precisely defined—and as the son of Mary.

In "The Cow" surah, we find a clear focus of Muhammad's understanding of this theme of divine preference. After affirming the particularity of God's providential care and instruction in the case of David, Muhammad goes on to insist that God is "bounteous to all beings." Then there is further identification of the fact of God raising some Messengers above others in rank. Muhammad proclaims Jesus, son of Mary, as the one to whom God gave "the clear signs" and confirmed with the Holy Spirit (K 2:81, 252–254). In another passage, Jesus is said to be a Spirit from God—language not used in the Koran of any other Messenger of God (K 4:168–169).

In the angelic annunciation to Mary, which we find also reported in the Koran, she is told that Jesus, "whose name is Messiah," is indeed a Word from God himself. He shall be high honored in this world and the next, "near stationed to God," a reference to Jesus' living presence with God in heaven in this period before the Last Day (cf. Acts 7:55).

This is also one of the passages wherein it seems that Muhammad accepts as authentic certain stories about Jesus found only in apocryphal New Testament gospels. In this case, the reference is to what has come to be called the "Arabic Infancy Gospel." An older English translation is as follows: "The following accounts we found in the book of Joseph the high-priest, called by some Caiaphas: He relates, that Jesus spoke even when he was in the cradle, and said to his mother: Mary, I am Jesus the Son of God, that word which thou didst bring forth according to the declaration of the angel Gabriel to thee, and my father hath sent me for the salvation of the world."[29] Muhammad's statement is that in the annunciation to Mary the angels further say of Jesus, "He shall speak to men in the cradle, and of age, and righteous he shall be" (K 3:40–44; 5:109–111; 19:30–31).

In the same Koranic passage, Muhammad cites as a revelation from God an incident found in the apocryphal "Infancy Story of Thomas," wherein Jesus as a five-year-old boy makes some soft clay and forms 12 sparrows from the clay. He claps his hands and cries to the birds to fly off. This they do, chirping as they fly.[30] Of greater historical and theological significance is the fact that Muhammad here fully acknowledges Jesus being given by God the power to "heal the blind and the leper, and bring to life the dead." The significance of this acknowledgment is heightened by the fact that Muhammad himself never claimed the power to perform such miracles. His role—in itself a wondrous miracle—was to communicate the Book Sublime that "could not have been forged apart from God" (K 2:21:10:38–39).

The fact that Muhammad appears to have drawn—briefly and, as it were, incidentally—from so-called New Testament Apocrypha does not alter the fact that his chief sources on the human level would seem to be oral versions of the canonical Jewish and Christian Scriptures that circulated in the Arabian peninsula in varying length and degrees of faithfulness from before his time.[31] The point to be stressed is the high religious, indeed theological, view of Jesus the Messiah that Muhammad gives in the various proclamations contained in the Koran.

The angels proclaim to Mary that God has chosen and purified her and has indeed chosen her "above all women." She was a just woman (K 3:38; 5:79). The Koran forthrightly affirms the virgin birth of Jesus and, in a Meccan surah, states that God "breathed into her of Our Spirit," at least in part as a consequence of her guarding her virginity. Mary became "one of the obedient" (K 3:42; 66:12; 19:16–20; 21:92). The birth of the child in her is said to be by divine creation and decree. The birth of the Messiah is described as occurring beside the trunk of a date-palm tree, by whose dates "fresh and ripe she was nourished" (K 19:23–26). Muhammad strongly rejects traditional Jewish criticisms of Mary's and of early Christian claims of her virginity in the event of Jesus' birth. He speaks of these criticisms as "a mighty calumny" (K 4:155; 19:29).

The angelic proclamations to Mary regarding her son to be born are thus that he shall be highly honored in this world and the next, and shall be close to God and righteous. He will be taught by God himself, taught "the Book, the Wisdom, the Torah, the Gospel," to become a Messenger to the Children of Israel.[32] He will confirm the truth of the Torah that preceded him, and yet will make lawful certain things previously forbidden. Muhammad hereby shows his awareness that Jesus identified and emphasized the best of his own Hebrew tradition, bypassing or rejecting what is not worthy of that best (cf. Matt. 5:21–48; Mark 12:28–34).

The Koranic passage then seems to move into a changed setting, wherein Jesus is depicted as an adult addressing his fellow Jews and, in particular, his own disciples. He asks them to fear God and also obey himself. Such appeal, we may recall, was also a part of Muhammad's call to his own hearers, especially in Medina. Muhammad's meaning may perhaps be best discerned from language used in the latter part of this passage, where Jesus' appeal is for persons to become his "helpers unto God." The Apostles are cited as responding, "we will be helpers of God" (K 3:40–46).

Both Mary and her son are said to have been divinely appointed as a sign for all beings (K 21:92). Jesus is specifically identified in another Meccan surah as a sign appointed by God for all humanity, even as he constitutes an act of mercy from God (K 19:21). He is a pattern, an example, for the Children of Israel (K 43:59). Jesus is described in another (apparently Medinan) surah as being the climactic figure in the series of Messengers sent by God to humanity out of which will emerge on the plane of human history the divinely appointed Prophecy and Book. Muhammad comments in the passage, almost incidentally, that among the Jews "some of them are guided, and many of them are ungodly." Jesus is the one to whom God gives the Gospel. At this point, Muhammad gives one of the strongest statements in appreciation of Christians to be found in the entire Koran. He cites God himself as affirming that he "set in the hearts of those who followed him [Jesus] tenderness and mercy" (K 57:26–27).

In this same passage, however, we find Muhammad insisting that monasticism is a Christian invention not prescribed by God. He acknowledges that the real intent of Christian believers in the institution of monasticism was to seek the pleasure of God, but their mode of observance of the institution was "not as it should be observed," probably an objection to their practice of celibacy. And in spite of the praise of Christians cited in the previous paragraph—perhaps emphasis is to be placed more on the gifting acts of God than on the responses of the receivers—Muhammad observes, again almost incidentally, that "many [Christians] are ungodly." In the concluding section, Muhammad turns to his own hearers and appeals to them to fear God and believe in his present Messenger to them: They will be given light to walk aright and forgiveness. After this proclamation of God's open door before the peoples of Arabia—God is All-forgiving, All-compassionate—Muhammad asserts in no uncertain terms that the People of the Book (Jews or Christians) are not in control of the bounty of God. The boundaries of his generosity remain in his hands (K 57:25–29). As to the prophetic authenticity of Muhammad, we note in another passage that Jesus himself is cited as giving good tidings of a Messenger who will come after him, "whose name shall be Ahmad" (K 61:6–7).[33]

We turn now to consider specific criticisms that we find in the Koran of what had become the mainstream of orthodox Christian Christology. Muhammad emphasizes that Jesus, even as the Messiah, the Word of God committed to Mary and a Spirit from God, was only the Messenger of God. "The Messiah will not disdain to be a servant of God," even as the angels stationed near to God do not disdain to be considered his servants. The Arabic word for servant here (*abd*) specifically means "slave," and the context was that of a slave-holding society. But from the passage, the meaning of the term is clearly that of subordination both obedient and dignified. The contrast is with rejection of the call to service of God, waxing proud before the Creator of all (K 4:168–171; 5:76–79). We are not to forget the common Muslim understanding of being in bondage to God as that which liberates from all other servitudes.[34]

Muhammad specifically emphasizes that the heart of his message is that God is One and not "the Third of Three." The word God is also not to be assigned to the Messiah, Mary's son. "It is not for God to take a son"; "God is only One God" (K 19:36; 4:168). In the lengthy passage in surah 5 that begins with God directly addressing Jesus, son of Mary, God asks Jesus when did he (Jesus) say to his contemporaries that they should take him and his mother to be gods, apart from God.[35] Jesus' response to God is given as "To Thee be glory! It is not mine to say what I have not right to. If I indeed said it, Thou knowest it, knowing what is within my soul, and I know not what is within Thy soul; Thou knowest the things unseen. I only said to them what Thou didst command me: 'Serve God, my Lord and your Lord'" (K 5:116–117; cf. John 5:30; 7:16; 8:28; 20:17). Muhammad then asserts that the association of aught else in the universe with God specifically warrants the punishment of God. "They are unbelievers who say, 'God is the Third of Three.' No God is there but One." Muhammad appeals to such persons to "turn to God and pray His forgiveness" for "God is All forgiving, All compassionate." Muhammad believes that he is divinely directed to say to the People of the Book that they "go not beyond the bounds in your religion" (K 5:77–79; 4:168).[36] It appears from a number of statements in the Koran that Muhammad thought both Jews and Christians were presumptuous in some of their religious claims, in particular their setting of boundaries regarding the ultimate salvation of persons in advance of the Last Day.

Perhaps the most controversial passage in the Koran regarding the person and life of Jesus is Muhammad's rejection in the fourth surah of the truth of the Jewish claim—the language implies a "claim"—that they "slew the Messiah, Jesus son of Mary, the Messenger of God." Muhammad's immediate retort to this "claim" is "yet they did not slay him, neither crucified him, only a likeness of that was shown to them . . . and they slew him not, of a certainty—no indeed; God raised him up to Him; God is All-mighty, All-wise." Muhammad goes on to insist that not a single Christian (here designated as the People of the Book) will disbelieve in Jesus according to this interpretation before he himself (the Christian believer) dies. And such persons will be witnesses against the Jewish claim in the Resurrection Day (K 4:155–157).

This passage has led many—including probably the great majority of Muslim interpreters—to believe that Muhammad is denying the physical reality of the crucifixion and affirming a mode of ascension (by the help of God) in place of the resurrection.[37] Many Western interpreters have surmised that Muhammad drew on Docetic or other Gnostic Christian teachings to come to this conclusion. It is not clear to what extent such variations of Christian faith were known in Arabia at the time of Muhammad, although his awareness of certain elements of apocryphal New Testament writings suggests that Muhammad was aware of a wide range of Christian views. Nevertheless, the passage does not really say that Jesus did not die on the cross. In fact, other passages in the Koran seem to indicate Muhammad's belief that Jesus indeed did die, including a specific affirmation allegedly made by Jesus to "the day I die, and the day I am raised up alive" (K 19:34). Another statement is as from God himself, speaking to Jesus of the event to come: "Jesus, I will take thee to Me, and will raise thee to Me, and I will purify thee of those who believe not" (K 3:48).

A modern Muslim scholar, Abd al-Tafuhum, interprets the whole range of these Koranic verses as affirming the death of Jesus upon the cross.[38] We must recall that the traditional Muslim understanding has been that Jesus, as the righteous servant of God, could not experience the defeat at human hands implied by such an ignominious death. But in the Koranic passages we have no denial of Jesus' physical death, but only a denial of the "claim" of Jews that they did it. The Koranic affirmation is rather that only God can kill the Messiah, in accord with "his mysterious purposes"; humans do not have the power (K 5:19–20). Elsewhere, after the victory of the Medinans at the battle of Badr in 624, Muhammad reminds his followers that it was in the deepest sense not their victory but God's. "You did not slay them, but God slew them" (K 8:17). This affirmation of the divine role at work behind human activity—a doctrine that was to become a highly significant element of historic Islamic faith—is evidently the key to proper understanding of the passage that we are considering (K 4:155–157). The Koran does not deny that the Jews desired to kill Jesus (although it was Roman soldiery who carried out the deed). Indeed, several passages in the Koran refer to historical Jewish mistreatment and even killing of their own Prophets (K 3:180; 4:154; cf. Matt. 23:37). But the Koranic affirmation is that God was behind and in sovereign control of the human event, even though not in such a way as to remove the human hand and will in the process.

This would seem to lead to the further conclusion that rather than ascension, a resurrection of Jesus by divine power is affirmed. We have noted several passages in the Koran that use precisely this language of God raising Jesus to himself (K 3:48; 4:156; 19:34). Thus even though the mainstream of Islamic tradition has believed that Jesus was carried away by God to heaven in his body of flesh, there to remain with God until the Day of Resurrection, the Koran does not precisely say this. To be sure, Muhammad, like the first Christian martyr Stephen or John Calvin (cf. Acts 7:55), believed that Jesus is now alive with God in heaven, as we learn from traditional accounts recorded in Ibn Ishaq's *The Life of Muhammad*.[39]

Some readers may object to this as too thin a basis for overturning centuries of Islamic interpretation. But the basis in the Koran for the traditional view is even thinner, and the interpretation here suggested has the merit of drawing the two great streams of Christian and Muslim prophetic understanding into closer harmony. Such theological and practical cooperation was certainly the devout desire of Muhammad's heart (cf. K 3:56). Whether we understand the Koranic affirmation to be of the ascension of Jesus or of his resurrection by the will and power of God, the intent of Muhammad's message is clearly to proclaim divine action at work in his Messenger Jesus the Messiah.

The Koranic views of Jesus the Messiah are thus exalted, but they never ascribe to Jesus the status of deity. There is never a tendency to displace God with Jesus as the Supreme Object of religious devotion. We have already noted the insistence that God knows what is in the soul of the Messiah, and not vice versa. It is God who knows the things unseen; the Messiah speaks only what he has been commanded (K 5:116–117; cf. Mark 13:32; John 7:16, 8:28). Yet there is guidance and light in the Gospel that God has given Jesus, son of Mary, and an admonition to the god-fearing. Muhammad asks the People of the Gospel to judge according to what God has "sent down" to them in the form of the Gospel (K 5:50–51).[40] "The likeness of Jesus, in God's sight, is as Adam's likeness." Like Adam, we are told, Jesus was created of dust. God simply said "'Be,' and he was" (K 3:52). Jesus the Messiah is thus affirmed to be of the created order, like other humans, or angels. But the God who raises Jesus to himself also sets his followers "above the unbelievers till the Resurrection Day" (K 3:48). The Koran says, in effect, that the spread of Christianity in the world is the result of God's strengthening of Jewish believers. We may recall that the Apostles of Jesus are cited, as those who respond to Jesus' call to be his helpers unto God. Their actual response is "We will be helpers of God." The enemy is presumably Jews who did not believe in Jesus as sent by God (K 61:14).

A credible item from tradition reports that when Muhammad entered the city of Mecca in triumph in the year 630, a fresco of Jesus and Mary was among others visible on the walls of the Ka'bah. He ordered all the paintings to be expunged except this one. This painting, it is said, was seen by an eyewitness as late as 683 C.E., when much of the Ka'bah was destroyed by fire and with it the painting.[41]

Most of what has been quoted from the Koran thus far comes from the Medinan period when Muhammad apparently for the first time came into contact with substantial and organized Jewish tribes or communities. Until the last years of his life, he had little or no comparable contact with Christians in organized community, and these were in relatively distant locations. This may be an important reason for the relatively more friendly attitude toward Christians than toward Jews generally found in the Koran. The people most hostile toward believers (Muslims) are said to be Jews and the idolaters, while "the nearest of them in love to the believers are those who say, 'We are Christians.'" This is because "they wax not proud," and "some of them are priests and monks" (K 5:85–86).[42] One primary concern of Muhammad in Medina, however, was the relationship of his own prophetic status, and the whole movement of which he was leader, to the historic Peoples of the Book. In Medina, these peoples were primarily represented by Jews, and it was evidently a surprise to Muhammad that most of these Jews refused to accept him as an authentic Prophet of God. Only a few Jews are said to have believed in Muhammad in this sense (K 4:49). Muhammad's assertion of Jesus as Messiah, as we have seen, only further alienated most Jews in Medina.

Muhammad's surprise, it seems, came because he fully acknowledges the divine validity of the historic monotheistic faiths that preceded him, although primarily in other parts of the world. Had God willed, we read in the Koran, he could have made one nation of all humanity, but God has allowed the present situation to try persons. And rather than dispute with one another, all should vie with one another in good works. (I may properly add that our contemporary world needs to hear and heed this advice for interreligious relationships.) All persons and peoples shall return to God, and he will tell all on That Day of the points at which they were at variance on earth. It has been God's way to appoint "a right way and an open road" for all humans, as to hearers in Arabia now. God chooses to bring to himself "whomsoever He will," but this process in its working is that "God guides to Himself whoever turns, penitent." God "accepts repentance from His servants and pardons evil deeds." Whereas the Jews have allegedly said, "God's hand is fettered" (again referring to what Muhammad sees as Jewish and Christian tendencies to limit the range of God's compassion to themselves and those who follow them in their institutions), Muhammad forthrightly asserts, "Nay, but His hands are outspread; He expends as He will" (K 5:52–54, 59, 72–73; 42:6, 11–12). Muhammad proclaims that "Surely they that believe, and those of Jewry, and the Sabaeans, and those Christians, whoever believes in God and the Last Day, and works righteousness—no fear shall be on them, neither shall they sorrow" (K 5:73). Muhammad's repeated appeal to the Peoples of the Book is that they "perform the Torah and the Gospel," and do the works of righteousness without which faith is not valid (K 5:70–73; 42:11; cf. James 2:17, 26).

Muhammad's word to the Peoples of the Book is that he has come also to them as a bearer of good news and a warning, as an authentic Messenger of God, one come after "an interval between the Messengers." This statement is made, in the Koranic passage, immediately after Muhammad's reproof of both Jews and Christians for claims (apparently understood by Muhammad as implying personal superiority and a favored status with God) that they are "the sons of God, and His beloved ones." Muhammad's response is first that their own history shows flawed action and God's chastisement. They are reminded of their common mortality, and that to God belongs all that is in the kingdom of the heavens and of the earth. The promised return of all to God on That Day implies, the text seems to suggest, that all in the created order share a basic commonality (K 5:15–23).[43]

Muhammad insists, using words allegedly from God, that his is no new message. It is no different from what came to their fathers of old. He himself is no "innovation" among the Messengers of God (K 23:70; 46:8). Therefore Muhammad makes his appeal to all: "Come now to what God has sent down, and the Messenger" (K 4:64). He evidently found it difficult to understand or justify the failure to respond on the part of those who from their background of faith and worship should have been the first to acknowledge the authenticity of his prophethood. Those to whom God had given revelations in the past should recognize this revelation given to Muhammad as they recognize their own sons (K 6:20).

As Westerners at the present stage of our historical development, we may wish to say that Muhammad was sociologically and psychologically naive to expect openness and warm acceptance from the Jewish tribes in Medina. From his own point of view, he is a charismatic Prophet like the Prophets of Israel's past, open-ended and pragmatic but simple in his language as he describes the essence of the tradition, not hesitating to give reproof and warning and promises of God's mercy and forgiveness. He tells Jews and Christians that they have broken the covenants that God made with them and that "they have forgotten a portion of that they were reminded of." He claims to make clear many things that Jews and Christians have presumably been concealing out of the Book. On the other hand, Muhammad asserts that through him a light from God has come, "and a Book Manifest whereby God guides whosoever follows His good pleasure in the ways of peace, and brings them forth from the shadows into the light by His leave; and He guides them to a straight path" (K 5:15–19).

Such language of sharp reproof, such claims of being the channel of direct revelation from God, even to the extent of correcting the Jewish (and Christian) tradition as generally known and publicly acknowledged, must have seemed to the Jews of Medina spiritually presumptuous to the highest degree. To be sure, Muhammad's message was not far different from the style and tone of their own Prophets in their time and setting. But the Jews of Medina did not live in that time and setting. All seemed to acknowledge that there had been an "interval between the Messengers." They were not, therefore, accustomed to be addressed by such persons. They depended upon the written Scriptures, of which the Jews in Medina must have possessed copies. Charles Le Gai Eaton, a contemporary Muslim of European background, informs us that Semitic peoples tend to be "legalistic by nature, and a certain literal-mindedness is characteristic of the Muslim."[44] Most Semites of the time of Muhammad evidently did not have a mentality open to revisions of the sacred text. But then, given our own long histories of at times slavish cleavage to the written word and related traditions, it would seem that neither Jew, nor Christian, nor Muslim has the right unduly to fault the Jews of Medina for their apparently excessive adherence to their own text, theology, and ways of worship.

Muhammad was, to repeat, a charismatic Prophet whose faith and religious experience gave him, he believed, the freedom and authority to function in the open-ended and pragmatic way characteristic of Hebrew Prophets vis-à-vis the religious, political, and cultural Establishment of their times. This way, we may suggest, is not entirely different in principle from modern historical criticism by devout believers. But to the Jews of Medina, Muhammad was not one of their own, and they were not accustomed to receiving Messengers of God critical of their tradition from one of *any* background, their own or others'.

In Mecca, Muhammad had had long experience of rejection of his message, but from polytheistic idolaters. He saw no rosy path for the Prophets of God. Indeed, he believed that every Prophet had a divinely appointed adversary—"Satans of men and jinn" (K 6:112). He recognized that Messengers of God before him were charged as liars and persecuted even as he, and had patiently endured these hurts until the help of God came to them (K 6:33). In Medina, the People of the Book, almost all of Jewish faith, like the Meccans, apparently asked Muhammad to produce miracles confirming his authenticity, such as bringing down a Book from heaven (K 4:152). His reply is actually multifaceted. For one thing, he reminds the Jews that their ancestors had asked Moses for a greater sign and were punished for their presumption (and later pardoned) (K 4:152–153). Muhammad repeatedly places the whole issue in the providence of God, affirming that had God willed, he could bring all to faith and send down whatever sign he wished. Muhammad is instructed, however, to give serious reply only to those who are open to hear (K 6:35–39). But the essence of Muhammad's reply is that the Koran itself—the divine revelation given through Muhammad—is a wondrous miracle, the like of which is surely not to be produced otherwise in his time. It is "a healing and a mercy to the believers" (K 2:21; 17:84; 21:107).

When no appreciable response was forthcoming from the Jews in Medina, Muhammad began to think along other lines. In a late Medinan surah, possibly the eighth or ninth year after the migration (*Hijrah*) to Medina, Muhammad reminds Muslim believers that the people of the Book have no power or control over the limits of God's bounty. It is in his hands; he gives it to whomever he wills. "And God is of bounty abounding" (K 57:29). Muhammad asks if these people of the Book are jealous of others in the wider ranges of humanity "for the bounty that God has given them." He becomes clearly angry when he perceives that the Jewish community in Medina seems to approve of the religious position of pagan "unbelievers" (and presumably also to support their partisan political stance) in preference to Muslims. Muhammad contends, rightly or wrongly, that the Jews, to whom God had given "a share of the Book," themselves believe in demons and idols (K 4:47–57).[45] And in this context of assertion that while some Jews are believers, "the most of them are ungodly," Muhammad begins to see the Muslims as the best community ever raised up by God in human history (K 3:106). Furthermore, he now affirms the divine victory of Islam on earth. He proclaims that God and his Messengers will assuredly be victorious, that the people who believe are the prosperous ones (K 58:21–24). God has sent his Messenger "with the guidance and the religion of truth" to the end that he [Muhammad] "may uplift it [Islam] above every religion" (K 61:9).

This atmosphere of partisan contention had, of course, both political and theological consequences. As we have seen in our consideration of the life of Muhammad, the political process ended in the complete victory of the Muslims and the total ousting of the Jews from the area. Theologically, the consequence was sharp criticism of alleged Jewish affirmations that Ezra is the Son of God and of Christian statements that the Messiah is the Son of God. Muhammad considers such confessions the perversion of proper faith in the One God and prays that God himself fight against them. He also claims that Jews and Christians have regarded their rabbis and monks as Lords without due subservience to God. Once again, Muhammad proclaims that there is no God but One, and all are "commanded to serve but One God" (K 9:30–31). And yet, in spite of all this acrimony, there is in the

Koran not a single word critical of Jesus himself, of Jesus the Messiah, the son of Mary, the Word of God, the Bearer of God's Spirit.

I should add at this point that, while Muhammad was clearly aware of the major activities and events of the public ministry of Jesus, he was apparently unaware of the richness and depth of the detailed teaching of Jesus as recorded in the Four Gospels of the New Testament. Muhammad, however, evidently believed that the content of Jesus' teaching (so far as he knew it) was both noble and true and that it was not only like his own message, but really the same.

A further item needs to be mentioned: Muhammad's understanding that God may abrogate, or cause to be superseded, previous revelations, and bring "a better or the like of it." Readers may recall the turmoil caused by the publication in 1989 (in the United States by Viking Press) of Salman Rushdie's book *The Satanic Verses* with reference to these passages. For Muhammad, such alteration lies within the prerogative of God's free and universal sovereignty (K 2:100–102; 16:102–104). Such divine freedom, to be sure, has occasioned not a little difficulty for Muslim interpreters over the centuries. This was especially so in the context of emerging belief in the Koran as the inerrantly inspired Word of God. In particular, the celebrated Verse of the Sword: "slay the idolaters wherever you find them" (K 9:5) is said to have canceled 124 verses that enjoined toleration and patience.

If, however, one is not bound by a doctrine of literal inspiration, this last statement, which is qualified in its immediate context by the direction to let "the idolaters" go if they repent, comes to be seen as less harsh in its particular historical situation. The time is probably the year 630 C.E., and the verse indicates an ultimate sanction against polytheistic idolaters in Arabia. The larger context is the emerging end of idolatry in all Arabia, and the message, or parts thereof, was evidently intended to be brought to Mecca and read to the people in public. This surah is the only one in the entire Koran that does not begin with the words "In the name of God (Allah), the Merciful, the Compassionate." Such omission may have seemed appropriate given the severe commandments against idolaters contained in this surah. But the time and situation suggest that such commandments had probably no need to be carried out.[46]

A final word at this point. Mahmoud Mustafa Ayoub, a Muslim professor of Islamic studies resident in the United States, has pointed out an important distinction in terms used in the original Arabic of the Koran. This has to do with Muhammad's objections to Christians calling Jesus the Son of God. There are two words in the Arabic of the Koran that are used to signify a filial relationship: *ibn* and *walad*. "*Ibn* ('son'), which is used only once in the Koran in relation to Jesus, may be understood metaphorically to mean son through a relationship of love or adoption (K 9:30). The term *walad*, on the other hand, means 'offspring' and thus primarily signifies physical generation and sonship." Professor Ayoub contends that the Koran "does not use the term *walad* to refer to Jesus. That is to say, the Koran nowhere accuses Christians of calling Jesus the *walad* offspring of God." If Ayoub is correct, it may be possible to conclude that Muhammad objected to Christian usage of the term Son of God primarily because it could too easily be misunderstood as implying the kind of sexual intercourse that he had heard of among pagan deities.[47]

It thus appears that Muhammad, and many later Muslim commentators, had the spiritual discernment and intellectual sophistication to perceive that the term "Son of God" was generally understood by Christians metaphorically as a relationship quite other than that produced by physical generation. But even in the allegedly single passage in the Koran where the Arabic *ibn* is used to denote Christian belief in Jesus' divine sonship, Muhammad—the text does not say that God (Allah) so proclaims!—is sharply critical. Muhammad was a radical monotheist.

Koranic Views of Humanity

The Koranic views of the nature, existence, and destiny of humanity are rooted in the conviction that God first created humans as bearers of a special dignity. The Koranic word is that "Surely We created man of a clay of mud moulded," whereas the jinn were created earlier "of fire flaming." Yet into the mud, once shaped, God breathed his Spirit, and God commanded the angels to bow before this human being. The angels in fact did so, all except Satan (Iblis), who is thereupon banished from the presence of God, but with a certain respite or conditioned freedom to work his will in the cosmos until the Last Day (K 15:26–42).

In what is perhaps the earliest surah in the entire Koran, the proclamation is that God "created Man of a blood-clot" (K 96:1–2).[48] In a later Meccan surah, the statement is made that God subsequently gave humanity "hearing, and sight, and hearts," all in the context of affirmation that the All-mighty, the All-compassionate "has created all things well"—and yet humans show little thanks (K 32:5–8). It would seem from another Meccan surah that Muhammad thought of the whole of divine creation in its initial form and quality as quite without any imperfection or flaw (K 67:3–4). In a later Medinan surah, however, in the context of statements of principles and rules regarding relations between the human sexes, we note the statement that "man was created a weakling" (K 4:32). This acknowledgment of human weakness with regard to control of sexual desire seems to be the one Koranic gesture in the direction of Augustinian so-called original sin.[49] In a very early Meccan surah, we find the proclamation that humanity was created "in the fairest stature," but then reduced to "the lowest of the low," except for "those who believe and do righteous deeds" (K 95:4–5). Affirmation here of humanity's original high stature does not, however, constitute a theological statement of likeness to God. In the Koran, there is nothing that may be compared to God (K 42:9; cf. Gen. 1:27; 5:1).

The reduction of humans to "the lowest of the low" seems, in the larger Koranic context, to be the consequence of human freedom and willfulness (K 5:54). In the face of the glory and majesty of God, the integrity of his creation, the generosity of his provisions for human usage, Muhammad evidently found disobedience and evil among humans a mystery and puzzle to marvel at (K 16:1–34). We have noted that, at times, Muhammad uses language that seems to deny secondary causation, as if the events of life are all the consequence of divine doing. Thus, in an early Meccan surah, we note the statement that humanity was created fretful (in Kenneth Cragg's translation: "with a restless anxiety"):[50]

> Surely man was created fretful,
> when evil visits him, impatient,
> when good visits him, grudging,
> save those that pray
> and continue in their prayers,
> those in whose wealth is a right known
> for the beggar and the outcast,
> who confirm the Day of Doom
> and go in fear of the chastisement of their Lord
> (from their Lord's chastisement none feels secure)
> (K 70:19–28).

This passage—which could also be considered an early expression of Muhammad's faith and ethics—in its first portion seems to ascribe responsibility for human ethical deficiencies to the Creator. The second portion stresses vitally important present exceptions, similar to what I noted previously in that "those who believe and do righteous deeds" are not to be counted among the "lowest of the low." Muhammad's view of humanity's ethical conduct as a whole was clearly not high; frequently repeated is the statement that many persons are evildoers. But such is the result of their turning their backs on their Maker, and "God desires only to smite them for some sin they have committed" (K 5:54). Koranic statements that, in brief, appear to indicate an absolute determinism in the operation of divine sovereignty do not give us the true thrust of Muhammad's faith and teaching. Exceptions and qualifications to statements apparently absolute in themselves appear almost at once in the text. Muhammad was concerned about proclaiming the sovereignty of God as unqualified *in potentia*, but *in actu*, God gives humans both freedom and responsibility.

The Koranic perception of human nature and existence may be summed up by saying that whereas the divine creation of all was originally good, the present existential situation of most of humanity is highly inadequate, to say the least. The paradox is that whereas human origin in God's intent and making was glorious, humanity in its present course of experiences is generally not of high quality. Perhaps both themes may be subsumed in the affirmation that God created humankind with the end of having mercy on them (K 11:120–121). As we have seen, the exceptions to the perceived general deterioration are "those who believe and do righteous deeds." These have accepted the mercy of God, have opened themselves to his work, so that (as taught by the long line of divine Messengers) they surrender to the will of God, and do it. Muhammad did not hesitate to identify by name examples in previous history of those—Jewish, Christian, and others— who strove to do the revealed will of God. In particular, he had great hopes for the community of Muslims in Mecca and Medina for whom he was divinely guided Messenger and later political leader. But Muhammad does not want to give the impression that even for him the whole reality of the present human condition is entirely clear. Realms of mystery remain. In "The Cow" surah, we note that before the creation of humans, the angels are said to be told by God that he intends to set a Viceroy (*khalifah*) of himself on earth, a statement elsewhere expressed by the affirmation that humans are given dominion over the rest of creation on earth. This affirms the high dignity assigned in the Koran to the original nature of humanity.

But the angels, with their foreknowledge, question God as to the wisdom of setting upon the earth "one who will do corruption there, and shed blood, while We proclaim Thy praise and call Thee Holy?" The answer of the Lord was: "Assuredly I know that you know not" (K 2:28; 35:36).

In many a passage, the Koran continues to affirm the paradoxical nature of the present human condition. Humanity was created severally as God's Viceroys on earth, given authority and the structured means to gain their livelihood (K 6:165; 7:1–34). But men and women rarely give thanks. In an eloquent passage, Muhammad describes how all things in the heavens and on earth were created to be subject and of service to humans, and God gives them all they ask of him. The blessings of God are innumerable. And yet "man is sinful, unthankful" (K 14:37–38; 31:18; 67:15). Even Muslims should not think of themselves as totally purified (K 53:34). Humans give little thanks for the wonders of their own physical and mental endowments. Indeed, they are said to be ever unthankful. Yet God "preferred them greatly" over many of the elements of his creation (K 23:80; 17:69, 72). No human being, however, is of itself immortal (K 30:19; 39:32).

I have noted statements that humanity was originally one community.[51] Muhammad affirms an ongoing solidarity of humankind. Muhammad states that in God's prohibition of willful murder to the children of Israel, the underlying principle is that killing another is as if one had slain all humankind. And whoever saves the life of one person in some way saves the life of all (K 5:35). The differing human languages and skin colors are portions and signs of God's creation. All persons share in the rhythms of life night and day, and among the signs of divine creation is the universally shared human quest for God's bounty. Yearning for the Divine seems to be part of every person's endowment and heritage (K 30:21–22).[52]

Muhammad also affirms divine process at work in the distinctions of rank in human societies, distinctions made for the testing of persons, for which each is to be held accountable (K 6:165). God has preferred some persons over others in provision of material goods. In these passages, we find not only statement of the divine origin of differences in wealth, but also a similar basis for distinctions between slave and free (K 16:73; 30:28).[53] Furthermore, we note the statement—evidently made with reference particularly to those Muslims who felt compelled to emigrate to

Ethiopia during the period of the Meccan ministry—that "Those who believe, and have emigrated, and have struggled in the way of God with their possessions and their selves are mightier in rank [spiritual?] with God; and those—they are the triumphant" (K 9:20). Muhammad also affirms that those Muslims who fought and spent of their possessions before the conquest of Mecca (i.e., during the hard years in both Mecca and Medina) are greater in rank than those who spent and fought afterward (K 57:11).

Against the Koranic affirmation of human solidarity must be placed the statements that each person shall ultimately give account precisely as they have labored, and that no one bears the load of another on the Day of Reckoning (K 53:40; 17:73). The Koran contains no doctrine of atonement. But the mercy of God and the open-endedness of human opportunities to believe and repent under God are stressed in almost every surah. Even in passages that stress the sovereignty of God in terms as strong as they are eloquent, Muhammad perceives humans as free and responsible. He insists that nothing within or without prevents humans from believing and seeking their Lord's forgiveness when the divine guidance comes to them. And such guidance, it appears, comes to all (K 91:1–10; 18:52). Humans have been granted a life long enough to "remember" and, to all persons, the Messengers of God, even as warners, have come (K 35:34).

The freedom of humans therefore does not mean that humans have been left to their own devices. I have noted the many references to inspired Prophets who came before Muhammad (K 12:108). But God works from within to expand human hearts that they may surrender and walk in a light from Him. Their hearts are softened to the remembrance (*dhikr*) of God (K 39:19–24). The remembrance of God, as we are informed by Kenneth Cragg, is "at once a title of the Koran and a vital element in Muslim religious practice."[54] The consequence is a kind of divine-human cooperation based on divine initiative. Muhammad is told that not only is God his Protector, but so also are the angel Gabriel and the righteous among the believers. The angels are specifically cited as his supporters (K 66:4). The end is a mutuality in divine-human relationship. Even as there is continued divine communication to humanity, so there should be appropriate human response in both prayer and work—or rejection. Human life is perceived in the Koran as properly a life of labor unto the Lord, who is both Goal and Rewarder. All shall encounter him on the Last Day (K 84:1–14; 53:40–44). Therefore the deepest meaning of human life, following upon faith and surrender to the Lord of the Worlds, lies in the practice of the religious life: "Prosperous is he who has cleansed himself, and mentions the Name of his Lord, and prays." For Muhammad, purification included purifying the soul, the inner self, and bodily extremities. It included the giving of one's wealth and accepting no bribes, and "seeking the Face of his Lord Most High" (K 87:14–15; 11:9–10; 92:17–20).

Muhammad's view of evil in human life and in the cosmos was not superficial. As noted previously, we do not find in the Koran a doctrine of original sin, but the present condition of some is seen as involving sickness in the heart, and hardness. Indeed, Muhammad recognizes that Satan tempts even every authentic Messenger or Prophet of God. The passage, in A. J. Arberry's translation, seems to suggest Muhammad's awareness that there may be a certain human "fancying" on the part of the Prophet in the midst of an otherwise faithful rendition of authentic divine revelation. Muhammad sees Satan as playing a role in distorting this human fancying and, at the same time, God works to annul that which Satan has cast into the mind of his Messenger.[55] It would seem that a far wider range of humanity experiences this "fancying," which constitutes especially severe trials for those whose hearts are hard—and sick. But the guidance of God is ever along a straight path (K 22:51–53). The worldview implied is that the cosmos is an arena where divine and demonic forces contend, and humans are tempted in their freedom. They may be grievously wounded and diseased as a result of their own choosing and consequent roles, but God is ever merciful and a straight guide to those who humble their hearts before him.

The Koranic picture, in sum, is that most people are ungrateful, even manifest adversaries of God. Humankind is "the most disputatious of things"; most persons lack knowledge. When God lets them taste mercy, they rejoice in it, but if some evil happens to them as a consequence of their own doing, they despair, because they do not perceive the hand of God in the process (K 16:4; 18:32; 12:68; 30:35). And yet, as we have seen, Muhammad had great hope for the community of Muslims whom he was nurturing, even in the midst of contention. He had no serious doubts of the rightness of his own role as Messenger of God, nor did he question the truth of his message. And we must recall that Muhammad's prophetic and political career in the final years at Medina manifests an almost unparalleled "success story." The Muslims in Medina and elsewhere shared in this "victory" in ways both external and internal. But the Muslims were intrinsically more the followers of God than of Muhammad. Something was happening in Arabia of far more consequence for human history and the cosmos than most contemporaries were aware. On this basis, we may begin to understand the astonishing energy and scope of Muslim expansion—and interiorization—in the years following the death of Muhammad.

The Position and Role of Women in the Koran

The Koran teaches that before God the ethical obligations of women and men are the same. God's treatment of them is the same. In a mid-Medinan surah, Muhammad stresses the obligations common to both men and women, namely, faith, obedience—to God *and* his Messenger—speaking the truth. He emphasizes the divine call to both women and men to be patient in endurance, generous in almsgiving, faithful in fasting, pure in their sexual relationship—to be "men and women who remember God oft." For such, God has prepared both "forgiveness and a mighty wage" (K 33:30–36). Without distinction of male or female, God will grant the means to live a goodly life, inner and outer, for whoever "does a righteous deed." Each shall receive recompense, a wage "according to the best of what they did" (K 16:99).

According to a very early Meccan surah, God created the male and female (K 92:4). Indeed, God created "all the pairs of what the earth produces," a reason to give glory to God (K 36:36). Muhammad suggests that God has placed "much good" in women (K 4:23). Nevertheless, even where Muhammad states that women have rights of honor that all are obligated to acknowledge as their divinely set due, he claims that men have been put "a degree above" women. In another passage, Muhammad states as a fact of life that men are "managers of the affairs of women," for the reason apparently that God has been more generous toward men in his bounty (in all categories?) and the latter have given of their financial means for the care of women. In this context, hearers are assured that a proper response of religiously righteous women is to be obedient, presumably also to their husbands. In fact, the passage goes on to state that husbands may admonish, banish to beds apart, and even beat their wives if they "fear" that their wives "may be rebellious" (K 2:228; 4:38).

We may properly recall, however, that both surahs in which these last statements are contained were composed in the Medinan period, that is, a number of years after the death of Muhammad's first wife, Khadijah. One wonders if statements of the superiority of men over women in any way could have been made by Muhammad during the lifetime of Khadijah. In fact, there is no evidence in or out of the Koran that they were. Muhammad owed his relative financial security to Khadijah's means and probably also to her continuing mercantile activity after their marriage. (His commitment to the prophetic call and an intensely disciplined religious life of prayer and proclamation, teaching and pastoral care would have left him little time for the oversight of Khadijah's presumed ongoing mercantile activity.) Theirs was evidently a highly successful achievement in distinct but cooperative and mutually respectful roles.

In the next section, on Muhammad's views of pagans, I note

the relatively low position of women cited as characteristic in pre-Islamic Arabia. I also note Muhammad's sharp criticism and vigorous rejection of the relatively common practice of burying unwanted female babies alive. He insists that persons who slay their children do so "in folly, without knowledge" of God's right guidance. Such persons work against God, they have gone astray from his will, and are losers in God's process of compensation (K 16:60–61; 6:137, 141). Muhammad insisted on the equal spiritual status of women before God and came to establish their legal rights in various ways.[56]

In Medina, Muhammad emphasized that men's relationships to women, including sexual access within the bounds of God's will, are in the context of their obligation to send good before them for their own welfare on the Last Day. They must fear God and know that they will meet their Maker then (K 2:220–223). Women, however, should have legal control, according to the Koran, of the dowries that their husbands pay at the time of marriage. They may inherit property that they receive as their proper share (K 4:3, 9).[57] A wife's word may be accepted against a husband's accusation if he has no witnesses (K 24:6–9). We note that in the case of known and proven fornication, both man and woman shall receive one hundred lashes—"let no tenderness for them seize you" (K 24:2).

If a woman fears ill-treatment from her husband, it is not wrong for the two to try to set things right between them. That is, a wife can initiate efforts at personal reconciliation. But historically, this passage (K 4:127–128) has not been interpreted by Muslims to mean that a wife can initiate proceedings for divorce. (In the twentieth century, it became possible for a woman to sue for divorce upon certain grounds in Egypt, Lebanon, and several non-Arabic-speaking Muslim lands.[58] The situation, however, has become more problematic in recent years, in large part because of the rise of more conservative forms of Islam.)

We have seen that Muhammad himself lived in an entirely monogamous marriage with Khadijah until her death after 26 years. The formal permission to Muslims to marry up to four wives was granted in the surah on Women, proclaimed in the fourth year at Medina, after the battle of Uhud. This was the battle in which a considerable number of Muslims were killed and provision had to be made for the widows and orphans of the fallen. Muhammad, with the full weight of Arab practice behind him, advised plural marriage as the best way to make provision for these needy persons. This provision was recommended on the condition that the husband treat his wives with full equality and justice. Otherwise, he should confine himself to one. He could also, it would seem, marry one or more of the slave girls whom he legally owned (K 4:3).

Actually, Muhammad acknowledges that Muslims will not be able to deal with perfect equality among their wives, however much they may wish to do so. But they must not differentiate so grievously among them as to leave any of them in uncertainty of mind (K 4:128–129).[59] Muhammad himself was dealing with a situation of concrete need, and he evidently had in mind a working arrangement that was possible and practicable.

Divorce is permitted in the Koran, in the context of faith and hope: faith that God is All-hearing, All-knowing; hope in that reconciliation is the preferred way. The language of the Koran at one point states that if a couple should separate, God will provide for the material needs of each (K 4:129). But the longer discourse on divorce in the surah of "The Cow" clearly states that it is the duty of a husband to make "honourable provision" for the material needs of a divorced wife, the affluent according to his means, the needy man according to his (K 2:226–241).[60]

The language in this passage just cited, as in other passages in the Koran, is consistently that of the husband's taking the initiative in the pronouncement of divorce, although there is no statement in this passage (nor in any other in the Koran, that I know of) that explicitly denies a wife's right to initiate divorce proceedings. There are, nevertheless, various regulations to temper this custom. Husbands must wait four months, keeping themselves sexually apart from their wives, before they may divorce them (K 2:226; 65:4). This rule is to ensure that no woman be divorced while pregnant by her husband. The verbal statement of the husband, twice pronounced (according to the Koran [K 2:228–229], but Muslim practice generally requires three successive declarations, at a month's interval, to make divorce irrevocable[61]), is sufficient for the action to be legal. During this time period, however, since the husband is free to change his mind, the wife may be retained in honor—or "released in kindness." But if the process is fully completed, the husband may not remarry his divorced wife until she has married another man and been divorced from him.[62] Islamic tradition, we should note, records that Muhammad said that of all things divinely "permitted," the most obnoxious in the sight of God is divorce.[63] Muhammad himself did not divorce any of his wives.

We read in a mid-Meccan surah that God created spouses for humans that they may "repose in them," and God set between them love and mercy. These are signs for a people who reflect (K 30:20). With these words, Muhammad unequivocally proclaimed marriage to be an institution of divine ordinance, necessarily constituting a spiritual and physical relationship. Tradition records that Muhammad said that the married state is the Muslim way and that he who deliberately turns away from this path is "not of us."[64] We have already noted Muhammad's conviction that the Christian institution of monasticism, in spite of his personal admiration for many monks, is not of God.

The sexual aspect of marriage was approved by, and important for, Muhammad and is specifically cited in the Koran as under divine approval. But in language that may not be pleasing to modern ears, Muhammad states that the women to whom male Muslims are permitted sexual access (i.e., wives legally married and female slaves legally owned) are their "tillage" (fields) to plough, and Muslim men may go to their tillage as they wish. But this permission is immediately followed by the admonition that such is part of the spiritual pilgrimage of every (male) soul. All is to be done in the context of proper Muslim fear of God, with awareness that every man will one day meet his God to give account of himself and his life (K 2:223). No mention is made in this passage of the female role (in personal awareness or spiritual consciousness) in the process of "tillage." Nevertheless, Muhammad clearly regarded the sexual relationship of men and women as bearing the most solemn ethical responsibilities before God. It was, however, the ethical responsibilities of males that he particularly stressed.

In "The Cow," permission is granted to men to go in to their wives (and/or female slaves) on the nights of the month-long fast of Ramadan (i.e., after sundown). Intercourse is forbidden from sunrise to sundown during this period.[65] This statement is immediately followed by the affirmation that wives are a vestment (protection, comfort, ornament) for their husbands, and the husbands are the same for their wives. The ideal, indeed the command of God, is a relationship of intimate and mutually responsible helpfulness (K 2:183).

There are statements in the Koran that reveal Muhammad's (and allegedly God's) concern for the sexual satisfaction and emotional contentment of wives. The context is the presumably God-given right of the husband to choose to whom of his wives and slaves he should go this night or that. The point is that the husband is to be concerned with a fair balance in such choices, to the end that "every one of them will be well-pleased with what thou givest her" (K 33:51). There is no hint, however, that the wives have a right to choose or take initiative in this matter. Men are not to go in to their women during their menstruation period; this is a time of pain for the women (K 2:222). Mothers are permitted to suckle their children for two whole years if they wish, or they may give the responsibility to a wet nurse if they prefer. During this period, it is the responsibility of the father to provide "honourably" for the physical care of the mother (K 2:233).

The principle governing the marital relationship—the most solemn of all human social compacts under God—was thus profoundly spiritual and physical and involved mutual responsibilities. The Prophet was uncompromisingly strict in his injunctions to preserve the purity of the relationship by confinement of sexual relations to the parameters being set down. As we have seen, men must preserve their chastity save with their wives and the female slaves whom they legally own (K 70:29–30). In a mid-Medinan surah, injunction is given that if anyone (a male) on coming to marriageable age is not able to afford marriage, he should live in continence until God gives him the means to marry (K 24:33). That females should live in continence before marriage goes without saying. In the Koran, any premarital sexual relationship is forbidden.

Adultery is forbidden as both socially indecent and an evil way before God (K 17:34; 25: 68–69). Anyone who commits adultery (or premarital fornication, by implication), whether man or woman, shall be scourged with a hundred lashes, as stated previously (K 24:2–3; 4:19–20). It is important to note that the man who commits adultery is considered as guilty as the woman. Muhammad thus took his stand in conformity with the Pentateuchal command in Leviticus 20:10, unlike "the scribes and Pharisees" who, in the passage in John 8:1–11, brought forth only the woman to be considered for punishment.[66] The way is left open, however, in these passages for the guilty to "repent thereafter and make amends." The presumption is clear as to their forgiveness and acceptance by God upon their fulfillment of these conditions, including the punishment. But in the Muslim community, a guilty fornicator shall marry none but a "fornicatress or an idolatress," the same stricture to apply to a woman found guilty (K 24:2–3).[67]

Any sexual relationship outside the structures permitted is considered indecent or lewd and is strictly forbidden. A point revealing something of Muhammad's spirit is the directive that if female slaves, once married, should be guilty of indecency, they should suffer only half the penalty inflicted upon free adulteresses (K 4:30). Incidentally, we read that it is Satan who entices persons into indecency, as, in the long run, his way leads to poverty (K 2:271). We should note again in this context that, for Muhammad, indecency involved both inner and outer aspects. He was always concerned for the whole person and never remained content with outward conformities (K 6:152).

Homosexuality is consistently decried in the Koran as wanton evil (K 7:79; 26:165; 27:56). All three of these citations are probably from the Meccan period, the latter two from a middle or even earlier time, indicative of Muhammad's perceptions from an early period of his prophethood. Tradition relates that Muhammad cursed men who act like women and women who act like men and ordered Muslims to drive them from their houses. He is said to have expelled such persons from the community. The second caliph (successor in the leadership of the Islamic community), Umar, a father-in-law of Muhammad, is recorded to have followed the same policy.[68]

The historic Islamic custom of the seclusion of women has its origin in a brief passage of the Koran wherein permission is granted to the Prophet's wives to be seen unveiled only by their fathers, their sons, brothers, brothers' sons, or by the sons of their sisters, or by the sons of their female servants or slaves. The presumption is that they are not to be seen by any other males, except of course their husbands. Mention is made in this passage of the possibility of believers being invited to the houses of the Prophet for a meal, apparently the only occasion when such permission to enter is given. As a specific precaution against believers' presumption—evidently a real temptation for some believers in the relatively open-ended ways of Muhammad's lifetime—persons receiving invitations are told not to come too early! Guests are told that if they should ask the Prophet's wives for any object, they should ask them from behind a curtain separating them. In a larger social context, prescription is given, as from God himself, for the wives and daughters of the Prophet, as for all believing women, to draw veils about their faces when they go outside their homes (K 33:53, 55, 59).

Muhammad evidently enjoined these practices as a result of his concern lest women be molested in the rough conditions of Arabic social life of his time, with the weight of pre-Islamic customs and attitudes still a powerful hindrance to his policies of reform. He evidently did not foresee the extent of personal restrictions that his prescriptions in this matter would bring upon generations of Muslim women in the centuries to come. One important factor in subsequent developments was indeed the partial reemergence of pre-Islamic Arab practices that caused a lowering of the tone of respect for women, beginning almost immediately after the Prophet's death.

Muhammad clearly did not envisage an overweening dominance of men over women. His 26 years of married life with Khadijah—or in fact the accounts of his later multiple marriages—give no indication of such an attitude or practice. For him, consistent practice of authentic religious faith was primary, and obedience in faith to God took precedence over all human relationships or ties. In a Meccan surah, he cites, as an example for believers to follow, the wife of Pharaoh who prayed God to build her a house in Paradise and to deliver her from Pharaoh and his work, and from the evildoers of her people. Mary, the mother of Jesus, is likewise singled out as praiseworthy for her chastity, faith, and obedience. In light of the discourse herein, it is significant that Muhammad seems to identify Mary's keeping of her virginity as the primary reason for God's breathing his Spirit into her. She thereby confirmed the "words of God" as recorded in the Scriptures ("His Books," K 66:11–12).

Views of Pagans

As noted, the prophetic career of Muhammad is particularly identified with two cities, Mecca and Medina. We also noted sharp differences developed in his public role and in the nature of his religious and political opposition in the two cities. We considered the Koranic views of Jews and Christians because they constitute major issues of the content of the Book, as of Muhammad's years in Medina. These issues also figured as major in the subsequent expansion of Islam beyond the borders of Arabia. It is well for us to consider, however, how Muhammad perceived the nature of the pagan beliefs and customs that constituted the practice of the great majority of persons in all Arabia during his Meccan ministry.

We have noted that Muhammad was adamantly opposed to polytheistic paganism in Mecca, particularly in its setting any form or fact on a par with the Creator, the Lord of the Worlds. Muhammad's criticism of paganism is sharp and radical, but with one significant reservation. He taught his followers not to use abusive words in criticism of the objects of pagan worship lest the pagan believers, in their ignorance, revengefully use similar language against God. Muhammad believed most pagans were simply ignorant of God (K 6:111), but then again on other occasions he seems to have credited some persons with certain knowledge of God and his ways (K 6:100–112). The pagan opposition to Muhammad in Mecca was expressed primarily through the wealthy and powerful within the city (K 43:30–32), the reasons for which I have already discussed. But Muhammad's view of the religious content of pagan faith was radically negative.

For Muhammad, polytheism as a worldview implies fundamental cosmic disorder (K 21:22). It is as if a person belongs to several part-owners who disagree among themselves (K 39:30). At one point, Muhammad asserts that pagans pray only to female beings—those worshipped in Mecca at that time appear to have been solely female: Lat, Uzza, and Manat (K 53:19–20). But he at once goes on to say that, in fact, these pagan believers pray only to Satan, who is a rebel accursed by God, as if the true nature of pagan religious posture were rebellion against the one God (K 4:117–119). At one point, Muhammad insists that the female deities are only names created by their worshippers, present and past (K 53:22). Worship of such deities at the Ka'bah is no more than whistling and hand-clapping (K 8:34). Then again, we find elsewhere language suggesting the real but dependent existence of such beings as jinn or devils. On the Day of Judgment, these beings will insist that they were unaware of the worship or service offered them. In either case, their worship constitutes no valid service before God (K 10:29–30). In another passage, we note the statement that the prayers of unbelievers are made in error (K 40:50–54). But we must not conclude from such language that the possibility of effective prayer to God is cut off for persons then for the course of this life. Unbelievers who turn and pray to the Lord of the Worlds have an open door before them: "Your Lord has said, 'Call upon Me and I will answer you'" (K 40:62; cf. Rom. 10:13). It would seem that such open-endedness is at the heart of Muhammad's faith and message and that other statements that appear logically inconsistent with this posture are properly considered as expressions of his tendency to overstate his case on occasion.

Muhammad insists that idols such as the golden calf the Israelites worshipped have power neither to hurt nor help (K 20:92; cf. 21:62). Pagans are said to have no Scripture; Muhammad challenges the Meccans to bring him a Scripture comparable to his own. The pagans respond that they belong to the community of their ancestors and follow in their ways. Muhammad insists, in turn, that the present word of God given through him is a "better guidance," and that faithfulness to tradition without moral discernment is an ancient excuse found everywhere (K 43:20–24; 37:156). Muhammad later asks his hearers in Medina to question tradition, asking whether their ancestors had adequate understanding or true guidance (K 2:165–166; 5:103). Certainly, the present mode of this tradition that asserts "There is nothing but our present life; we die, and we live, and nothing but Time destroys us" is utterly inadequate (K 45:23–24; 23:82). For Muhammad, rejection of the Hereafter and the Judgment is tantamount to rejection of God.

Some passages in early Meccan surahs suggest Muhammad's message was winning its way, especially with persons already prepared, those who fear and worship their Lord in secret (K 35:8–19; 36:10; cf. Matt. 6:4, 6, 18). Muhammad was clearly aware of these persons' existence and evidently aimed his early ministry in their direction. Once he felt called to make public proclamation of his message, however, he clearly came to regard himself as the Messenger of God to the whole of society.

Muhammad's objection to pagan concepts and practices was clearly based on ethical as well as religious grounds. He considered various taboos regarding the eating of flesh and other foods meaningless. Like Jesus before him, he was concerned for sin both inward and outward, and like the early Christian church, he tried to simplify and limit the range of taboos. Only carrion, the blood of animals, and the flesh of swine came to be forbidden to believers. They may eat of all else—especially of the fruits of gardens or the fields—but not wastefully or greedily. Let the name of God be pronounced over that which is to be eaten. Muhammad acknowledged the religious authenticity of the various prohibitions on food given the people of Israel, but simplified the rules of living for Muslims (K 6:117–121, 135–148; cf. 15:28–29).

More significantly, however, Muhammad was vehemently opposed to the pagan custom, which the pagans believed their various deities ordained, of burying alive female children deemed superfluous (K 6:137, 141). Something of the compassionate spirit of Muhammad is revealed in the statement in an early Meccan surah in which on the Last Day the buried infant, upon being raised, is asked for what sin she was slain (K 81:9).

Muhammad knew that a primary reason for the slaying of daughters was the poverty of parents. He forthrightly rejects this excuse on the basis that God will provide for the material sustenance of both parents and children. Such confidence in divine providence, however, is not to be left solely to God. The context immediately after charges believers to be just and fair in commerce and in all interpersonal relationships with orphans (implying the needy of every kind), to fulfill the believers' covenant with God, whose basic principle is that God has forbidden killing people except by legal process or in just war. Such respect for the life that God gives all must also include inward and outward self-control with regard to any sexual indecency toward others (K 6:151–154).

Pagan attitudes toward women at times led to dark anger and inner choking on a parent's part if given news of the birth of a daughter. Muhammad regards such parental response as ingratitude toward the generous provision of the All-mighty, the All-merciful, who is the Creator of daughters and of sons. And he mocks this attitude, since it is coupled with the worship of angels on whom the pagans themselves have bestowed female attributes (K 43:14–19). Such experience with the attitudes and practices of Arabian paganism was clearly a part of the background that led Muhammad to commit himself to force to eliminate it from Arabian life throughout the peninsula.

The Ethics of the Koran

Our study to this point has made clear the central importance of ethical endeavor in the Koranic concept of authentic religion. The ultimate destiny of a person depends on what she/he earns; all are exhorted to work for the supreme triumph of Paradise (K 37:59). Recovery from ethical failure, however, would seem always to be possible for those who repent and amend their lives (K 5:43). The Koran proclaims continuing open-ended prospects before God for all humanity, because God is All-forgiving, All-compassionate— even as he purifies whom he will (K 24:10, 21–22). The Koran offers no theological interpretation of how such mercy may be cosmically possible; there is no concept, for example, of vicarious atonement. Muhammad's views of the sovereignty of God possibly would have made such an inquiry presumptuous, if not blasphemous. God is sufficient, of bounty abounding, and he will arrange for whoever fears him to have a way out of dilemmas (K 3:167–168; 65:3–5; 2:18; cf. 1 Cor. 10:13). We note only that God calls for humans to make effort, to "struggle," and God acquits of their evil deeds those who believe and turn to do righteous deeds. Furthermore, God's generosity is such that he will recompense these persons for "the best of what they are doing" (K 29:6), up to ten times the original, while payment for evil is no more than tit for tat. (It is important to note, however, that, to Muhammad, human punishment in Gehenna, an apparently permanent condition, does not appear to constitute a disproportionate payment, that is, infinite suffering for finite transgression. In the Koran, the open-endedness of God toward all humanity seems confined to this world and to this cosmic time period.)

God is sufficient for all human needs, and his will is not to be questioned. In principle, the ethics of the Koran are based on the absolute will of God—as received through his Messenger Muhammad—in contrast with the moral code received from "the customs of our forefathers." It is clear that application of the principle did not prevent Muhammad from carrying on certain customs from the pre-Islamic past into his overall ethical teaching. The process, however, was clearly selective and Muhammad was the one who selected. He believed himself to be chosen of God to convey the content of the will of God to his Arab contemporaries.[69]

A few instances in the Koran suggest possible atoning value for people's good deeds. For example, in giving alms to the poor, it is better for persons to give without publicity, although it is excellent to give alms even when publicly proclaimed. But to act in accord with the better way is said to acquit that person of his or her evil deeds (K 2:273). One verse states flatly that good deeds will annul evil deeds (K 11:116). Another passage affirms that whoever forgoes retaliation—an eye for an eye, and so forth, as prescribed by God in the Torah—as a freewill offering will find it to be expiation (K 5:49). But in the larger context, the way of the Koran is to emphasize the sovereign mercy and forgiveness of God apart from any rationale. It appears unwise, therefore, to draw significant theological conclusions from a few verses alone. Far more frequently we read: Who can forgive sins save God alone?

There are also a few references to the need for human penances and making amends. It is forbidden a believer to kill another believer. If a Muslim should kill a fellow believer by mistake, he is to set free a believing slave as penance and pay appropriate compensation to the slain person's family—unless they forgo receiving such payment as a freewill offering on their part. If the responsible believer does not have the financial means to make payment, he is to fast for two months in succession (evidently in the mode of Ramadan fasting, that is, during daylight hours). But whoever kills a believer willfully, "his recompense is Gehenna, therein dwelling forever" (K 4:94–95).

For those who divorce their wives by declaring them to be their mothers (a practice disapproved of by Muhammad) and then retract their words afterward—an act necessary for the process of forgiveness—the penance enjoined is the freeing of a slave. If the man does not have the means to do this, he is ordered to feed 60 poor people. If he cannot afford this, he is to fast for two successive months (K 58:3–4; 33:3–4).

The spirit of the Koran as a whole, however, is not that of a bargaining religion. The awesome majesty of its perception-concept of God quite removes it from any such trivialization of spirituality. In the concluding verses of the longest of surahs, "The Cow," Muhammad prays to his Lord with language of the heart comparable to the noblest of Hebrew Psalms:

> Our Lord
> take us not to task
> if we forget, or make mistake …
> Do Thou not burden us
> beyond what we have the strength to bear.
> And pardon us,
> and forgive us,
> and have mercy on us;
> Thou art our Protector.
> And help us against the people
> of the unbelievers.

Muhammad proclaims in another Medinan surah that no believer would ever be pure apart from God's free and generous mercy, but God purifies whom he will. In the text as we have it, Muhammad follows these statements with injunctions for believers who have means to continue to give to their kinsmen, to the poor, and to "those who emigrate in the way of God" (referring, no doubt, to the Muslim emigrants in Ethiopia). He commands them to pardon and forgive others, and then asks if they do not wish that God should forgive them. The language seems to suggest that if believers refuse to forgive others, such refusal could somehow block divine forgiveness from working effectively in their own lives. But God is All-forgiving, All-compassionate (K 24:22–23).

An Arabic term frequently used in the Koran to describe believers (*taqwa*) seems to carry the double meaning of fearing God and warding off evil (as in K 2:2).[70] The Koran contains ethical prohibitions, but the emphasis in its ethical teaching is on the positive. A very early Meccan surah describes the right path for believers, those who are "Companions of the Right Hand." The right path is especially:

> The freeing of a slave
> or giving food upon a day of hunger
> to an orphan near of kin
> or a needy man in misery.

The persons walking this path will "counsel each other to be steadfast and counsel each other to be merciful" (K 90:9–18). Prosperous in this life, as in the life to come, is the person "who has cleansed himself, and mentions the Name of his Lord, and prays" (K 87:14–15).

We read that restraints from the Lord are particularly laid upon those who honor not the orphan or "urge not the feeding of the needy." Those who love wealth inordinately and greedily devour the inheritances of others shall experience a scourge of chastisement even in this world. They shall certainly receive the chastisement of God when the Lord comes on the Last Day (K 89:15–20). In another Meccan surah, we find that not to urge oneself and others to feed the needy is a sin comparably heinous to not believing in God the All-mighty (K 69:34–35; 74:44–45). The servants of God, however, who fulfill their vows and live in awed awareness of the Last Day give food to the needy, the orphan, the captive. This is an important part because "the beggar and the outcast" have a "right" to the wealth of believers (K 70:21). But this service is especially for love of God, in response to his person ("the Face of God"), certainly not in expectation of recompense from the recipients. Sufficient for the givers is the reward of the wondrous Garden, they who remember the Name of their Lord "at dawn and in the evening and part of the night, bow down before Him and magnify Him through the long night" (K 76:5–25).

Clearly central in Muhammad's motivation was the consciousness of his own past reception of benefits, awareness evidently brought into recollection by the inner workings of God's revelation. In an early Meccan surah revealed when his worldly prospects were low indeed, Muhammad was told that the Lord had not forsaken him, does not hate him. His latter portion will be better than the former; he will be satisfied with what the Lord gives. Then he is reminded of his own past:

> Did He not find thee an orphan, and shelter thee?
> Did He not find thee erring, and guide thee?
> Did He not find thee needy, and suffice thee?

Therefore, Muhammad is told:

> As for the orphan, do not oppress him,
> and as for the beggar, scold him not;
> and as for thy Lord's blessing, declare it (K 93:1–11).

This theme of compassionate concern is repeated frequently in various contexts. The covenant that God made with the children of Israel was so that they should serve none other than God and:

> be good to parents, and the near kinsman,
> and to orphans, and to the needy;
> and speak good to men, and perform the prayer,
> and pay the alms.[71]

The Hebrews were not to shed the blood of their own people nor turn any of them out of their dwellings (a wrong of which apparently some Jews in Medina were guilty). It is noteworthy that Muhammad inserts into this listing of ethical obligations belonging to the divine covenant with Israel—a covenant that could be viewed as separatist and partial—a stricture of concern for the wider reaches of humankind (K 2:77–78).

As the community of Muslims became more carefully organized in Medina, we note concern expressed that women receive a proper share ("apportioned") of what their parents or kinfolk leave as inheritance. Orphans and the poor, and other kinfolk, should be provided for. And people should speak kindly to them (K 4:8–9; 6:153; 2:218; 4:2–3). Muhammad proclaims that true piety lies not in the niceties of worship. Authentic worship is:

> to believe in God, and the Last Day, the angels, the Book, and the Prophets, to give of one's substance, however cherished, to kinsmen, and orphans, the needy, the traveler, beggars, and to ransom the slave, to perform the prayer, to pay the alms. And they who fulfill their covenant when they have engaged in a covenant, and endure with fortitude misfortune, hardship and peril, these are they who are true in their faith, these are the truly godfearing (K 2:172–173).

These citations make clear that, for Muhammad and the early Muslim community, faith and works, especially in behalf of others, were inextricably intertwined. But like the prophets of the Hebrew Old Testament, Muhammad had deep concern for the individual's inner self, for human thoughts and attitudes, for their intent and motive. The right way to come to God is with a pure heart (K 26:89). Paradise is for whoever comes to God with a penitent heart (K 50:31–34). God will take people to task not for a slip in their oaths, but for what their hearts have earned. God is All-forgiving, All-clement, but all shall be questioned on the Last Day regarding matters of hearing, sight, and the heart (K 2:225; 17:38). God changes people's condition only when they change that which is within their hearts, a work that God helps them do

(K 13:11; 15:47). In a Medinan surah, Muhammad states that there is no fault to be found in mistakes, "only in what your hearts premeditate"—yet, again, God is All-forgiving, All-compassionate (K 33:6). In a late Meccan surah, Muhammad urges his hearers to forsake both the outward sin and the inward, which another passage specifically associates with "indecencies," that is, with sexual indiscretion of thought, word, or deed—wrong-doing that was apparently keenly offensive to Muhammad and is often cited in the Koran among the Prophet's sharpest admonitions. God himself is not only the First and the Last, he is also the Outward and the Inward (K 6:120; 7:32; 57:3). Repeatedly proclaimed is the fact of the full knowledge of God, who knows not only what persons do, but also what they think, and there are consequences in this world and the next. But God accepts repentance from his servants (slaves) and pardons evil deeds of every kind (K 42:23–24). Therefore God's servants are characteristically sincere of heart (K 37:40, 129, 160) and humble-minded (K 2:42).

In "The Cow," Muhammad cites God as instructing the children of Israel that interior work becomes possible for the humble-minded. They are to seek God's help in patience and prayer (K 2:40–43). In various passages, all persons are exhorted to refrain from walking on the earth exultingly, for such conduct is wicked and hateful to the Lord (K 17:39). Then we note the daunting words that God does not love those who exult, who are proud and boastful. He does not love such as are niggardly toward the needy in the world (K 28:76; 4:41). We are to recall, however, that this term "love," in the Koran, more often than not means "approval" or "approbation." It is never intended to proclaim a hard-faced God who shuts the door of opportunity in this world to those who would repent and return to fellowship with their Maker in faith and obedience. Muhammad's concern is to proclaim that the most serious of consequences in this world and the next follow those who are wrongfully proud, who scoff at or revile others (K 28:39; 40:75–76; 49:10–11).

One particular element in this concern of Muhammad's was that believers should not be impudent or presumptuous in the presence of God *and* his Messenger. This is the first part of the well-known passage in which believers are told not to raise their voices above the Prophet's nor be loud in their speech to him. Yet Muhammad goes on to insist in the same passage that believers are indeed brothers (and sisters). For this reason they are not to find fault with each other, certainly not to revile one another with nicknames. The names of persons are important—in the Semitic linguistic context (K 49:1–5; 10–12).

The good tidings of Muhammad's proclamation are for those who believe *and* strive to do good deeds. Such preaching is never intended to slight the central importance and necessity of faith in God, the All-merciful. Those who reject faith consider the signs that God sends through his Messengers or through events in history or nature to be lies (K 2:23; 7:145; 18:105).

The concept of reward is a significant aspect of the Koranic teaching on ethics. As we have noted, reward from God is neither mechanically given nor arithmetically measured: the Lord prefers to repay good double or even tenfold (K 4:44; 27:91; cf. Matt. 5:12). Muhammad emphasizes that those who believe in God and the Last Day and do what is right—prayer and almsgiving are sometimes specifically identified as central to what is right—shall receive an immense reward with their Lord, in part in this life. "No fear shall be on them, neither shall they sorrow" (K 2:59, 104, 108, 275, 278). Such persons receive guidance from their Lord; it is they who prosper, who are the successful even in this world (K 2:1–4; 23:1–10; 3:141). As for those slain in the way of God, as we have seen, they are not to be called "dead"; they are living.

> Who ever obeys God and the Messenger—
> they are with those whom God has blessed,
> prophets, just men, martyrs, the righteous;
> good companions they!
> That is the bounty from God; God suffices
> as One who knows (K 4:71; cf. 13:20–26).

Those who have bought error with the price of rejecting divine guidance find that their commerce has not profited them. God has taken away their light, leaving them in darkness. "Evildoers do not prosper" (K 2:15–16; 10:18; 12:22). Muhammad wishes his hearers to take a longer view of present human life—as of the Hereafter—and not presume upon the bounty of the Lord. Appropriate consequences follow, and the timing of consequences is in the hands of God. Hence the appropriate life posture of believers is fear of God, with personal modesty, an awed sense of the working of his ways of recompense, all encompassed with deep gratitude for the compassionate mercy and generous providence of God.

Muhammad preferred to proclaim the fact of reward from God as a reality both in this world and the world to come. But when pressed for a comparison, he did not hesitate to slight the life of this world and to stress the superlative excellence of the reward of the Hereafter. "Forgiveness and mercy from God are a better thing" than whatever riches may be amassed in this world (K 3:139–142, 151–152). "The enjoyment of this world is little; the world to come is better for him who fears God" (K 4:79). Believers will be tested with "something of fear and hunger, loss of goods and crops, even of their lives." But God is with these who are patient. "The mighty triumph" is to be received into large gardens beneath which rivers flow, to dwell there forever. This is the reward of those who obey God and his Messenger (K 4:16–17).

The Koran lays great emphasis upon the wider social responsibilities of every adult believer, and in particular upon the financial duties of those possessing means. (It is important to note again in this context that Muhammad always refrained from equating the religious community who acknowledged him with God's more inclusive parameters in past or present.) Frequent in the Koran are the admonitions to spend on others that which God has bestowed (K 2:3, 192). The alms tax *(Az-Zakat)* is obligatory for those who have the means, but in the

Koran the context is primarily religious, and the term thus means a religious offering to God and a contribution to human need. Commerce and business should not divert anyone from remembrance of God, that is, to keep the times of prayer and to pay the poor due (K 2:40; 24:37). In an early Meccan surah, we read that a characteristic of the god-fearing who will receive their reward is that they gave the beggar and the outcast a share in their wealth. This statement is made immediately after note of the primary characteristic of the believers (good-doers) of those early, devout days. We read "Little of the night would they slumber, and in the mornings they would ask for forgiveness." This is to say that prayer and aid to the needy are like twin polarities of the daily life of the god-fearing, and to receive such aid is the right of the needy (K 51:15–19; 70:24). In the context of repeated proclamations that all that is in the heavens and the earth belongs to God, Muhammad admonishes believers to be proponents of justice—which is a primary way to be witnesses for God. They are to work for justice even though it be to the (presently appearing) disadvantage of themselves or their kinspersons. In the context, it would seem, of a court case, believers are to be impartial, whether the other persons in the case be rich or poor (K 4:130–134).

There are numerous statements in the Koran that God allows (honest) trading (the very repetition implies encouragement to mercantile activity), but forbids usury. Indeed, we read that God shall war against usurers, a term that is still generally understood in contemporary Islamic lands even to forbid accepting interest on savings deposits.[72] And if one's debtor be in difficult circumstances, the creditor is directed to "let him have respite until things are better." The admonition immediately after says in effect that it is better to give freewill offerings—which may suggest that it would be better in general for creditors to remit a debt (K 2:275–280; 3:125; 30:38). God approves the generous, and we are told that he will replace that which his servants expend. Indeed, the promise is that "God will multiply such a good loan (to God) in manifold ways as the likeness of a grain of corn that sprouts seven ears, in every ear a hundred grains" (K 2:192; 34:35–38; 2:246, 263). Of course, this was not expected to be taken literally, but as an example of the generosity of God. This was intended to be a community of grateful believers who live in awe of their Maker even as they strive to help others.

The teaching of lending good loans to God—that is, giving to the needy of the earth, with confidence that God will ultimately multiply reward for such—was assuredly well developed in the Meccan period (K 64:15–18). But in Medina, Muhammad's responsibility and concern for the entire community gave a new emphasis to his teaching on almsgiving. He was concerned not only for the quantity, but also for the manner of giving. Those who give of their wealth should not follow up such freewill offerings with critical words or other injury to the recipients. This would void their good effect upon the giver. Respectful words and forgiveness toward recipients are "better" for the givers, for "God is All-sufficient, All-clement" (K 2:264–269). The exigencies of the situation evidently made open and public giving necessary, but Muhammad insisted that, if possible, it is "better" to give to the poor in secret. Muhammad added—with how much theological implication?—that such secret giving will, before God, acquit the givers of their evil deeds (K 2:273–275; cf. Matt. 6:2–4).

Much or most of the fulfillment of social responsibilities enjoined during the Medinan period was carried out through what we would call the agency of state, the informal bureaucracy of Muhammad's closest followers and military leaders. The theocratic community of which Muhammad was both religious Prophet and politico-military ruler—as if he were a younger and physically more vigorous Moses—increasingly gained authority and firmness of structure. In Muhammad's lifetime, the administrative structure remained relatively simple and his direction largely personal. Apparently, any suppliant had personal access to the Prophet, and he believed it his duty to be the final (human) level of appeal in judging any case or reconciling disputing parties (K 49:1–10).

In the case of distribution of the booty won in caravan raids or battle, these spoils of war are said to belong to God *and* his Messenger. From these gains, however, it appears that Muhammad proclaimed one-fifth of the total for his own disposal, that is, for the state—on behalf of "near kinspersons, orphans, the needy, and the traveler." But Muhammad and his fellow leaders apparently monitored the whole process of distribution so that the rich could not take an unfair share (K 8:1, 42; 59:6–10). We may recall that, in the early Medinan years, Muhammad was particularly concerned for the welfare of the economically destitute Muslim emigrants who fled with him from Mecca to Medina, and for other fugitives who later came to join the community, from Mecca or elsewhere.

Fighting in the cause of God came to be put in the same moral and religious category as contribution of means. True believers strive with their wealth and their lives for the cause of God (K 49:15). This situation began with the Medinan period, for, as noted, in the Meccan period, believers were forbidden to resort to arms for their faith (except for legitimate self-defense). In Medina, the principle was first established that Muslims may fight in the cause of God against those who fight against them, but they must not begin hostilities. "God loves not the aggressors." But Muhammad came to believe that the Meccans' persecution of Muslims was morally worse than the killing that would ensue if the Muslims resisted, then moved beyond allowing armed resistance to permitting attacks. He came to believe that idolatry must be extirpated from Mecca and from all Arabia—by persuasion, if possible; by military means, if necessary. The growing community of Muslims was urged to support and participate in the military campaigns necessary to achieve this purpose. (If the opposition, however, desisted from persecution, turned to faith in God as One, and followed in the practices enjoined therein, no ill will would remain. Individual wrongdoers were to be handled separately.) The overarching reality is that God is All-forgiving, All-compassionate (K 2:187–191; 8:39–40).

Muhammad thus proclaimed to the Muslims that warfare is

divinely ordained, even though it is personally hateful. Indeed, it is even suggested that those who turn away when fighting was prescribed for them, as in the case of the children of Israel in the time of Saul and David, are evildoers in God's sight (K 2:210–215, 247). The alms that Muslims are required to give are also for those who are in need because of their fighting or other activity in the cause of God. Muhammad's sensitivity is revealed in his insistence that it is the responsibility of people of means, as of the state, to be aware of and seek out such of the needy who do not importune others to meet their needs. Muhammad speaks forthrightly of divine punishment for those who are greedy and keep their wealth to themselves in the face of these human needs (K 2:272–275; 3:175; 4:41–42).

The frequent admonitions in the Koran to obey God *and* his Messenger, and also those in positions of authority with him, are thus to be understood as appeals for the dedication of life and means to the expansion of the Muslim community by military means (K 3:126; 4:62, 82, 85; 9:41). In a late Medinan surah, however, as a part of the vow that women fugitives from Mecca or other parts of Arabia were expected to make, a significant qualification is offered: Obedience to the Prophet is incumbent only in that which is honorable or right (K 60:12). As with Muhammad's frequent use of the term (in English translation) "haply," we note again his tendency to refrain from making absolute statements except that God is One, All-forgiving, All-compassionate. I would suggest that these "qualifications" indicate that Muhammad did not always expect his language, even in the Koran, to be taken as literally as most believers have done. Can we not say the same of the Judeo-Christian Bible? Jesus himself espoused and practiced a selective use of Scripture and the early church largely followed his example with their development of lectionaries for public reading of Scripture in church service (Matt. 5:17–48; Mark 12:28–34; Gal. 5:14). One of the most needed conditions for constructive dialogue and better relations in general among Christians, Jews, and Muslims[73] would seem to be less certainty of the perfection of our respective Scriptures.

The presence in the Koran of these "qualifications" is a helpful guide in the interpretation of some of the very strong language occasionally to be found in the Koran, especially with regard to the fate of unbelievers in this world and the next. In battle, the Muslims are ordered, with their angelic helpers, to smite the unbelievers "above the necks" and "every finger of them." God himself is said to be involved in primary fashion in this work of slaying unbelievers, because they had broken covenant with God and his Messenger. Upon such persons the retribution of God is terrible; the chastisement of the fire awaits unbelievers. And yet the text goes on to command Muhammad to say to the unbelievers that if they yield—to God *and* his Messenger is the implication—God will forgive them what is past (K 8:12–18, 39, 63; 2:187–189).[74] The larger context is that a Messenger from God has come out of the Arabs, one of themselves, one who grieves over the suffering of persons, who is anxious for their welfare, "gentle to the believers, compassionate" (K 9:129; 48:28–29). Muhammad seems always to leave a door open for persons here on earth, whether the context be discussion of the mind of God toward unbelievers or the attitude of Muslims toward others. His deepest conviction was that his Message is most reasonable, no different in content from the Torah and the Gospel that had been given to humanity before him (K 9:1–20; 5:50–53). It is supremely a Message of mercy and forgiveness, an open door to all humanity.

The goal of ethical action in the Koran is especially to create one nation, one people out of many, a nation that calls all persons to goodness. It invites all persons to honorable living and forbids all dishonor or wrongdoing (K 3:100). The goal is the creation of a community that is also a state, one that provides the conditions most favorable to the achievement of goodness in human living. This is the ideal of Islam, but whether or not statehood is achieved, believers must individually and collectively strive to do good. What God commands—such as to judge justly in human dispute, to restore in proper condition whatever others have entrusted to one's care—is good in itself (K 4:61). Repeatedly, believers are told that to work for justice is to be a witness for God, to be fair in one's dealings with others is close to the heart of one's duty to God. Believers are enjoined to work for justice, even when it appears to be against their own interests or those of their parents or other kinfolk. God has promised those who believe and do deeds of righteousness both forgiveness and a great reward (K 5:11–12; 4:134).

Those who fear God also restrain their anger against fellow humans and pardon their offenses, even as they continue to be generous in almsgiving, whether they personally experience prosperity or adversity. It is the good pleasure of God that people work at reconciliation and setting things right in human life (K 3:127–128; 4:114).

Muhammad notes God's prescription in the Torah of an eye for an eye, "a tooth for a tooth, and for wounds retaliation." He states, however, that the Word of God is now that whoever forgoes this right will find it an expiation for him. If believers have been hurt by others, they are permitted to return such injury in like measure, but it is better to be patient with these others. Muhammad is instructed to be patient and is told that such patience is only possible with the help of God. Muhammad is aware of the divine law that the consequence of evil is evil, but he wants to say that the process is somehow flexible, open-ended. Whoever forgives others and works to put things right in human relationships will receive special reward from God (K 5:48–49; 16:128–129; 42:35–38; cf. Matt. 5:38–42). The way for believers is to overcome evil with good, done in the context of faithfulness in prayer. The good deed has greater power even to make a loyal friend out of one with whom there had been enmity (K 13:20–21; 29:97; 41:34; cf. Rom.12:17–21).

Injunctions to goodness, to kindness, are frequent in the Koran. God has been good to believers, indeed to all; the proper response is a religious life, worshipping God and doing what is right to others. Believers are instructed to make provision for their wives and for divorced women. Generosity toward one another is the right way for Muslims (K 20:132; 28:77; 2:234–242).

The proper relationship between believers is to be protecting friends to one another, the men and the women, all in an honorable way, all in the context of a lifestyle of prayer and almsgiving—with obedience to God and his Messenger. Orphans who have been adopted are to be considered brothers (and sisters) in the faith and dependent clients (K 8:73; 9:73; 33:5). Symbolic of this relationship of mutual respect and helpfulness is the command for believers to exchange a greeting from God—"blessed and sweet"—when they enter each others' houses (K 24:61). The bond of faith is prior to all other kinds of human relationship. It is, for instance, the command of God that all beings be kind to their parents. But if they try to lead believers into idolatry, they are not to be obeyed. They are to be honorably treated in this world, with gratitude for their upbringing, but the way to follow is that of those who turn to God the All-sufficient, All-laudable (K 29:7; 31:13–14).

Muhammad's injunction to Muslims was to be stern with disbelievers, either as individuals or as communities. It is wrong, he says, to take for friends a people with whom God is (then) angry or to love (approve of) those who oppose God and his Messenger (K 58:15, 22; 53:30). Muhammad sees the departure of Abraham from his kinsfolk in Mesopotamia as indicative of (currently) irreconcilable faith positions—with resultant enmity "until you believe in God Alone." Yet even here Muhammad shows his customary open-endedness, for he quotes Abraham as saying to his father, "certainly I shall ask pardon for thee." It is thus Muhammad's hope that God will yet establish "love" between believers and those with whom they are currently at enmity (K 60:4, 7–9).

A further qualification is that Muslims should not take hostile action against unbelievers who resort for refuge to a people who have a compact with the Muslim community, nor against those who come seeking peace "with hearts constricted," in repentant mode. Furthermore, if any of "the idolaters" seeks protection from the Muslims even without profession of faith, Muhammad is directed to grant such protection until the individual has opportunity to hear the words of God (K 4:90–93; 9:5–19). This language seems to tell us something of the procedures for religious instruction that were instituted within and without Medina as the community of faith expanded before Muhammad's death.

These passages, however, also contain clear directions for Muslims to slay idolaters "wherever you find them," unless they "repent and perform the prayer and pay the alms" as authentic tokens of faith. Then they become "brothers in religion." Muslims should not take as friends Jews and Christians who make a jest and sport of the faith of Islam. They should not choose their own fathers or other family members as friends of the heart if they "prefer unbelief to belief." Muhammad does not specifically say that Muslims should fight with members of their own families who do not profess their faith,[75] but as for Jews and Christians "who have been given the Book" and do not practice the religion of truth, Muslims should fight them until they pay the assigned tribute readily and humbly (K 9:23, 29).

We may note that this last citation is immediately followed in the Koranic text by Muhammad's sharp criticism of Jews for claiming that Ezra is the Son of God and of Christians for saying that the Messiah is the Son of God. Muhammad further asserts that Jews and Christians have exalted their rabbis and their monks as "lords apart from God" although they were commanded to serve only One God. Indeed, "there is no god but He." Here, too, Muhammad seems to cite "the Messiah, Mary's son" as unduly exalted in Christian theological faith.[76] God has sent his (present) Messenger "with the guidance and the religion of truth, that He may uplift it above every religion." Muhammad refrains from any criticism of the Messiah himself, here or elsewhere, but he goes on to accuse "many of the [Jewish] rabbis, and [Christian] monks" of greed and extortion of material goods from believers, so as actually to keep them from following the way of God (K 9:30–35).

A further prohibition is that Muslims should not marry idolatresses—presumably polytheistic pagans—until they believe. Similarly, Muslim women should not marry men who have not yet come to Islamic faith (K 2:220–221).

I have already discussed the teaching of the Koran with regard to sexual morality in the section on women. It is sufficient to repeat that sexual relationships were strictly forbidden outside the structures of responsibility established in the Muslim community; anything else was "indecent and hateful, an evil way" (K 4:23–29). As we have seen, Muhammad was severely critical of lewdness of thought, word, or deed. The overall ethical posture of the Koran, however, is non-ascetic. Celibacy and the monastic life are not approved; God has only forbidden "indecencies, the inward and the outward." Further details are not given, but Muhammad himself and the early Muslim community were resolutely opposed to the kind of debauchery seen in the Roman Empire at the height of its pagan power. Prostitution, male or female, was forbidden and apparently did not exist at all in Medina at that time.

Muslims should not be prodigal, but may and should enjoy the good things in this world. They may eat, drink—wine was later forbidden, except in Paradise!—and wear that which God provides. They should not forbid such things to self or others (K 7:29–31). Muhammad himself and other Muslims are directed ("God loves not any man proud and boastful") not only to be modest in their bearing in public, but also to keep their voices low at any time, for "the most hideous of voices is the ass's." Such bearing is also enjoined as the proper mode of prayer, whether in public worship or in private devotion. All are urged not to be loud in their prayers, "nor hushed therein." They should seek a way of moderation between the extremes of loudness and silence (K 31:16–17; 17:110–111).

As noted earlier, the whole ethical life of Muslims is to be interfused with thanksgiving to God. They are to be thankful to God, at least in part because God recompenses those who are thankful. The very fasting prescribed for daytime during the month of Ramadan is to the end that persons be thankful. The text is clear in its prescriptions and prohibitions surrounding the event such that even this period of daylight fasting is not intended to create an ascetic pattern, not to be severe. For "God desires ease for you" (K 2:147, 181; 7:141; 28:73; 54:35).

This last citation is not to be understood as if "an easy life" was to be the proper expectation of Muslims. They are to toil and persevere in good works, be patient and "do deeds of righteousness; for them awaits forgiveness and a mighty wage." They are to seek God's help in patience and prayer, put their trust in their Lord (K 11:14; 22:148; 29:59). In a very early Meccan surah, Muhammad is commanded not to give of himself, thinking to gain the more on this material plane, but to be patient before his Lord. Patience clearly meant to Muhammad a sturdy constancy in face of whatever befalls persons in this life. Those truly guided by God experience, even in this life, awareness of true relationship to God; they know also that their ultimate destiny is with Him (K 74:6; 31:16–17; 2:150–151). Believers should therefore do the best they can (K 64:15).

It is in this context that the permission of God for believers to engage in trade is to be seen, although God forbids usury, as noted previously (K 2:276–277; 3:125). (Usury, at that time, could double or redouble the amount originally lent [K 3:125]). Muhammad also commands believers in the strongest terms to forgive outstanding debts that may be classified as usury (K 2:278–280). Indeed, he goes on to say that if any debtor should be financially in difficulties, the Muslim creditor should allow him time to repay "till things are easier." The larger context of these passages is that Muslims may rightly seek the bounty of God in this life, but Muhammad contrasts those who pray for good in this world alone with those who pray for good in the world to come (K 17:68; 2:196–198). The latter receive their proper portion in this life as in the life to come. The discussion of both permission to seek wealth and prohibition against usury is placed in the context of strong injunctions to generous giving on the part of believers.

Other restrictions are laid upon traders. As noted, they must not let sale of goods nor commerce of any kind divert them from remembrance of God or constancy in prayer, or from paying their due to the poor. These words, we should note, follow closely upon proclamation that "God is the Light of the heavens and the earth," that he "guides to His light whom He will"—in part through signs or similitudes (metaphors) given humanity. The passage does not say that such divine guidance or (implied) revelation is given only through the special Messengers of God. The more generic use of the term "guidance" here and in other passages of the Koran suggests that every believer may experience the guidance of God. They are evidently given a light whereby they may walk aright, along with God's forgiveness. Muhammad seems to have envisaged for believers a personal relationship with God, enriched with graces different from his own perhaps only in degree and leadership role. Muslim orthodoxy over the centuries, to be sure, has in large measure confined divine revelation to what is given to God's Messengers—practically speaking, to what is written in the Koran, and, in very secondary measure, to the *hadith* of tradition. Muhammad himself, however, was evidently readier throughout his prophetic ministry to respect the religious role of believers. There is considerable evidence that there was much discussion between him and the people, especially, no doubt, with reference to practical matters of public policy, but also, we may surmise, with reference to other matters; that is, more personally religious and ethical issues (K 14:34–38; 57:28–29).

Traders are strictly enjoined to give full measure and a true balance in weighing goods for customers. They are not to be corrupt, nor to be harmful to others in any sense. Their ongoing mercantile career is not to bring about the impoverishment of the people as a whole. These injunctions, we may note, are as pertinent to contemporary societies as to Mecca in the second decade of the seventh century! In a later Medinan surah, we learn that central to the whole work of God in the world in sending his Messengers—of whom Adam was the first!—was that humans may uphold justice. The Messengers bring both the Book and the Balance, affirmation that fair judgment is a central quality of the revelation, as of the conduct, of God (K 26:181–183; 57:25). Muhammad insists that Jews and Christians do not have a monopoly on the bounty of God (evidently a reference to Judeo-Christian claims of special divine provision for themselves). It is in God's hand to give to whom he will, even as his generosity is abounding. Humans contend for "wealth and children," boast about obtaining them, "wear" them as personal adornment, but tend to forget that the present life is only of secondary value, "a sport and a diversion," no more than "the joy of delusion" (K 57:18–20). Believers endure patiently whatever befalls them. Muhammad's message is good news to such persons, who are humble before God and whose "hearts quake" when the very name of God is mentioned. They are faithful in prayer and contribute to the common cause from what God has provided them (K 3:150–154; 22:36).[77]

The Koran's theological position is not to be equated with the Protestant ethic or the later synthesis of the Calvinistic-Puritan theology of work from which modern capitalism developed. There are commonalities, such as the sober dedication to be found in both traditions in their early periods. In the Koran, economic activity is permitted by God, and the principle affirmed that, with certain exceptions, God will bless believers with material provisions and, indeed, the Lord himself works to promote their mercantile activity (K 17:68). The Koran does not seem to glorify work as such, but it is clearly viewed as part of the religious task of believers.

The worshippers of God keep their commitments and covenants (with God and with one another). Note, however, the statement that "God will not take you to task for a slip in your oaths," a statement immediately followed by insistence that God *will* take believers to task for commitments made with oaths. Expiation is prescribed for breaches thereof, such as the feeding of "ten poor persons with the average of the food you serve to your families, or to clothe them, or to set free a slave; or if any finds not the means, let him fast for three days." This statement of proper expiation is then followed by a command to "keep your oaths." The point of this "back and forth" language seems to be Muhammad's abiding concern to retain the integrity of the human word, on the one hand, and an equally strong desire not to burden believers with absolute or unqualified strictures, on the other. Therefore believers are told not to make oaths that are a

hindrance to the quality of their religious life or their relationships with fellow humans (K 76:34; 5:91–92; 2:224–225). Indeed,
in certain cases (especially, it would seem, in matters of relationship with wives), God grants to believers absolution for their
oaths (K 66:1–2). How teaching of this kind was actually applied
in the community we do not know.

The Koranic teaching on sin appears to find its source in the
choices that persons make—especially between turning to or
from God, the Lord of the Worlds. There is no concept here of
original sin or sin inherited from ancestors. People are responsible themselves for what they do and are. If believers fear God,
they will be given a criterion (*Furqan*), guidance by which they
may discriminate between good and evil. In this process, God forgives and people are cleansed, inwardly and outwardly, from the
consequences of their wrongdoing (K 8:29; 2:50; 9:15), although
believers should not consider themselves already complete or
perfectly purified (K 53:34). Muhammad does not appear to
assign to pagans comparable keenness of ethical discrimination,
but the Koran implies that all humans are capable of making
basic moral distinctions. The expression "men possessed of
minds" appears to refer to persons across a broad spectrum of
humanity (K 53:23). Certainly, evil and good are not alike and
equal, and so the distinction between them is discernible. The
difference between the corrupt and the good, however, is ultimately not of human making (K 5:100; 4:34; 8:37). What this last
statement means the Koran does not say. There is no detailed
account therein of "Paradise Lost."

No fault is ascribed to the mistakes that persons make unin-
tentionally, only to what their hearts "premeditate." One verse
states that God shall turn, return, in mercy only to those who do
evil in ignorance, then promptly repent. This verse, however, is
prelude to warning against "deathbed repentance," that is, carrying on an evil lifestyle with intent to repent just before dying. God
is not to be tricked, Muhammad is here affirming, but such a statement does not alter the primary fact that God is *All*-compassionate.

The repeated Koranic assurances of the open-endedness of God toward those who would turn and repent are the primary reality of the Message (K 36:6; 4:21).

Believers are restricted only from eating "carrion, or blood outpoured, or the flesh of swine." This contrasts with the more extensive prohibitions of goods previously laid upon Jews, evidently by God himself. Furthermore, if anyone eats that which is forbidden without intent to transgress, "God is All-forgiving, All-compassionate" (K 6:146–147; 16:115–120; cf. Acts 15:20; 1 Cor. 8:4–13). Central is what is in the heart, and because God knows what is in people's hearts, let them be fearful of Him—who is yet All-forgiving, All-clement. (K 2:236; 53:25).

A distinction is made in the Koran between the more and the less in quantity and in quality. It seems that if persons avoid "the heinous sins that are forbidden," God will not only acquit them of their wrongdoing, but admit them into Paradise by "the gate of honour." There are degrees of good and evil in human conduct that the Lord will appropriately reward or punish (K 4:35; 53:33; 6:133). The greatest of evils is to reject the overtures of God. The theological expression of this rejection is to ascribe "partners" to God, but the heart of the matter is human rejection of proffered relationship with the Lord of all Being (K 4:40; 6:156–157, 162–163; 18:14). But comparably wrong is to fail to feed the needy (K 69:34–35) or not to pray (K 74:44–45).

Divination is in the category of sacrificing to idols, an abomination, part of Satan's work, and is forbidden. Such practice looks for guidance from spiritual forces other than God (K 5:3, 92; 2:216).

Muhammad was concerned with the wide-ranging effects of the good and evil that humans do. But his concept of divine justice to be manifested on the Last Day enabled him to say that, in the final analysis, any person who commits sin commits it only against himself or herself. This is not to say that sin is not also or even primarily against God, for he is the one who punishes. God, however, is supremely All-forgiving, All-compassionate to whoever "does evil, or wrongs himself, and then prays

God's forgiveness." The door of God's mercy is ever open here upon earth. But whoever rejects the proffers of God's mercy earns the consequences of his or her own wrongdoing (K 4:110–111; 6:168).

The drinking of wine in moderation was apparently at first permitted in the early Muslim community and later forbidden. In the Koran, we find only the prohibition. Wine is cited as an abomination like the shuffling of divining arrows, but, in one passage, Muhammad proclaims as a message direct from God the fact that there is "heinous sin" and also practical uses in both. "But the sin in them is more heinous than the usefulness" (K 2:216; 5:92). Believers are not to consume their goods "in vanity," a term evidently indicative of gambling as of unduly luxurious living (K 4:33; 17:29).

Murder is severely proscribed, especially among believers. Whoever slays a fellow believer willfully is to be in Gehenna forever. If, however, the cause of death be unintended error, various methods of compensation are cited, all quite within reason for the time and place (K 4:33–34, 94–95). We note also another significant passage wherein God's ancient commandments to the Children of Israel cite their communal responsibility to retaliate with appropriate penal action in the case of willful murder of any human being. Muhammad proceeds to identify the solidarity of all humankind as a deeper reason for the heinousness of willful murder. For the community not to take appropriate penal action "for a soul slain, nor the corruption done in the land [herein a widening of communal responsibility for the quality of its social life!], shall be as if he had slain mankind altogether." And whoever "gives life to a soul"—presumably the meaning is to refrain from murder even though there may be just cause for anger— "shall be as if he had given life to mankind altogether" (K 5:35; 2:174–175). This wider perception of human solidarity is thus also to be seen as integral to the anthropological perspectives of the Koran.

In the context of strict prohibition of willful murder, Muhammad allows a "right" to slay, evidently a reference to legitimate warfare or the judicial process of the community. The text, however, seems to allow also a limited measure of personal vendetta to relatives in the case of a family member unjustly slain. The community may even assist in this action. In the same passage, but earlier, we note again Muhammad's strong language regarding the grievous sin of the traditional Arab practice of infanticide. Economic need, "fear of poverty," is no excuse. Muhammad proclaims as the word of the Lord, a veritable divine promise, that God will provide for the economic needs of his people, for both children and parents. The text in larger compass seems to view this divine promise as operative both within and beyond the boundaries of the Muslim community (K 17:32–33).

Muslims are instructed to control their anger and to pardon the offenses of fellow humans, for they themselves know that they have the way open—indeed, it is the way approved by God—to pray forgiveness for their own wrongdoing. It is God, of course, who is the ultimate forgiver (K 3:128–129). The treatment of thieves prescribed in the Koran, however, is severe. The community is told to cut off the hand of a thief, male or female, as a recompense for their deed, as the punishment that God himself deems right. The text immediately after this pronouncement allows that God, who is All-forgiving, All-compassionate, will turn in forgiving mercy toward the person who repents after wrongdoing and makes amends (K 5:42–43). Since such divine response does not presume the restoration of the hands of repentant thieves prior to the Last Day or earlier physical death, this prescription is one of the few instances of Koranic law wherein, from an early period of Islamic history, secular courts intervened at times in the process of judicial administration in the direction of less severe modes of punishment.[78]

Muhammad allows that God has given more material good to one person than another, but Muslims are not to covet what others may have received. They may ask of God in prayer to serve their needs from his bounty, which needs God already knows. The passage affirms the right of all, both men and women, to receive an appropriate share of what their economic activities have earned. As always, Muhammad is concerned for economic justice, even though such does not mean for him total equality in wages or property. He is willing to give specific instructions with regard to bequests (K 4:1–15), but consistently refrains from detailed controls of economic activity (K 4:36). Muhammad, as we have seen, was aware of greed as a human problem and had much to say to the community after greed for spoils led to Muslim defeat in the battle at Uhud in 625 C.E. (K 3:150–153). But in the absence of total equality of goods in the community, Muhammad was concerned about personal attitudes. Envy was as much a problem as covetousness.

There is a significant passage in a late Medinan surah that reaches its summation in strictures to believers not to find fault with one another, nor insult one another with bad names. One wonders, however, whether Muhammad's word in the preceding verse that no people or person should "scoff at another people (or person) who may be better than they" refers to actual moral superiority of others. Or does the language imply socioeconomic superiority, such as was apparently the meaning of the old English expression, one's "betters"? In either case, to be sure, the stricture was critical of envy—and suspicion, or spying upon one another, or backbiting (K 49:11–12).

We read also that God loves not (approves not of) the proud and boastful, who hoard their wealth and urge others to be comparably greedy and niggardly. Also guilty are those who spend in the way of conspicuous consumption, to show off their wealth and power to others (K 4:42–43). With these words, Muhammad proclaimed to the wealthy and powerful of Medina, as he had done earlier in Mecca, that they, too, are under divine scrutiny and will be judged according to their several situations and conduct. As we have seen, in the Koran, election to faith is no guarantee of ultimate salvation in the Hereafter. In a Meccan sermon, Muhammad used the strongest language to indicate the disastrous consequences to be experienced by those who were exultant in the earth without right and were proud (K 40:75). Believers were also not to speak any falsehood. This last commandment is given in the same sentence as a stern warning to shun the abomination of idol worship (K 22:31–32).

I have noted a number of references in the Koran to the "guidance" of God, and Muhammad disclaiming any right or authority to give "guidance" to believers (K 28:56). Such right is the prerogative of God alone. This gives us significant insight into the relationship of early believers with the Prophet, and reveals the measure of inner freedom to make moral judgments that Muhammad believed God had given all believers, indeed all humanity. The Prophet urges believers to turn inward and look after the state of their own souls. To cope with their personal needs in daily life, they have available both divine protection and divine guidance. No other person can hurt them if they are "rightly guided." This passage, however, is but one of many that assert or imply the responsibility of all humanity to discern and follow the guidance of God (K 5:104). The implication is clear that God—as he wills or permits—makes this guidance inwardly available to all persons.

This affirmation of God's universally available guidance enables us to see the role of the ever-growing Koran in the life of the community during Muhammad's lifetime. I have noted injunctions to believers to obey God and his Messenger. But no statement in the entire Koran asserts "this form of the Book" to be the whole of the divine Message. The same must be said of whatever *hadith* came to have authoritative force in the community. Muhammad's faith understanding, from its earliest expressions, affirmed the universal presence and work of the Lord of the Worlds, and specifically the fact of legitimate Prophets and of authentic divine Messages in other times and places. Thus neither the teaching nor other directions of Muhammad, even at the highest level of his pan-Arabic glory, constituted the whole of the divine Message. Muhammad believed himself to be the bearer of true revelations from God, but he was not telling "the whole story." If believers and others are in charge of their own souls, they are responsible, on the basis of their possession of the criterion of right and wrong given them by God, to judge for themselves what they should do and do it. The emerging Koran, and the presence of the Prophet himself, are but one part of that which is available to Muslims, or others, as the basis for this moral judgment.

The Koranic affirmation is of interior freedom and divine guidance (personal revelation) made available to all. This should keep us from ascribing a strictly legalistic mentality to Muhammad, to the Koran, or to the early community. There is, of course, a notable instructive and corrective role for Prophets—blessed be their names!—but the process of moral judgment is expected to work in the context of constructive, creative tension between Prophet and community, between individual and community, all in the presence of the living God. As a Christian, I would affirm the same truth as applicable to the Judeo-Christian Bible and Church. Neither the Bible nor the Koran was intended primarily to be a Book of Law, even though they contain what came to be particular laws. I believe that my study of the ethical teaching of the Koran has revealed it to be quite other than strictly "legalistic" in form or content. We may perhaps also find therein a basis for responsible scriptural hermeneutics of the Koran as a whole that is closer to the principles and procedures of modern Western historical-critical methodology than has been previously realized.[79]

This is not to deny the truth of H. A. R. Gibb's statement that the practical bent of the Islamic community, and its tendencies of thought, expressed itself in the fact that its earliest academic activity was in law rather than in theology. Certainly, its schools and systems of law are among the most significant institutional expressions of historic Islam. The Koran came to be understood by many Muslims, perhaps most, as a book of laws. Together with the commentaries provided by the words and deeds of the Prophet (*hadith*), it was accepted generally as an infallible source of divine truth.[80] Kenneth Cragg has even written that the Koran communicates God's Law; it does not reveal God himself.[81]

This probably goes too far, however. Proper definition of

terms is an issue. As Cragg himself later wrote, law in Islam is often denoted by a term of earlier usage than *Shariah*, namely *Fiqh*, or "understanding." *Shariah* itself is the "way," or right path of human action, whether ethical or ritual.[82] The theology of the Koran, of Muhammad's preaching, is relatively simple in its thought and speech. To be sure, the style is never weak, certainly not in expressing the Prophet's primary emphasis on the fact and necessary worship of God. But even as the fact of God and his proper worship never lost their central place or role in Muslim life, there came to be an increasing emphasis on practice, on practical ethics, in the early community. I suggest that in the preaching or teaching of Muhammad, and in the daily life of the early community of believers, there was less "legalism," in the literal sense of the word, than either modern Western interpreters or historic Islamic jurists have often implied.

Our study of the ethical content of the teaching of the Koran has revealed that its intent and largely its format are not strictly or primarily "legalistic." Koranic ethical injunctions, with very few exceptions, are not given in the systematic or detailed format of literal legalism (K 4:1–33). The emphasis is most often on general principles, with certain specific instances of application occasionally given, of what is right and wrong according to the will of God. But since this will has been revealed through God's Messengers to the whole of humankind in the past—mostly in the same mode and content, Muhammad generally implies, as his own discourse—this will can be presumed to be universally known, at least to some degree. This presupposition of faith is no doubt one reason why, for Muhammad, true faith is a mode of remembrance. The Prophet understands his divinely given Message, the Koran, as the Reminder (*Al-Dhikr*), even as it is the Criterion (*Al-Furqan*) and the Guidance (*Al-Huda*). Indeed, Kenneth Cragg has suggested that the term *Dhikr* is wholly synonymous with the title of the Book itself: Koran.[83]

In fact, one may properly compare the mode of Muhammad's ethical teaching in the Koran with that of the Apostle Paul, especially in the letters generally recognized as authentically Pauline.

In Paul's longer letters, he devotes usually the last chapter or two to a statement of what he believes to be the mind of Jesus Christ—and therefore the will of God. This is, however, neither legalism nor a legalistic system. It is to set up certain guidelines, actually rather simple structures, to guide and correct believers who themselves are expected to receive guidance from God and personally discern his will (cf. Rom. 12:1–15; 13; 1 Cor. 2:14; 12:1–14; Phil. 2:1–18; Col. 1:9). In both Paul and the Koran, the responsible judgment of believers is always seen as having a proper role in ethical perception and endeavor.[84]

IV

HISTORICAL AND THEOLOGICAL EVALUATION

The primary intent of this book has been to provide for non-Muslims the essential content in structured form of what Muslims believe to be the supreme (for many, the infallible) manifestation of divine revelation and human living under God, which are the Koran and the life of Muhammad. I have noted that there is a distinct priority assigned by Muslims to the Koran as *the* external Criterion of their faith and practice.[1] Indeed, as we have seen, much of what we may discern as historically authentic items in the life of Muhammad derives from the Koran. Items derived from the *hadith* and other forms of tradition (*sunna*) that are without basis in the Koran may have, in many cases, played a significant role in the development of popular Muslim piety over the centuries. But, as discussed in the second chapter, there is considerable variation in the historical authenticity and reliability among the numerous *hadith*—and popular practices—in the many nations where substantial numbers of Muslims reside.

I may also add, as Alfred Guillaume has written, that the Koran is nearer to biblical Christianity than the system of Islam as it has developed over past centuries.[2] Likewise, we may say that the New Testament, or, more particularly, the Synoptic Gospels, are closer to the Koran than the system of Christianity as it has developed over the same period. As preparation for dialogue to come, therefore, I offer this focus on the content of the Koran as "the best" of Islam. Some concluding observations, however, are in order.

I write this section with memories of having attended with my wife a conference of Christian Muslim relations in Chicago, Illinois, in April, 1993, and also the 1993 Parliament of the World's Religions, held that year in Chicago from August 28 through September 5. Our experiences at these conferences and more recent readings suggest to me the need to repeat briefly here what I tried to do, also briefly, in chapter 1; that is, to identify the major areas of contact between Muslims and Christians from the very beginnings of Islam. My experience with modern and contemporary Muslim apologists, however, has been to hear or read these contacts described as essentially originating with the Western incursions into the Middle East in the Crusades. This process is seen as moving then into a new phase with modern Western colonial expansion after 1800.

As I have noted, this mode of description has often been used to create the image of Islamic lands as being largely the victims of the military and economic power of the Christian West. The longer story gives a much more complex picture: the almost unimpeded sweep of Muslim military forces out of Arabia into Palestine, Syria, Egypt, all across North Africa to the Atlas Mountains, over into Spain and, even though for but a brief period, into central France and soon the island of Sicily—this entire military conquest was of lands with centuries-long backgrounds of Christian faith. Apart from Spain and Sicily in continental Europe and contemporary Israel in Palestine, all these lands are currently again under Muslim political control. But of the greatest historical importance is the fact that the former Christian populations of the North African littoral and the Middle East were in very large measure converted to the Islamic faith over the passage of time, with some compulsion, "whether discrimination or economic handicap or often no other choice," and have remained so until the present.

In the Middle East, Christians were reduced to minorities, usually ethnically, religiously, and culturally defined. Such have been the Coptic Christians in Egypt, Greeks and Armenians in Asia Minor (modern Turkey), Assyrians in Iraq and Persia (Iran). Only they have been able—with decreasing success—to retain their Christian faith and social identity against the powerful pressures to join the dominant and "successful" Islamic majority.

This situation remained largely unchanged for the first four centuries of Muslim rule after the initial invasions. That is, there were no major military confrontations between Western European Christians and the Muslim rulers until the beginnings of the reconquests of Sicily and Spain. The Normans of southern Italy were able to restore Christian control of Sicily in the years from 1060 to 1090, and the land has remained largely Roman Catholic. The restoration of Spain to Christian political control began in earnest in the eleventh century and came to its conclusion with expulsion in 1492 of all Moors (Muslims) and Moros (Jews) who were not willing to renounce their faith. We should note, however, that the beginnings of Christian reconquest of Sicily and Spain in the eleventh century were coterminous with the beginnings of the Crusades.

Jerusalem had come under Muslim military control in 638, six years after the death of Muhammad. But with only brief intervals as exceptions, Muslim rulers allowed free access to Christians on religious pilgrimage. Increasingly, popular piety in Western Europe had placed great value on both relics and pilgrimages, and no source of relics, pilgrimages, or goal of worshipful pilgrimage could surpass a visit to the Holy Land and the city hallowed by the life, death, and resurrection of Jesus Christ. Jerusalem had already become a special object of pilgrimage for Christians from both East and West during the reign of Constantine (312–337 C.E.). Such pilgrimages became more numerous in the eleventh century in spite of unusually painful economic sufferings experienced in western Europe in the early part of that century (reportedly, 48 years of famine out of the 70 years from 970 to 1040.)

These untoward events, however, were in some measure counterbalanced by an economic revival concurrent with fresh spiritual and intellectual upsurges of energy experienced all over western Europe in the latter part of the eleventh century. These developments represented a distinct change from the general lethargy in western Europe during the previous five to six centuries after the fall of the Roman Empire. "Forest lands were being cleared, frontiers pushed forward, and markets organized, and the Muslim predominance in the Mediterranean was being challenged by Italian shipping."[3] The Norman conquest of England in 1060 showed that a western European state of modest size was capable of planning and executing a major military undertaking. As one aspect of all this eleventh century activity, western Europe was now in a position to take action against any sustained interruption of access by Christian pilgrims to the city of Jerusalem.

This brief account of the background of the Crusades is not to be understood as "justifying" them. The Crusaders' conduct, even in Europe, was at times utterly cruel and irresponsible, as when largely undisciplined groups of peasants in the first Crusade massacred Jews in cities of the Rhine Valley and elsewhere. Their reckless pillage en route brought about fierce reprisals by national or local authorities, particularly in Hungary and the Balkans. But of the greatest significance for subsequent Christian-Muslim relations was the capture of Jerusalem by the Crusaders in June 1099. Apparently, all its Muslim and Jewish inhabitants—men, women, and children— were "put to the sword." The testimony of contemporaries was that blood ran in the streets of Jerusalem as high as the bellies of horses.

The role of the Seljuk Turks and their heirs in the Ottoman Empire was perhaps the most significant element in subsequent Christian-Muslim relations from the eleventh century into the twentieth century. The appearance of the Seljuk Turks as a military power in the Middle East created a distinctly new situation. After conversion to Islam in their homeland in the steppes of central Asia, this Turkic linguistic group pushed south and westward, in large measure to escape the repeated forays of Mongol horsemen from the east.[4]

The Seljuk Turks were one of the Muslim *Ghazis* (fighters for the faith) who, from at least the early ninth century, had begun to transform themselves from marauding wanderers into settled states. They began their conquest of Asia Minor with their military victory over Byzantine forces at Manzikert in eastern Anatolia in the spring of 1071. The Eastern Roman emperor Romanus IV Diogenes had assembled a large army to check what were increasing Seljuk raids and incursions into Byzantine-ruled territory. The Byzantine troops fought valiantly, we are told, but were defeated, and Diogenes himself was taken prisoner.

The subsequent Turkish conquest and occupation of Anatolia was a relatively extended process, but the eastern frontier of the Byzantine Empire was now undefended, and Turkish horsemen were able to ride into Anatolia unhindered. The Byzantine military forces were soon driven from all but the western coastal regions and, by 1092, the Greek city of Nicaea, perilously close to Constantinople, the capital city of the Byzantine Empire, had fallen into Turkish hands. At this point the Byzantine emperor Alexius I Comnenus appealed to the West for help, sending envoys to the Roman Catholic Council of Piacenza in 1095, where they received a warm welcome and promises of military aid. Pope Urban II and his advisors evidently hoped that this aid would serve to heal the de facto breach between the great Eastern and Western churches. It would seem also that knowledgeable persons in the West had come to realize that the expanding military activities of the Muslim world were a serious danger to the Western and to the Eastern churches.

We need not discuss further the complex history of the Crusades. We should note, however, that Nicaea was recaptured from the Turks in June 1097 by combined Byzantine and Crusader forces. The Crusader army then began the arduous task of crossing south and eastward across arid and mountainous

Anatolia. They were able to achieve a major victory over Turkish opposition at Dorylaeum in July and from there made their way to Syrian Antioch. The Crusaders reached Antioch in October of the same year. They began at once a siege of this great city with its fortifications of a circle of walls and were able to achieve a breakthrough on June 3, 1098. The Crusaders followed their victory with a massacre of all the Muslim inhabitants and, as we have seen, the same gruesome policy was carried out after the successful siege of Jerusalem in July 1099.

But the Crusaders did not leave any substantial forces in Anatolia proper and, from about the year 1220, the Muslim lands to the east of Anatolia were again thrown into turmoil as a result of fresh attacks from the Mongols. Refugees of every class streamed westward into the relative safety of Anatolia and the protection of Turkish military rule. This was the first large-scale immigration of Turkic-speaking civilians into the territory of the former Eastern Roman Empire. By the first decades of the fourteenth century, Asia Minor had become a collection of large and small states, all ruled by Turkic-speaking military leaders, but now with increasing numbers of civilians of similar ethnic background destined to create a groundswell of change, both linguistic and religious.

The Seljuk Turks, operating under a series of different dynasties, culminating in the rule of the Ottoman family, thus emerged as the dominant military, political, and increasingly cultural, religious power/influence in the land. In the year 1354, they invaded the European portion of the now greatly weakened Byzantine Empire, captured the Greek city of Adrianople in 1361, and finally took Constantinople in 1453.

The fall of Constantinople marked the end of the Byzantine Empire and, from this, their new capital, the Ottoman Turks gradually expanded their rule over the Balkan lands of southeastern Europe. In the next century, during the early Protestant Reformation, victorious Turkish forces came for a time to the very gates of Vienna. The borders of Turkish rule were later to be pushed to the south after the fifteenth century, but Turkish control of the Balkans was to remain in force until the end of the First World War in 1918.

To return, however, to internal developments within Anatolia, at the time of the first Turkish incursions into Asia Minor in the eleventh century, the population was predominantly Armenian-speaking in the eastern part, Greek-speaking in the western sections. Both groups were Christian. This land and people had constituted a major part of the geographical and cultural heartland of the Christian faith in the Greek-speaking Eastern Mediterranean and Middle East. The Byzantine capital city of Constantinople, located at the western edge of Asia Minor, which we should now designate as Anatolia, depended more on this territory than on Greece itself for its supportive population and the basis of its religious and cultural life.

Ottoman Empire records maintain that, by the sixteenth century, Anatolia had become largely Turkic-speaking and about 90 percent Muslim in its religious faith, a very excessive claim. It is safe to say, however, that this period of history involved change with extraordinary significance for both the Middle East and the larger world. In reflecting on some of the available data, we should first note that the Ottoman record figures are greatly exaggerated. Reports of European travelers continued to speak of substantial Christian communities in the land. Indeed, not a few groups, especially Christians of Armenian and Greek ethnic background, continued to retain their traditional forms and practices of Christian faith, and their language and culture, into the twentieth century. In any case, the Turkish conquest of Anatolia did not mean a major destruction of the previous population, nor did the influx of Turkic-speaking civilian refugees mean the displacement of that population. What occurred was a large-scale "Islamicization of Anatolia," a process that in fact extended with varying degrees of rapidity and thoroughness from the eleventh century to the present.

This process occurred within a large variation of government policy and pressures to move Christians to convert to Islam. Certain socioeconomic advantages were connected with conversion. The head tax levied upon all non-Muslims then no longer needed to be paid, certain mercantile opportunities were opened, and more openings and higher ranks in government service became available. Furthermore, the pre-Ottoman structures of government under the rule of Rum Seljuks became the format for the development of high levels of Islamic civilization. The Seljuks had become heirs of the important shift that occurred in Islamic personnel and policy under the rule of the Abbasid family, which took over the Damascus-based sultanate of the Umayyads in 750 and established a new capital in Baghdad. This shift was a geographical, ethnic, and highly significant religio-cultural move from the previous Arab dominance in the early expansion of the Islamic Empire after the death of Muhammad. There was now an increasing presence of Persians and Turks and soon Afghans, Indians, and others in the leadership of the far-flung Islamic Empire in the East. These peoples inevitably brought into the mix the heritages of their own civilizations, including religious and larger cultural elements. The increasing power and influence of Shi-ite forms of Islamic faith in Persia (Iran), Iraq, and Syria were, at least in part, a consequence of the shift.

As participants in this process, the Seljuk Turks in Anatolia came to build splendid mosques and schools (*madrasa*) for the training of religious leaders. They built mausoleums of beauty and dignity, and fine residences for the families of their leaders in the capital city of Konya (Iconium) and in other cities and towns of Anatolia. There was clearly a powerful cultural and socioeconomic attraction—surely, also religious attraction in some times and places—in accepting the Islamic faith and, in time, the language of what had been in the beginning a small minority of Turkish overlords. The subsequent immigration of Turkish civilian groups brought into the mix those of nomadic background and also those more accustomed to settled life in towns and cities. The Seljuk family itself had originally been the captains of Turkish nomadic bands who served as mercenary soldiers. Intermarriage between those of Greek and Turkic-speaking background was no doubt a phenomenon of increasing importance.[5]

The invasions and subsequent rule of the Turks in Asia Minor (Anatolia) have been in some ways the most significant events touching Christian-Muslim relations in the entire second millennium C.E. Another example of historically significant Turkish activity is the role of the Janissaries.

The Turks, in their earliest forays into Asia Minor, were horsemen unaccustomed to fighting on foot. The attempts of the Ottoman leader Orkhan to create a disciplined army from men of this background largely failed. As a result, on the advice of a Turkish general, a system was created in 1330 whereby a select number of boys were taken from Christian families in Turkish territory and given a special course of training. The majority of these youths—legally identified in Turkish as *kapikullari,* or slaves of the ruling sultanate—were trained as soldiers in military barracks. Those who evidenced ability for high office were sent to a school attached to the sultan's palace. Here the boys were instructed in the highest levels of Muslim humane studies, which included the Persian and Arabic languages, music, and practical (military) arts and crafts. The boys at all levels were taught the faith of Islam by ulama, the Muslim equivalent of clergy, specifically religious leaders in every Islamic community. Those destined for military service came to be enrolled as *yeni cheri* (Turkish for "new troops").

The majority of these youths were later selected from territories in the European Balkans, which increasingly became subject to Ottoman rule after 1389.[6] This forced levy of the most promising youths of Christian families was at first greatly resented by their parents and others. But in time, this corps, which in English came to be called Janissaries, became not only a highly effective military force but also one into whose ranks Christian parents, according to some sources, often sought to have their boys enrolled. The perquisites accruing to these posts conveyed not a few economic and other advantages to the families of the Janissaries. It is necessary to note, however, that this theme of the willingness of Christian parents to have their sons enrolled in the corps is strongly contested by some scholars as part of the mythology that has crept into Western scholarship on the Ottoman Empire. These soldiers were not permitted to marry (though the order was not celibate; concubinage was allowed) and thus there were no children legally able to inherit the high positions of their fathers. The Turkic "establishment," the in-group that remained at the top levels of the whole Ottoman imperial system, was able, in this way, to draw on the finest talent available in every part of their territorial control without "diluting" their own "religious purity." There was essentially no change in the Muslim faith of this Turkic in-group throughout the entire period of their control.

The Janissary system was thus highly effective in retaining "religious purity" among the Turkic overlords and loyalty to Islamic faith among the larger population vis-à-vis potential Christian influences of a troublesome kind. This is not to say, however, that there were no problems over the five hundred year history of the corps. In fact, the Janissaries were a particularly turbulent lot in their relationship with their Turkic overlords from an early period until the dismemberment of the corps in 1826, which followed a disorderly period of 20 years and an unsuccessful revolt of the Janissaries. The long history of a troubled relationship, however, did not alter the military effectiveness of the system of Janissaries vis-á-vis "enemies" of Ottoman rule within or without the empire. The system came to be seen throughout the larger Islamic world as a model method for retaining Muslim political and religious control over disparate peoples and faiths. It also served to create in the European Christian West long-lasting negative images of Muslim practices in the Muslim relationship with Christians.

We must bring this Turkish story, incomplete at best, to a close with a consideration of events in the twentieth century. One way to begin is to quote a statement found in the sixteenth edition of *The New Encyclopedia Britannica*, in a major article entitled "The Islamic World." The author, Marilyn R. Waldman, associate professor of history at Ohio State University, describes in one phrase the historic experiences of the Armenian peoples in

Turkey in the twentieth century as that of a religious minority that "suffered and shrank." Such is all that the author has to say about the matter![7]

It would be difficult to find a more egregious example of the distortion of historical data from their true nature and proportions than this depiction of the Turkish massacres of Armenians within the Ottoman Empire from 1894 to 1922. These were actually the first examples of large-scale genocide in what became a century notorious for such events. There is a remarkable book—and not a few others!—that gives both the larger picture and more than a little personal detail of the Armenian experiences in that period. This is the memoir of an Armenian Protestant pastor and community leader who is said to have "miraculously" survived the massacres and deportations of the Armenians in Turkey. A publisher's note—not a blurb—at the beginning of the volume gives in one sentence a fair account of the actual events of the time in saying that the author "reveals a human being grappling with evil and malign powers almost too great to be borne or understood; and throughout there emerges the agony and frustration of an entire nation facing obliteration."[8]

The tragedies of those days take on a particularly sinister aspect in that the massacres were indeed initiated, though not solely perpetrated, by secret police or other instruments of government gone mad. As examples of the latter, we can recall the governmental policies and actions of Josef Stalin in the Soviet Union in the 1920s and 1930s, Adolf Hitler in Germany in the 1930s and 1940s, Pot Pol in Cambodia after World War II, and Saddam Hussein against the Kurds in the north of Iraq or the Marsh Arabs in the south in more recent years. We must not forget the genocidal slaughter in Rwanda and Burundi in Africa in the mid-1990s.

The tragedies in Turkish territory were greatly enhanced by the participation on a large scale by the civilian population, who consisted, as Muslims, of a variety of ethnic backgrounds: Turks, Kurds, Circassians, Chechens, Zazas. One of the first examples of massacre was the slaughter of about 1,500 men out of an

Armenian population of seven thousand in the city of Severek in eastern Turkey during a week of terror beginning Sunday, October 27, 1895. This terror included the destruction of Armenian churches and schools, the pillage of homes, the rape of young women. Most of the remaining Armenians in Severek were temporarily imprisoned and then released to face the winter without the opportunity to regain the materials stripped from their homes.

The order to commit or allow this kind of massacre came from Sultan Abu ul-Hamid (1876–1909), the titular head of the Ottoman Empire, called the Great Assassin by many at the time. The years 1894–1896 were especially the "years of massacre, rape, and plunder." During this period, as a result of the orders of the sultan to attack at different times in different places, more than 300,000 Armenians are said to have died either in the massacres or from accompanying starvation and disease.[9]

A second focus of massacre occurred in April 1909 in the city of Adana in south-central Turkey, not far from Tarsus, the birthplace of the apostle Paul. This massacre, in which 30,000 Armenians are said to have been killed, was evidently planned by the Young Turks Committee for Union and Progress, who hoped to put the blame on Sultan Hamid and thus bring about the overthrow of his rule and the destruction of the entire format of imperial government. The Young Turks, the core group who ultimately succeeded in this overthrow, later came under the leadership of Mustafa Kemal Ataturk.

Evidently, economic, religious, and cultural differences contributed to these Turkish genocidal actions against the Armenians. To be sure, these Armenians had lived as ethnically and linguistically distinct Christian communities in various parts of Anatolia, especially in the eastern areas, for centuries before the arrival of the Turks. The Armenians, like the Greeks, were on the whole better educated—they comprised many craftsmen, tradespeople, teachers, doctors and nurses, clergy—and were generally more prosperous than the Muslim population. A significant example was the city of Marash in central Anatolia, where in 1913, the year before the beginning of the First World War, more than 40,000 Armenians lived and were said to be "wealthy, flourishing, well educated." In the surrounding cities and towns, including Zeytoon to the north, an approximately equal number of Armenians were dwelling. Relations between Turks and Armenians had been peaceful, even cordial in some cases, for a number of years. Indeed, because of their personal abilities and relatively better educational backgrounds, some Armenians had come to occupy high positions in civil government, although never to the extent of altering the firm Turkish control of key positions and of the basic policies of government.

Marash had also become a remarkable center of Armenian Christian activity. The members of the Armenian Apostolic Church had "six splendid churches, many grammar schools, and a large high school, and the Catholic Armenians had two most inspiring churches." There were three Armenian Evangelical churches, with memberships ranging from eight hundred to 1,500. There was a theological seminary founded by Americans, a girls' college, and five orphanages operated by German, English, and American missionaries, which cared for 1,500 Armenian orphans and widows. Christians in 1914 still constituted over 20 percent of the population of Turkey.

This apparently idyllic picture was radically shattered by the advent of World War I. What began with both Turkish and Armenian men being drafted into military service on an equal basis turned in 1915 into a "terrible year of massacre, deportation, robbery, pillage," the beginning of the annihilation of the Armenian people in Ottoman territories. Behind this radical change in government policy lay the decision made by the Turkish government early in 1915 to deport all Armenians from the territories of the empire. The term "deportation" became largely a euphemism for a "final solution" by whatever means available. The means became particularly frightful as a result of Armenian military resistance—temporarily successful—that included the killing of several hundred Turkish troops who had been sent to Zeytoon to begin the process of "deportation."[10]

The Turkish decision to deport all Armenians from the land was the aftermath of a relatively long and tragic history. The Armenian minorities in eastern Anatolia had long suffered disabilities under Ottoman rule, but we may properly identify some specific events following the treaty signed at the congress of Berlin on July 13, 1878. This treaty ended the Russo-Turkish war begun in 1876 by Russia and concluded militarily with the defeat of Turkey in January 1878. One important element of the treaty—hateful to the Turks, especially for the 300 million rubles of indemnity it was forced to pay Russia—was the requirement that the Turks introduce reforms in their treatment of Armenian minorities in eastern Anatolia and of Orthodox Christians in the Rumelian provinces of Bulgaria.

That the Ottoman Empire was in a condition of final decline, especially outside Anatolia, became increasingly clear as the nineteenth century came to its close. A series of independent non-Muslim governments were founded within the empire, based on revolts, for example, in eastern Rumelia (in 1885), in Crete (in 1890), and elsewhere. These events raised hopes at least for civil rights and local self-government among the Armenians in the eastern *vilayets* (provinces) of Anatolia. The Armenians had long enjoyed the freedom to form their own schools and thus create better educated, professionally skilled communities than the Turks, who were the majority in Anatolia as a whole. But this demographic fact made the Armenian position in Anatolia permanently vulnerable in a sense not applicable to those parts of the Ottoman Empire where the populations were predominantly non-Turkic-speaking.

Two Armenian revolutionary committees, which had ties of communication and support with Armenian communities in Europe, were formed. In 1894, two factors led the Armenians to rise in revolt. One was persecution by Kurds to the East. The Kurds had unwisely been given special patronage by Abd ul-Hamid, who as sultan was nominally the absolute monarch of the empire. The second factor was the severe measures that the Ottoman Empire's representatives had been accustomed to use for some time in collecting taxes. The revolts were put down by Turkish troops, but with such frightful bloodshed that the governments of England and France intervened and compelled the Ottoman government to accept a program of reforms the two countries prepared for Turkish treatment of the Armenians in the eastern provinces of Anatolia.

The Turkish government, at least from this time (1894), regularly defended its treatment of Armenians with the allegation of Armenian armed rebellion against the legitimate authorities of the empire. In response to this allegation, it may be noted that the Kurds within the Ottoman empire, themselves Muslims, had risen in revolt against the government in 1830, in the early 1840s, during the Crimean war (1852–1853), in the late 1870s, and in 1880, actions severely repressed by the government, but never leading to the policy of extermination that came to be exercised against the Armenians. Actually, the vast majority of Armenian subjects in every part of the empire were consistently loyal to Turkish rule and laws throughout the nineteenth and twentieth centuries. They only very rarely resorted to physical reprisal, primarily because of the behavior of the Turkish soldiery in support of the excessively unjust misgovernment of local officials. Until the outbreak of the First World War in 1914, the Turks were outnumbered by the combined total of other nationalities in the empire—Armenians, Greeks, Kurds, Arabs, Albanians, Assyrians, Circassians, and Jews.[11]

Turkish misgovernment was characterized by legal discrimination in cases between Muslims and non-Muslims, by highly arbitrary methods of tax collection, and by exorbitant degrees of taxation in many cases. Armenians were forced to provide "free winter quarters to the nomadic Kurds and to their flocks, often for four to six months each year." As early as 1883, the British vice-consul in eastern Anatolia, Harry Charles Eyres, reported to his superiors on the "utter corruption and incapacity of the authorities" and, in 1884, that "the courts of justice are a mere farce. They are neither more nor less than engines for extorting from litigants for the benefit of officials."[12]

The conduct of the Turkish soldiery had become the cause of international dismay, especially after the savage repression of Bulgarians following the latter's rebellion in April 1876. In the case of treatment of Armenians, however, the policy of the Turkish government seems to have moved, at least from the mid 1890s, steadily in the direction of extermination of Armenians either by massacre or by forced emigration, which more often than not turned into massacre in practice. The Turkish soldiery—usually aided by local officials and police—generally followed a pattern of killing, looting, burnings, and rape.[13] The British historian Arnold J. Toynbee wrote in 1916 in *The Treatment of Armenians in the Ottoman Empire, 1915–1916* about the larger picture as follows: "an atmosphere of horror, which breathes through all the eye-witness accounts, had settled down over the provinces of the empire."[14]

The Turks refused to carry out their promises of reform and when, in 1896, the British government of Lord Salisbury tried to enforce Turkish compliance, it failed to get cooperation from either France or other European powers. As a result, the Armenians were left without support from outside. In desperation, the Armenian revolutionaries, hoping to compel the attention of the European powers, seized the Ottoman bank in Istanbul, a primarily European financial institution. The result was once more a defeat of the revolutionaries by the Turkish government troops and a bloody reprisal unchecked by the European powers. Such, then, was the general situation at the beginning of the First World War—a background of mutual distrust, resentments, fears, and hatreds between the Turkish government and peoples of the Ottoman Empire and the Armenian communities in their midst. To cap this situation, during the early battles of the war between Turkey and Russia on the Caucasian front, the Armenians were apparently guilty of subversive activities behind the Turkish lines, endangering major lines of communication between the government and its troops facing the Russians. The Turkish government's response was to initiate, early in 1915, a general "deportation" of Armenians from the empire, a program wherein, as noted, "atrocities were committed on a large scale."

The military situation vis-à-vis the Russians did not go well for the Turks, and General Antranik, said in some sources to be a Russian general of Armenian ethnic extraction, was able to take his troops into eastern Anatolia. He evidently permitted Armenian soldiers under his command to revenge the atrocities committed earlier by the Turks in their deportation program. This became known as the "Christian Army of Revenge," although the atrocities committed under this banner were allegedly on a "far smaller scale" than those committed by the Turks.[15] It is estimated that, between 1915 and 1917, well over 600,000 Armenian and many Chaldean Christians were massacred by Turks. Over 600,000 more Armenians were deported. The latter figure is to be understood as including the massive exodus of Armenians who survived the war and emigrated to other countries after the treaty of Lausanne in 1923. This treaty forced one and a half million Greek Orthodox to leave Anatolia in exchange for Turkish Muslims in Greece.

The year 1923 thus saw the end of this frightful story. Almost all Armenians, leaving behind their personal belongings, uncompensated for their equities in real estate and other property, left Turkish territory as it came to be defined within the postwar boundaries agreed to by the Allied Nations. The Greek Christian communities, which had largely resided in western Turkey, were also compelled to leave with comparable loss of property. Such was the conclusion necessitated, the Allied Powers had evidently concluded, by the consistent victories of Turkish military forces after the war over attacks from within and without present Turkish territory. Armenians of the Armenian Republic in former Tsarist Russia had allegedly made a number of raids upon Turkish frontier villages but were compelled by the victories of the Turkish army to accept the terms of a treaty signed on October 13, 1921, between Russia, the three then relatively independent Caucasian republics, and the Turkish government, with its capital in Ankara.

The position of the Greeks in Turkey had greatly worsened as a result of a series of unwise military moves. Military hostilities between Greece and Turkey continued for four years after the formal conclusion of World War I. For the Turks, this latter was the armistice treaty of Mudros signed on October 30, 1918, only a dozen days before the formal armistice of Versailles. The victorious Allies, however, found it difficult to come to agreement among themselves over implementation of the terms of peace of Mudros. As part of this confusion in policy, a Greek army was landed in Smyrna on the west coast of Turkey on May 15, 1919, as the Allied means to establish peace throughout the land. The debarkation took place under the protection of British, French, and American fleets. The Greeks began their military occupation with massacres of Turkish civilians committed without hindrance from the fleets looking on. The occupation itself and the conduct of the Greek troops created great anger throughout Turkey. As a result, even though the Turkish government itself was passing through the throes of transition from the rule of the sultanate to a republic under Mustafa Kemal Ataturk, local organizations were created in western Anatolia to defend Turkish independence against the Greeks. Mustafa Kemal was the man chiefly in control of these activities, which consisted largely of smuggling in arms and ammunition and the organization and training of personnel for military action.

The Greek army took the offensive on July 10, 1921, and was able to push the Turkish troops east of the Sakarya River, which flows into the Black Sea about 85 miles east of the Straits of Bosporus. In response, the Turkish government made Mustafa Kemal generalissimo of the Turkish army, and he at once brought the Turkish forces together to resist the Greeks. After a series of battles lasting 20 days, he was able to force the Greeks to withdraw to the west of the river, where they remained, still technically within Turkish territory.

The Greeks found it difficult to learn a basic military truth of the Middle East, namely that the Turks, when properly equipped and under able commanders, are almost unbeatable by comparably sized forces. In early 1922, the Greeks asked the supervising Allied governments for permission to occupy Istanbul, a request that was refused. Then on July 30, 1922, the Greek high commissioner in Smyrna, Aristeides Sterghiadis, proclaimed the autonomy of the territory in Anatolia that was under occupation by the Greek army. This action was evidently motivated by the intent to continue war with the Turks on Anatolian soil by creating a Greek national movement supported by armed Greek civilian troops. On August 10, 1922, the Allies proclaimed their neutrality in this territorial provocation and possible Turkish military action.

The Turkish government did respond and its military forces began their offensive on August 26, 1922, against the Greek army remaining in Anatolia. The Greek army was routed and almost completely annihilated as a military force. The Turkish army then began its notorious march from the province of Ushak (125 miles east) to the city of Smyrna, the primary center of Greek residence. En route, it destroyed, largely by fire, the largest and most prosperous towns in western Anatolia. Once again, "atrocities were committed on a large scale," and nearly a million people, mostly Greeks and Armenians, are said to have been made homeless. The Turkish army entered the city of Smyrna on September 9 and burned its central portion on September 13. Large numbers of the Christian population fled as best they could.

The Turkish military victories created a dangerous situation for the Western Allies, especially Great Britain and France, who proceeded to various diplomatic acts to check further moves by the Turkish army. The Allies were anxious to preserve the freedom of the Straits of Bosporus and to maintain peace within the remaining so-called neutral zones of western Anatolia, the area around Istanbul, and eastern Thrace. As a major British move, Prime Minister David Lloyd George announced publicly on September 16, 1922, that the British dominions, Yugoslavia, and Romania had been asked to promise military support in the event of Turkish violation of the freedom of the Straits. The Turks

resented what they took to be the threatening tone of this proclamation and began to move their troops toward the neutral zones.
France and Italy withdrew their troops, leaving the British alone.
The very real danger of further advances by the Turkish army
compelled the British and French to resolve their differences
and, on September 23, the principal Allied powers invited the
Turkish government in Ankara to a peace conference, an invitation that both the Ottoman government and the Turkish nationalist forces under Mustafa Kemal accepted. The latter were, by
this time, the real power of government in Turkey and met with
the Allies in a preliminary conference on September 29.
Hostilities were concluded by a military convention signed at the
town of Mudania on October 13, the same day of the signing of
the treaty ending hostilities between Russia and Turkey.

The settlement creating the boundaries and largely the international relationships of Turkey extant today was effected by the
Treaty of Lausanne, signed on July 24, 1923. By this time, the
nationalist government was the sole Turkish power and representative. The sultanate was abolished. The house of Osman experienced the end of its seven-centuries-long rule of the land. The
caliphate, a title denoting primarily religious leadership, was permitted to remain in the Osman family, as a symbolic gesture that
lacked any political significance in the new secular state being
forged under Mustafa Kemal Ataturk. The treaty of Lausanne
granted the Turks almost all their demands, except that of including the city of Mosul in their territories.

The exchange of populations under the treaty of Lausanne
allowed a very minor presence of Greeks in Istanbul and its envi-
rons. Their rights and those of other Christian minorities in
Turkey were to be the same as those secured for other minorities
in Europe by the postwar treaties already in force. The fate of the
Armenians, however, was left to the discretion of the Turkish
government, provided the means were peaceful. As we have
seen, deportation in toto was the final result for the Armenians.

One specific consequence of this series of events in and
involving Turkey from 1885 to 1923 was a drop in the number of

Christians in Turkish territory from more than three million at the beginning of the period to no more than 100,000 at the end. The remnant consisted largely of diplomats and tradespeople with their families confined to Istanbul, Izmir (Smyrna), and the new capital of the government in Ankara. A change occurred, however, with the inclusion of Syrian Antioch and its ancient Greek Christian patriarchate into Turkish territory in 1939. The number of all Christians adherents in Turkey, however, was estimated to be about 100,000 in the mid-1980s, according to *The Europa Year Book* of 1993 (Vol. II). The number of Muslims in Turkey was cited in *The World Christian Encyclopedia* as 45,018,800 in the mid-1980s. *The CIA World Fact Book* of 2000 gives the total population of Turkey as 65,666,677, the percentage of Muslims (mostly of Sunni faith) as 99.8 percent, of Christians and Jews together as 0.2 percent. The number of Jews in Turkey, most of whom are Sephardic, was cited as 24,000 in 1980. Their number has been steadily diminishing because of emigration to Israel.[16]

What has been called the "Islamicization of Anatolia" thus began with the first Turkish military incursions after the defeat of Byzantine forces in the battle of Manzikert in 1071, and concluded in as thorough an "ethnic cleansing" as any nation has known.

To sum up the historical situation, the furthest reaches of Muslim expansion by military conquest in the first century after the death of Muhammad (632 C.E.) extended across north Africa through Spain—and Sicily—to central France in the West. In the East, the extent was into what is now Pakistan, northern India, and Bangladesh, and across the southern steppes of Asia into western China. Of very great historical and religious significance is the fact that, except for countries at the periphery of this vast sweep (France, Spain, Sicily, India, China, and, later, most of the Balkans), Muslim military and political control from Morocco through Pakistan and Bangladesh has remained intact. Malaysia, Brunei, and Indonesia are included in this category of Muslim political and cultural dominance, and, since the breakup of the Soviet Union, so, too, have been the largely Muslim nations of the southern steppes of Asia. Especially in the Middle East and all across North Africa, the large-scale Islamicization of former Christian peoples has also remained intact until the present day. Furthermore, some scholars and specialists allege that, after the Second World War, concerted efforts have been made by Muslim governments, especially in the Middle East, to eliminate altogether the presence of Christian churches and communities in their midst.

These historical reminders are not intended to be polemical or defensive. They are not intended to justify the Crusades, Western colonialism, or contemporary Western petro-diplomacy with its use of military and financial power. They are not intended to justify the Orthodox Serbian "ethnic cleansing" in Bosnia-Herzegovina or Kosovo.[17] They must be mentioned, however, to "even out the playing field." Neither Muslims nor Christians are solely victims—or victimizers. No one of us is innocent or pure, not one side, not one land, not one person. This discussion, therefore, cannot properly be held on the basis of the moral superiority of one side or the other.

Powerful forces are at work seeking to "demonize" the other in contemporary Christian-Muslim relations. Both sides have reasons, even of massive significance, for legitimate complaint. But our respective faiths and practices have their better sides, and the best of our representatives believe that the God whom we both worship is calling us to peace, to reconciliation—with perhaps varying modes of repentance—to mutual respect, and even to cooperation. The place to begin is with what each side acknowledges as its own best. The other side should study with care what that acknowledged best is. The intent of this book, to repeat, is to inform fellow Westerners, especially fellow Christians and Jews, what the acknowledged best of Islam is in terms that they can understand with relative ease.

I conclude this study with a few words about the "place" for peace, reconciliation, and mutual respect between Christians and Muslims. Much of the early part of this chapter attempts to delineate the terrifying consequences of the lack of peace between these two in the contemporary world. The Christian population of the world is estimated at 1,833,022,000, the Muslim population at 971,328,700. These two together constitute over half of the estimated world population of 5,480,010,000.[18] Peace between these two massive constituencies constitutes, therefore, a major hope for the welfare of much of humankind.

The Swiss Roman Catholic theologian Hans Küng has been expressing with great force what he believes to be the vital connection between ecumenism and world peace. He understands the term ecumenism in this context as a wider ecumenism that includes relationships not only among Christian churches, but also with and among other religions in the world. Küng contends that mutually respectful and adequately informed ecumenical dialogue for the first time in human history "has now taken on this character of an urgent consideration for world politics. It can help to make our world more livable, by making it more peaceful and more reconciled."

As part of the conclusion of his massive collaborative work on *Christianity and the World Religions*, Küng writes as follows:

> There will be no peace among the peoples of this world without peace among the world religions.
>
> There will be no peace among the world religions without peace among the Christian churches.
>
> The community of the Church is an integral part of the world community.
>
> Ecumenism *ad intra*, concentrated on the Christian world, and ecumenism *ad extra*, oriented toward the whole inhabited earth, are interdependent.
>
> Peace is indivisible: it begins within us.[19]

Hans Küng continued to emphasize this theme as one of the major contributing participants in the 1993 Parliament of the World's Religions. He had been asked more than a year in advance to prepare a document, which came to be named *The Declaration of a Global Ethic* and was signed by almost the entire assembly. The Parliament was not meant to be a legislative body, and the document, while it had been circulated for comment to a number of the religious leaders before the public meetings, was not open to revision. But the great majority of those present at the Parliament on September 4 wished to accept the document as their own and insisted on the right to affix their signatures.

This nine-page, 5,000-word *Global Ethic* document was thus able to express with noteworthy accuracy what the assembly members from many places and religious traditions thought and felt. Hans Küng had somehow intuited months in advance that the Parliament as a whole would develop with an emphasis on practice of religious faith rather than on theological or confessional content. Remarkable also was his perception that the basis for a shared ethic already existed. He had sensed that the participants in the Parliament (of whom this writer and his wife were two) would come, in spite of the great variety in external name and form of their historic faiths, sharing a common set of core values in their ethical teachings. He recognized that even though these values are yet to be lived adequately in heart and action, they are already known and can serve as the basis of a global ethic. The Parliament agreed, even if its forms of agreement were "unofficial."

A very few words from the *Global Ethic* document may be in order here. Actually, some theological or larger cosmic truths affirmed in the document seemed to cause no more difficulty for the many participants than the ethical ideals. One is the opening affirmation, both ecological and theological, that we humans are all interdependent, not only as one human family, but also as beings dependent on the well-being of all living beings. Hence we must have respect for what is a community of living beings. This theme of mutual respect was repeated again and again by many speakers during the Parliament and could be called perhaps the central theme and feeling of the whole. In the *Global Ethic* document, this feeling was expressed through an early reference to the Golden (Silver) Rule that is a part of the ethical tradition of several historic faiths: "We must treat others as we wish others to treat us." The document goes on to say that "We make a commitment to respect life and dignity, individuality and diversity, so that every person is treated humanely, without exception."

The phrase "treat others, all others, humanely" was central to the ethics of the document. In Hans Küng's language, we must have patience and the mentality of acceptance of others, be able to forgive. We must "open our hearts to one another, practicing a culture of solidarity and relatedness." Within our one human family, "we must strive to be kind and generous. We must not live for ourselves alone, but should also serve others . . . No person should ever be considered or treated as a second-class citizen, or be exploited in any way whatsoever. There should be equal partnership between men and women. We must not commit any kind of sexual immorality. We must put behind us all forms of domination or abuse."

The *Global Ethic* document calls for universal commitment to a "culture of non-violence, respect, justice, and peace. We shall not oppress, injure, torture, or kill other humans, forsaking violence as a means of settling disputes." There is call for strenuous effort to create a "just social and economic order." Characteristic of such an order will be to "speak and act truthfully and with compassion, dealing fairly with all, and avoiding prejudice and hatred. We must not steal. We must move beyond the dominance of greed for power, prestige, money, and consumption to make a just and peaceful world."

The document concludes that "Earth cannot be changed for the better unless the consciousness of individuals is changed first. We pledge to increase our awareness by disciplining our minds, by meditation, by prayer, or by positive thinking . . . Therefore we commit ourselves to this global ethic, to understanding one another, and to socially-beneficial, peace-fostering, and nature-friendly ways of life. *We invite all people, whether religious or not, to do the same.*"[20]

The reason for bringing to bear this material from the 1993 Parliament of the World's Religions and its *Global Ethic* is probably apparent. Most of the discussion in the earlier sections of this chapter revolves around ethical issues. The earlier chapters of this book are inevitably grounded in historical events, as in scriptural and theological-faith matters. Intelligent and profitable Christian-Muslim dialogue in the days to come—and these days will come, perhaps sooner than we realize!—will have to depend on participants who are well informed in matters of history and faith, of Scripture and theology. But I suggest that in these days to come, dialogue will be engaged with ethical issues in a sharper and more passionately intense way than ever before. I have focused in this chapter on relations between Turkey and the West, and, in the process, issues of ethics and practice have loomed large. Rightly so, I believe. To discuss relations between Iran and the West, we could hardly avoid the role of the U.S. Central Intelligence Agency (CIA) in unseating the government of democratically elected Premier Muhammad Mossadeg in August 1953, restoring the Shah to power after only a few days of absence. Similarly, it would be inappropriate to focus on aspects of the Khomeini revolution displeasing to Western powers without full and fair disclosure of the role of Western petrochemical corporations in Iranian politics earlier in the century.[21] At this writing, we shall have to forego exploration of the labyrinthine background activities behind the Iran-Iraq war of the 1980s, or the Gulf War of the early 1990s, and we are not yet able to pursue the many-stranded background activities leading to the war in Afghanistan or the invasion of Iraq.

Some readers may feel that I have put in this chapter too much emphasis on negative aspects of Christian-Muslim relations over the many centuries of our histories, but both sides have been guilty of superior attitudes, arrogance, and corresponding conduct toward each other in these centuries. I have intended to create, in each, some humility in self-reflection. The bulk of this book has been committed to giving Christians a carefully informed and very largely positive view of the life of Muhammad and the content of the Koran, as a data basis for a respectful, appreciative understanding of these primary sources of Muslim faith and practice. If readers will combine the knowledge gained from study of these materials with due personal and cultural humility, we shall have a factually solid and spiritually valid foundation for ongoing dialogue that may issue in peace and cooperation beyond any degree that we have known.

I should like to conclude with a word about spiritual validity. I believe that the central issue for Christians is to be able to recognize and acknowledge the presence and work of the living God not only in the life and work of the Prophet Muhammad, or in the Koran, but also in historic Islam. This is not to bring to the fore issues of infallibility or of absolute perfection. Muslims may handle these issues as they wish. Most Christian critical thinkers have quite abandoned claims to absoluteness or infallibility in their theological work or in their confessions of faith.[22] But we must be able to recognize what the late Roman Catholic theologian Karl Rahner called the traces of the divine presence and work outside our historic Christian church as an institution. Rahner charged us with having looked at other religious traditions too ineptly and with too little love to perceive these traces.[23] Rahner insisted—and he has carried with him in this the majority of Roman Catholic critical scholars and many others—that God in freedom offers the divine self to all humans in their freedom. He does affirm a special history of divine revelation, which is recorded in the Old and New Testaments of the Bible, but he goes on to state that "revelation in such essential purity" is not found only there. At least a part of that revelation may be found in comparable purity elsewhere within the collective history of humankind and in the history of its religions.[24]

And, finally, Christians are compelled by their own biblical witness to look more broadly in appreciation of "others," even though some popular and academic Christian opinion has been slow to do so. The Bible, right from its beginning, gives as its setting the divine creation of the whole universe and of a primal couple who are identified as the ancestors of the whole of humankind. The book of Genesis begins with God's creation of "man" and "woman," not with the Israelites. The New Revised Standard Version translation rightly translates the Hebrew word *adam* as "humankind" in the passage in which God expresses his intent to create them "in our image" (Gen. 1:26, 5:1–2). The promise that God made to Eve, who was often cited by early Christian theologians as the mother of all humanity, has historically been identified as the first of the biblical covenants (Gen. 3:15).

The second major covenant recorded in the book of Genesis is that with Noah and his family, who are cited as preceding the call of Abraham and, of course, preceding the establishment of the people of Israel as a distinct community. This covenant is five times denoted as a promise of the Creator not only to all humans, but to "every living creature of all flesh that is upon the earth." The sons of Noah and his wife are said to be the ancestors of all peoples, and the covenant of divine-human relationship and mutual responsibility is with all (Gen. 9:8–19). On the basis of this Noachian covenant, the later Jewish rabbinical tradition came to acknowledge the existence of a universal divine rule extending over all nations, one that had specific implications for potential divine blessing and, indeed, the "salvation" of the nations (gentiles). We Christians need to take careful note of the fact that from the first century of our common era, Jewish theological thought in its mainline rabbinical stream has always "left the door open" for the salvation of the whole world on the basis of this Noachian covenant. Among contemporary Roman Catholics, Raymond (Raimundo) Panikkar, following the French theologian Jean Daniélou, has used the term "cosmic covenant" to denote the universal scope of this covenant with Noah.[25]

These two universal covenants constitute the larger background and context specifically for God's call of Abraham and the charge to create a particular people to fulfill particular purposes. But the particularity or narrower scope of this call and covenant with Abraham and his descendants is specifically stated to be effected only for a universal restorative purpose, that "in you all the families of the earth shall be blessed" (Gen. 12:3; cf. Gen. 18:18, 22:18, 26:4, 28:14). This is one way of saying that a later more particularized covenant does not abrogate or replace the early universal covenants.

This faith-understanding of the continuing theological validity of the older universal covenants is an integral element of the faith of Israel.[26] Some Christians—possibly the majority—perceive the covenant in Jesus of Nazareth as abrogating the old rather than reforming it.[27] But the teaching of Jesus, particularly as recorded in the Gospel of Matthew, like Jeremiah's, forthrightly affirms selective reform and a deeper interiority and rejects wholesale abolition of the past (Matt. 5:17–48). The ideal Christian, or "scribe who has been trained for the kingdom of heaven is like the master of a household who brings out of his treasure what is new and what is old" (Matt. 13:52).[28] Nowhere in the teaching of Jesus recorded in the four Gospels of the New Testament, or in the whole of the Old Testament, is salvation denied the nations because they are not of Israel. The apostle Paul drew from this Judeo-Christian tradition the inescapable conclusion that the living God had revealed his self and his will in some measure to all peoples (Rom. 1:19, 2:14–16). And as the noted German-American theologian Paul Tillich was wont to insist, we cannot separate, although we may distinguish, the revealing and the saving work of God.[29]

Christians therefore have solid biblical basis for a fresh and appreciative look at Muhammad and Islam, as particularized expressions of the presence and work of the living God in the world, in the whole of his creation. I should like to add that I work from the standpoint of the Logos theology as seen in the Johannine literature of the New Testament and developed in the church fathers of the second and third centuries of our era. That is, I follow the apostle Paul in his affirmation of the preexistence of Christ Jesus, who existing in "the form of God" may be presumed to have served the purposes of God in his work as the universal Word (Phil. 2:6; John 1:1) prior to his manifestation as Jesus of Nazareth. The light-life he gave was "the light of all people . . . the true light that enlightens everyone coming into the world" (John 1:4, 9).[30]

In the second century, Justin Martyr (ca. 100–165) taught that the divine Logos (Word) appeared in fullness only in Jesus Christ, but that a "seed" of the Logos had been scattered among the whole of humankind long before its (his/her) manifestation in Jesus of Nazareth. Every human being, therefore, possesses in his or her mind a seed of the Logos. This terminology allows an appreciative and critical approach to noble pre-Christian (we may add "post" in the sense of later than the Jesus of history) figures. Thus Justin wrote of noble pagans such as Socrates, Heraclitus, and others of like spirit among pre-Christian Greek philosophers and lawgivers as worthy of the name "Christian," even though their knowledge of the Logos was imperfect and they often fell into contradictions. One of the most seminal of Justin's statements on this theme of the wider presence and work of the Logos of God in the world and throughout human history is that whatever has been well (i.e., beautifully and truly) said among all humans belongs to the Christian heritage. Even amidst our imperfections, the Logos is in every human being.[31]

Irenaeus (fl. 185), writing a generation or more later, carried on this tradition of faith-understanding with his conviction that God is one and the same to all humans and has aided the human race from its beginning by various providential orderings. Irenaeus wrote that the Logos has always been present with the human race, that, from the beginning, the Son has revealed God to all to whom, and when and how, God wills. Indeed, God has made a number of covenants with humankind.[32] That is, the divine presence is universal, but the scene of human receptivity is blotched and requires authentic spiritual discernment that the Word may be rightly discerned and obeyed.

Clement of Alexandria (ca. 150–215), the first Christian who may properly be called a scholar in the technical sense of the term, gave further specificity to the Logos theological tradition. He taught that "all authentic understanding or wisdom is sent by God and that the true teacher of the Egyptians, the Indians, the Babylonians and the Persians, indeed of all created beings, is the first-begotten Son, the Fellow-counselor of God. . . . Philosophy was given to the Greeks as a covenant peculiar to them; many are the different covenants of God with men. . . . The Lord is upon many waters (Ps. 29:3); his beneficence is not limited to particular places or persons."[33] The graphic focus that Clement gives in his depiction of the many covenants that God has with humans, the potentially universal presence and work of the Logos of God, reveals the broadly compassionate and inclusive spirit characteristic of what was the mainstream of Christian theology in the second and third centuries of our era. It also puts to shame the narrower and more exclusive spirit that has characterized not a few Christians in later centuries even to the present time, persons who in many instances have arrogantly insisted that theirs is the only authentic Christian position.

The Christology of Muhammad as revealed in the Koran is admittedly not that of the Nicene or Chalcedonian creeds.[34] I will not repeat here what I have already cited from the Koran on this theme. What I would like to say in summation is that in the present climate of critical opinion in the Christian world community, there is much reason to be grateful, that is, theologically respectful and appreciative, for what Muhammad does reveal of his views of Jesus Christ. (He believed, it would seem, that they were also God's.) Our "present climate of critical opinion" is no longer that of the Reformation and early post-Reformation period when lengthy confessions of faith by both Protestants and Roman Catholics seemed accompanied by expectations that believers would accept as equally true every single part, sentence, or even word of these confessions. The expectation, even demand, was then for total conformity. In our present critical climate, we no longer consider such conformity possible or even desirable. And if we compare the Koranic views of Jesus Christ with those of a number of "critical" scholars of our own day, Muhammad appears to be closer to the New Testament gospel accounts, as they stand written, than do these more liberal (some would prefer to call them "radical") scholars of Christian self-designation.[35]

The issue at times concerns language used, especially if more attention is given to surface differences than to fundamental intent. It has been noted over many centuries, for example, that there is no doctrine of the "atonement" in the Koran, at least as that term has been used historically by Christians to denote the role of Jesus Christ in effecting the divine forgiveness of human sin. It is too often forgotten in our popular parlance that, according to New Testament usage, this work of the Messiah is ultimately the work of God (cf. 2 Cor. 5:18–19). For Muhammad, the role of God is absolutely central in the forgiveness of human sin. As previously noted, every surah but one in the entire Koran begins with the phrase "In the Name of God, the Merciful, the Compassionate." For Muhammad, this divine forgiveness is really the central element in the content of his message, even if he accompanied it with various warnings that forgiven persons cannot presume on God's forgiveness without consequences. How God's mercy and forgiveness are cosmically viable, Muhammed prefers to leave as a mystery. But very much like Christians, he acknowledges the roles of many "agents" of God in his divine work, including numerous Prophets, above all, the "exceptional and exemplary" Prophet, the Messiah, the Word of God, the Bearer of the Holy Spirit, Jesus the Christ, the Son of the virgin Mary. This Jesus the Messiah is God's revelation for humankind and a mercy from him, before whom angels should prostrate themselves in obedience. May we not ask, is there not something of "atoning" significance in all this?

Finally, is it really true that the Koran denies the death of Jesus on the cross? Perhaps so; the text as it stands can certainly be read to this effect and historically has commonly been so understood by most Muslims and Christians. A recent writer, however, quoting from contemporary Arab (Muslim and Christian?) and Western sources, contends that the passage under consideration (K 4:155) intends not primarily to deny the death of Jesus, but to deny the power of humans "to vanquish and destroy the divine Word, which is forever victorious." This is to say that like certain New Testament sayings, the death of Jesus as a central element—along with the resurrection—of the Christ Event, cannot be rightly seen except as somehow also a part of the providential orderings of God himself (cf. John 19:11 and especially Acts 2:23). The Koranic denial is "a denial of the human intention and ability to crucify and defeat God's exemplary apostle." That is, the worldview of the Koran is finally that God is "in charge," even though it also affirms a measure of human freedom. Humans are not able to "destroy" the Messiah of God. Such is the affirmation of both the New Testament and the Koran.[36]

Pakistani Christian scholar Daud Rahbar, writing more than a generation ago, called for a "genuine word of love for Muhammad from the followers of Christ. In my own way as a Christian, I have tried to speak that word."[37] Key Christian figures throughout the middle and latter part of the twentieth century—beginning in a massive way with the generous words of the Roman Catholic Church's Second Vatican Council[38]—have tried to do that very thing. Some of the finest theological writing of our generation has come from the pen of Anglican Bishop Kenneth Cragg, who writes of Islam—and of Muhammad—with a depth of sympathetic understanding and affection hardly to be equaled previously.[39] As I have heretofore written, my own judgment is that I see Muhammad as:

an authentic Prophet of God, even though, like other Prophets both before and after the time of our Lord, neither morally perfect nor doctrinally infallible [I plead for the compassion of Muslim brothers and sisters as I write these words again]. And the movement which is called Islam I regard as an instrument of God in the history of salvation with at least some of the thankful affirmation and cautious qualifications that I make of the movement that is called Christianity. I believe therefore that as Christians we are obliged under God to incorporate this evaluative understanding into our faith-concepts both of the nature of the Church of Jesus Christ and of the missiological imperatives which are an integral part of its life and work.[40]

ENDNOTES

Preface

1. Note the description of the views of *seven* Christian Islamic scholars—(Eastern) Orthodox, Protestant, and Roman Catholic—who "have attempted to 'include' Muhammed by affirming his prophetic stature" in David A. Kerr, "'He walked in the Path of the Prophets': Toward Christian Theological Recognition of the Prophethood of Muhammad," in *Christian-Muslim Encounters*, Yvonne Yazbeck Haddad and Wadi Z. Haddad, eds. (Gainesville, Fla.: University Press of Florida, 1995), pp. 426–446.

2. See Richard H. Drummond, *Toward a New Age in Christian Theology* (Maryknoll, N.Y.: Orbis Books, 1985), *passim*. Cf. Ewert Cousins, "Judaism—Christianity—Islam: Facing Modernity Together," *Journal of Ecumenical Studies* 30:3–4 (Summer-Fall 1993), pp. 415–425; S. Mark Heim, "Mapping Globalization for Theological Education," et multi alii, "Fundamental Issues in Globalization," *Theological Education* 26:Suppl. 1 (Spring 1990), pp. 5–112. One should note the emergence of a similar mentality in the formerly Indian, now Pakistani, Muslim scholar and journalist Mawlana Wahiduddin Khan (b. 1925). See Irfan A. Omar, "Islam and the Other: The Ideal Vision of Mawlana Wahiduddin Khan," *Journal of Ecumenical Studies* 36:3–4 (Summer-Fall 1999), pp. 423–438. It seems proper also to note the relatively thorough and indeed sympathetic account of the developments and changes in Roman

Catholic views of Islam from before Vatican II to the end of the twentieth century by the German-English missionary and specialist in Islamic
studies, Christian W. Troll, SJ. Father Troll particularly stresses as significant the life and work of two French scholarly priests, Jacques Jomier
and Robert Caspar, especially the latter. "Changing Catholic Views of
Islam," in *Islam and Christianity*, Jacques Waardenburg, ed. (Leuven,
Belgium: Uitgeverij Peeters, 1998), pp. 19–77.

3. A contemporary Muslim scholar, a professor and fellow of King's
College, Cambridge University, affirms that while the Koran in Islam's
first half century "existed in a form largely similar to the text we possess
today, its status among believers in that early period was not necessarily
comparable to what it later became . . . concurrently, the Muslims of this
first century or so were generally quite receptive to the religious lore of
Judaism, Christianity and the other great religions of the new Muslim
empire." Tarif Khalidi, *The Muslim Jesus* (Cambridge, Mass.: Harvard
University Press, 2001), pp. 18–19. Khalidi elsewhere asserts that
Christianity and Islam have a need for complementarity. He further
asserts that Jesus "remains a towering figure in his own right—one who
easily, almost naturally rises above two religious environments, the one
that nurtured him and the other that adopted him." Ibid., p. 45.

I

1. Leighton Ford, "Friends and Enemies," *Hopeline* 5:1 (March
1991), p. 3. Cf. an even more irenic approach expressed by a Muslim
scholar teaching in the United States, Zayn R. Kassam, "Reflections on
Teaching Islam at a Liberal College," *Council of Societies for the Study of
Religion Bulletin* 29:3 (September 2000), pp. 66–70.

2. Ibid.

3. The quotation is from Arthur J. Arberry, *The Koran Interpreted*
(New York: Macmillan, 1955), I, p. 232. Unless otherwise indicated, subsequent quotations from the Koran will be from Arberry's version. This
work has been cited by numerous specialists in Islamic and Arabic studies, such as Alfred Guillaume and Kenneth Cragg, as the best translation
into the English language.

4. This sense is significantly translated by Mohammed Marmaduke
Pickthall, no. 2:257 in his enumeration of verses, in the following way:
"Allah is the Protecting Friend of those who believe." *The Meaning of the
Glorious Koran* (New York: New American Library, 1961).

5. The German scholar Rudolf Frieling notes that frequently in the

Koran Allah uses (is quoted as using) the so-called plural of majesty as a self-designative pronoun ("We"). He insists, however, that if such usage is an appropriation of the royal plural, traditionally used by kings and queens, it is "merely a formality and has no other meaning or content." Indeed, Frieling further claims that taken literally the usage "contradicts the exclusive uniqueness of Allah." *Christianity and Islam* (Edinburgh: Floris Books, 1978), p. 78.

6. Cf. Aurelius Augustinus, *St. Augustine's Confessions* I, 1: "fecisti nos ad te et inquietum est cor nostrum, donec requiescat in te."—Thou hast made us for thyself, and our heart is restless until it rests in thee.

7. We may recall that Martin Luther in his Smaller Catechism regularly introduces various items of faith affirmation with the phrase "We should so fear and love God."

8. Frithjof Schuon, *Understanding Islam* (Baltimore: Penguin, 1961), pp. 18, 65, 91, 116, 141. Schuon indicates a further aspect of the interiority of Muhammad by quoting an extra-Koranic saying of the Prophet (*hadith*). With reference, for example, to the eating of food, as in every religious tradition, overeating is considered a sin in Islam, but to eat proper foods and in due quantity, in the context of thankfulness to God, is not wrong but a "positively meritorious action." But in a well-known saying of the Prophet, the latter said he "loved women, not that he loved food." As Schuon points out, "love" in this case moves into areas of profound appreciation of spiritual qualities that, together with commitment and responsibility, take us far beyond the physical. Ibid., p. 28. A contemporary Pakistani Muslim scholar and journalist has emphasized in the strongest way that "Islam's fundamental basis is its spiritual dimension; it is the connection that exists between the creation and the Creator." This is to focus upon the *inner jihad* (the Arabic term means "striving," but it has been popularly and historically often interpreted as "holy war"); this inner aspect we shall see later to be the preference of Muhammad. Irfan A. Omar, "Islam and the Other: The Ideal Vision of Mawlana Wahiduddin Khan," *Journal of Ecumenical Studies* 36:3–4 (Summer-Fall 1999), pp. 432, 437–438.

9. Kenneth Cragg, *The Mind of the Quran* (London: George Allen & Unwin, 1973), pp. 163–164.

10. Ibid.

11. Cf. Frederick M. Denny, *Islam* (San Francisco: Harper & Row, 1987), p. 87. Denny also notes that "the Koran itself contains many statements and examples of religious experience."

12. "Acts of barbarism can be stopped," letter by John Healey. Reprinted in the *Des Moines Register* (April 8, 1991), p. 8A.

13. Perhaps the bloodiest, as well as the most perfidious, violence in the entire range of the Crusades was perpetrated by Christians against Christians. This was the capture by the Crusaders, in cooperation with Venetian traders, and plunder of Constantinople in 1204 as a part of the Fourth Crusade (1202–1204). As the treasures of Constantinople were plundered, no booty was more eagerly sought than the ancient Christian relics of the city's churches, relics that were brought back to enrich, but even more to give "heightened spiritual authority and power" to the churches of Western Europe. An English specialist, however, in studies of Muslim views of Christians and Christianity over the centuries has contended that the Crusades were "peripheral to the Muslim world as a whole." Hugh Goddard, "Christianity from the Muslim Perspective: Varieties and Changes," in *Islam and Christianity*, Jacques Waardenburg, ed. (Leuven, Belgium: Uitgeverij Peeters, 1998), p. 214. This view of Goddard's is strongly substantiated by the contention of Bernard Lewis that "when at the end of the eleventh century, the Western crusaders occupied Palestine and captured Jerusalem, their presence and their actions aroused hardly a flicker of interest in the surrounding Muslim countries . . . During the two centuries of the crusader presence in the Levant, the Arab historians of the time devote remarkably little attention to them, while other writers—literary, political, theological—hardly mention them at all." Bernard Lewis, *The Middle East: A Brief History of the Last 2,000 Years* (New York: Scribner, 1995), p. 236.

14. Hendrik Kraemer, *World Cultures and World Religions* (Philadelphia, Pa.: Westminster, 1960), p. 19.

15. Ibid., pp. 30, 37. Cf. Lewis, *The Middle East*, op. cit, pp. 55–61.

16. Irving Howe, in reviewing V. S. Naipaul's book *A Bend in the River* for the *New York Times Book Review* in 1979, writes as follows about the writer's struggles with the persons and the problems of living in "Third World" countries: "He is free of any romantic moonshine about the moral charms of primitives or the glories of blood-stained dictators. Nor does he show a trace of Western condescension or nostalgia for colonialism." Quoted in *Newsweek* (November 16, 1981), p. 104.

17. Quoted from Naipaul's 1977 report of his year-long visit in India, entitled, "India, A Wounded Civilization." Quoted in "The Dark Visions of V. S. Naipaul," by Charles Michiner, *Newsweek* (November 16, 1981), p. 115.

18. V. S. Naipaul, *Among the Believers: An Islamic Journey* (New York: Knopf, 1981), p. 132; cf. the frequent references to violence, or assassination attempts, against Islamic rulers in Annemarie Schimmel's *Islam* (Albany, N.Y.: State University of New York Press, 1992), passim. A contemporary Muslim scholar, Tarif Khalidi, professor of Arabic at Cambridge University, writes that as a consequence of the "series of dramatically victorious conquests" that led to the formation of the early Islamic empire, there came "sudden and vast wealth, on a scale hardly imaginable to the conquerors, many of whom had been raised in a frugal, often subsistence-level Arabian environment." Tarif Khalidi, *The Muslim Jesus* (Cambridge, Mass.: Harvard University Press, 2001), p. 22.

19. Naipul, *Among the Believers*, pp. 131–143. The title of this chapter in Naipaul's book is "Killing History."

20. For an attempt to see the history of Western colonialism with some sense of fairness and balance, see Stephen C. Neill, *Colonialism and Christian Missions* (New York: McGraw-Hill, 1966), passim.

21. Paul F. Knitter has recently emphasized that a necessary element of authentic religious dialogue is to acknowledge the "fruitfulness" that characterizes all religions—perhaps we may more safely say "all major religious traditions"—in the world. This is to say that all these religions have borne significant fruit historically—in terms of ethical and cultural uplift and of personal interior satisfaction in human life—to gain and retain the allegiance of many thousands, indeed millions, of persons over long centuries. Such fruit-bearing, even if not perfect, requires, Knitter contends, the respect of others. "Ideally," he writes, "we come to the conversation from a position of richness, not impoverishment." The aim of interreligious dialogue is thus to enrich each other, to change and be changed, on the foundation of this prior reality of mutual respect. Leonard Swidler, John B. Cobb Jr., Paul F. Knitter, Monika K. Hellwig, *Death or Dialogue: From the Age of Monologue to the Age of Dialogue* (Philadelphia: Trinity Press International, 1990), pp. 22–26. The well-known British colonial officer John Bagot Glubb, writing a generation ago, after a lifetime "spent, mostly out-of-doors, in practical activities in the Arab countries," has shared some notable observations on this theme: "Muslims are often kind and gentle people. The equalitarian nature of their society, their geniality and helpfulness to their neighbours, the tender-hearted compassion shown by their women and their passionate love of children make them a very lovable community. It may be added, however, that the indigenous Christian

communities who live among them show the same qualities." Glubb wrote thus, saying also: "I am happy to be a Christian, but I have also loved Muslims." John Bagot Glubb, *The Life and Times of Muhammad* (New York: Stein and Day, 1970), pp. 9, 389–390.

22. Simon Jargy, *Islam et Chrétienté* (Geneva: Labor et Fides, 1981), p. 10. Quoted by Mohamed Talbi, "Possibilities and Conditions for a Better Understanding between Islam and the West," *Journal of Ecumenical Studies* 25:2, p. 162. It is well to note in this context that a statement as from Muhammad himself is "oft-cited" in *hadith* (traditions) over the centuries that "Jesus is the closest of prophets to him (Muhammad)." Khalidi, op. cit., p. 60.

II

1. Koran 29:48. As in the previous chapter, quotations from the Koran are from the translation by A. J. Arberry, as is also the numbering of surahs, or chapters, and verses. References to the Koran, as distinguished from quotations, are indicated in the text simply by the letter K and appropriate numbers.

2. This fact of the existence of versions containing more and less material does not warrant our assuming that the text prepared under Uthman, the third caliph or successor (as politico-military but not prophetic leader) to Muhammad, contained spurious matter. It is highly unlikely that the Koran as we have it contains anything other than what Muhammad himself proclaimed. See also F. E. Peters, *Muhammad and the Origins of Islam* (Albany, N.Y.: State University of New York Press, 1994), p. 261.

3. The treatment of this problem by Alfred Guillaume in his *Islam* (Baltimore, Md.: Penguin, 1962) is particularly good. See his chapter entitled, "Apostolic Tradition," pp. 88–110.

4. Muslim custom seen as obligation is called *sunna*, literally "the trodden path"; as written record, it is *hadith*. Cf. Kenneth Cragg, *The Call of the Minaret* (New York: Oxford University Press, 1956), p. 98.

5. Cf. John Alden Williams, *Islam* (New York: Washington Square Press, 1963), pp. 44–45; Annemarie Schimmel, *Islam* (Albany, N.Y.: State University Press, 1992), pp. 52–54.

6. Cf. H. A. R. Gibb, *Mohammedanism: An Historical Survey* (London: Oxford University Press, 1950), pp. 72–87.

7. Williams, op. cit., p. 45.

8. I shall henceforth specify as from tradition any item that is derived from the use of *hadith* as source.

9. This latter name means "praised one" (*Muhammad* means "highly praised") and, in Muslim tradition, the Prophet is thus linked to the promised comforter of John 14:26. Alfred Guillaume, *New Light on the Life of Muhammad* (Manchester, England: Manchester University Press, 1960), p. 19.

10. J. B. Bury, *A History of Greece* (London: Macmillan, 1931), p. 740.

11. A significant example of the working of this process is seen in the case of Britain, where a high level of Roman civilization had developed and was long maintained, beginning with the invasion of Britain by Julius Caesar in 55 B.C.E. Within a generation, however, after the withdrawal of Roman troops in 410 C.E. for the sake of the defense of Italy, England succumbed to the invasions of Germanic tribes, the Angles and Saxons, and quickly lost much of its distinctly Roman character and quality of cultural as well as politico-economic life.

12. Philip K. Hitti, *History of the Arabs* (London: Macmillan, 1953), p. 111.

13. Guillaume, *New Light on the Life of Muhammad*, op. cit., p. 27.

14. Cf. John Bagot Glubb, *The Life and Times of Muhammad* (New York: Stein and Day, 1971), pp. 35–37.

15. See Edward Atiyah, *The Arabs* (Harmondsworth, Middlesex, U.K.: Penguin, 1958), p. 21.

16. The term *hanif* was apparently a loan word in Arabic, borrowed from the Aramaic through the Nabataeans. Cf. Hitti, *History of the Arabs*, op. cit., p. 108.

17. Ibn Ishaq, *The Life of Muhammad*, with introduction and notes by Alfred Guillaume (London: Oxford University Press, 1968), p. 99.

18. Alfred Guillaume, *Islam* (Baltimore, Md.: Penguin, 1962), pp. 9–10.

19. Cf. Hitti, *History of the Arabs*, op. cit., p. 96. Sir John Glubb uses the term "bedouin cavalier" to denote this ideal figure and asserts that these qualities were brought to Europe by the Arab invaders and contributed significantly to the development of medieval chivalry there. Glubb, *The Life and Times of Muhammad*, op. cit., pp. 26–28. Glubb adds, however, that the Arab knight did not aspire to be gentle, nor did he abandon the concept of revenge.

20. With regard to pre-Islamic Arab ethical concepts and practices, see Toshihiko Izutsu, *Ethico-Religious Concepts in the Quran* (Montreal: McGill University Press, 1966), pp. 45–116, 252.

21. Mohammed Marmaduke Pickthall, *The Meaning of the Glorious Koran* (New York: New American Library, 1961), p. x. See the detailed

account of the *Hanifs* in F. E. Peters, *Muhammad and the Origins of Islam* (Albany, N.Y.: State University of New York Press, 1994), pp. 121–132.

22. Ibn Ishaq, *The Life of Muhammad,* op. cit., p. 82. Ibn Ishaq relates that she employed men on a profit-sharing basis.

23. The fact of the birth of six children after Khadijah had, according to the tradition, become 40 years of age raises some doubt about her age at the time of marriage. Perhaps Muhammad was actually younger than the age of 25 traditionally given for his time of marriage. The discrepancy of 15 years is probably true.

24. Cf. Deut. 5:6, 26:5; Ezek. 16:1–7.

25. Pickthall, op. cit., p. ix.

26. Williams, op. cit., p. 47.

27. W. Montgomery Watt, *Muhammad: Prophet and Statesman* (London: Oxford University Press, 1961), p. 14.

28. Guillaume, *Islam,* op. cit., pp. 27–28.

29. Cf. Williams, op. cit., p. 48.

30. Cf. Ezek. 3:18–21.

31. I have followed here the translation of Pickthall, op. cit., p. 94, for K 81:24.

32. Hitti, op. cit., p. 113. Montgomery Watt adds that, on some occasions, Muhammad experienced a kind of physical pain in his entranced state, op. cit., pp. 18–19.

33. Williams, op. cit., p. 49. Ibn Ishaq relates that Waraqa was in fact a Christian. Waraqa may have so understood himself, but there is no evidence, as we have noted, of an organized community of Jews or Christians in Mecca during the lifetime of Muhammad.

34. Pickthall, op. cit., p. xi; cf. K 69:40–43.

35. The term "slave of Allah," which is frequently used of Muhammad in the Koran, is intended more to suggest the majesty of God than the servility of his bondsmen. Muslims think of bondage to Allah as "liberating from all other servitudes." My own experience in Muslim lands coincides with that of Count Keyserling, who wrote of the proud dignity of demeanor that characterizes Muslims, a dignity deriving in no small measure from this sense of belonging to a Lord so majestic as Allah. Count Hermann Keyserling, *The Travel Diary of a Philosopher* (New York: Harcourt, Brace, 1925), vol. 1, p. 206–209. It should also be noted that, in the New Testament, Paul's designation of himself, which is generally translated as "servant of Jesus Christ," is in Greek, "slave of Jesus Christ." Cf. Rom. 1:1; Gal. 1:10; Phil. 1:1; Titus 1:1.

36. The early biographer Ibn Ishaq, who was sympathetic to the Shia position, gives the name of Ali (the leading figure, after Muhammad, for Shi-ite Muslims) as the first male to accept Islam, but it is very possible that Abu Bakr, who became the first caliph, was first. Cf. Williams, op. cit., pp. 50–51; Guillaume, *Islam*, op. cit., p. 32.

37. Cf. K 43:23, 30. One of the derogatory charges made against Muhammad was that he had received his message from a Christian slave who was among the earliest converts. This slave, incidentally, is said to have suffered cruel persecution in Mecca for his commitment to Islam.

38. Cf. Williams, op. cit., p. 51–52.

39. In Surah 5:85–86, we find the statement that the most affectionate friends of believers (Muslims) will be found to be those who say they are Christians. This surah is traditionally regarded as of the Medinan period, but it is possible that the verse was, at least in part, motivated by the treatment received by the Muslims in Ethiopia. Cf. Guillaume, *Islam*, op. cit., pp. 33–34.

40. Cf. Pickthall, op. cit., pp. 226–227.

41. Cf. Hitti, op. cit., pp. 98–99; Guillaume, *Islam*, op. cit., p. 35; Watt, op. cit., p. 26. There is some difficulty, however, about the translation of the Arabic in 53:19–20.

42. The privations experienced by the Muslims at this time are related in moving detail by Ibn Ishaq. See Guillaume, *New Light on the Life of Muhammad*, op. cit., pp. 42–43.

43. Muhammad is sent to *a* nation (K 13:28); cf. K 10:48: there is a messenger for every nation.

44. Whoever obeys the messenger obeys God (K 4:83). Cf. Matt. 11:28–30; Luke 6:47. There is a passage, however, in the Koran where it is suggested that obedience to the Prophet is not absolute but obligatory only "in what is right" (K 60:12).

45. Cf. Pickthall, op. cit., p. 300.

46. The term "seal" may mean "final" or, more probably, what is an important part of Muhammad's teaching elsewhere, the "confirmation" of the prophets who had been before him.

47. "He used to tell her of his troubles." Williams, op. cit., p. 56. Michael Cook asserts that the trip to Ta'if was primarily to find protectors, as were other preachings at fairs at this time. Michael Cook, *Muhammad* (Oxford: Oxford University Press, 1983), p. 18. See Karen Armstrong, *Muhammad: A Biography of the Prophet* (San Francisco, Harper Collins, 1992), pp. 136–138.

48. Muslim tradition relates that the Jewish expectation of the Messiah led the pagan Medinans to accept Muhammad as the very prophet-judge of whom the Jews of Medina had warned. For the Jews had threatened that they would be able to kill the pagans with the Messiah's aid when he came. The pagans apparently resolved to forestall this eventuality by getting him on their side first. Williams, op. cit., p. 57.

49. Pickthall, op. cit., p. ix.

50. Williams, op. cit., p. 49.

51. The Koran relates (69:44–47) that, if Muhammad had lied concerning Allah, He would have destroyed him.

52. Pickthall, op. cit., p. 405.

53. Williams, op. cit., p. 59.

54. Williams, ibid., p. 57. Cf. K 10:47.

55. Guillaume, *Islam*, op. cit., p. 40.

56. The second caliph, Umar, took the step, which had not been authorized by Muhammad and was specifically in disregard of earlier treaties, of compelling all Jews and Christians to leave the Arabian peninsula, although with the safety of their persons and transportable goods guaranteed. Cf. Hitti, op. cit., p. 169.

57. Pickthall, op. cit., p. 32.

58. Guillaume, *Islam*, op. cit., p. 41.

59. The charter bound all Muslims to joint responsibility in the military service of the community, guaranteed them its protection, and made Allah and His Prophet the final arbiter of all disputes.

60. Cf. Arend Th. van Leeuwen, *Christianity in World History* (London: Edinburgh House, 1964), pp. 246-247; Kenneth Cragg, *The Event of the Quran* (London: George Allen & Unwin, 1971), pp. 133–135.

61. See K 2:217, where it is stated that idolatry (or persecution) is worse than killing. Cf. Fazlur Rahman, *Islam* (Garden City, N.Y.: Doubleday, 1968), p. 15.

62. The Muslims had compounded the injury by capturing a richly laden caravan.

63. Pickthall, op. cit., pp. xx–xxi.

64. In order to conciliate and win over the Jews, Muhammad adopted a number of Jewish practices such as the fast of Yom Kippur. Possibly the early Muslim custom of prayer facing Jerusalem was begun for the same reason. Cf. Bernard Lewis, *The Arabs in History* (London: Hutchinson University Library, 1960), p. 42; Pickthall, op. cit., pp. 45, 69.

65. Guillaume, *Islam*, op. cit., p. 44.

66. Hitti, op. cit., pp. 104–105.

67. The Qaynuqah were mostly goldsmiths.

68. Ibn Ishaq, *The Life of Muhammad*, op. cit., pp. 463–464.

69. Guillaume, *Islam*, op. cit. p. 48. Karen Armstrong gives a more detailed account of these events. Karen Armstrong, *Muhammad: A Biography of the Prophet*, op. cit., pp. 206–210. For an insightful interpretation of the dilemma of all the Jewish tribes in Arabia during the time of Muhammad's prophetic and political career, see W. Montgomery Watt, op. cit., pp. 188–194.

70. Two of these men, Khalid ibn al-Walid and Amr ibn al-As, were to become important military leaders in later Muslim conquests.

71. Some accounts cite the *casus belli* as no more than the murder of a Muslim by a Meccan in a private quarrel. Cf. Lewis, *The Arabs in History*, op. cit., p. 46.

72. Cf. Pickthall, op. cit., p. 365.

73. H. A. R. Gibb, "Islam," in *The Concise Encyclopedia of Living Faiths*, R. C. Zaehner, ed. (New York: Hawthorne, 1959), p. 179. Muhammad evidently knew that external pressures may subdue evil but cannot in themselves transform it. Cf. Kenneth Cragg, *The Mind of the Quran* (London: George Allen & Unwin, 1973), pp. 94–95.

74. Pickthall, op. cit., pp. xxiv–xxv.

75. Gibb, *Mohammedanism*, op. cit., p. 31.

76. *Mushrik* refers to him who commits *shirk*, literally "association" in the sense of ascribing to other than God the prerogatives that belong to him alone, in short, an idolater. Cf. Kenneth Cragg, *Sandals at the Mosque* (London: SCM Press, 1959), pp. 151, 153.

77. Gibb, *Mohammedanism*, op. cit., p. 30.

78. Williams, op. cit., pp. 59–60.

79. Cf. Lewis, *The Arabs in History*, op. cit., p. 43.

80. In K 58:13, there is reference to a practice of paying alms before having access to the Prophet. Perhaps this practice was a device to limit callers as well as to preserve the dignity of the occasion.

81. Williams, op. cit., pp. 72, 73. Cf. Arthur Jeffery, *Islam: Muhammad and His Religion* (New York: Liberal Arts Press, 1958), pp. 27–28.

82. Hitti, op. cit., p. 121.

83. This practice ceased shortly after the death of Muhammad, and Sunni Muslims regard the caliph as temporal ruler and the imam as the

spiritual. Shia believers (largely confined to Iran, Lebanon, Iraq, and Pakistan), however, give more inclusive authority to their imams. Cf. Joseph M. Kitagawa, *Religions of the East* (Philadelphia, Pa.: Westminster, 1960), p. 247.

84. Pickthall, op. cit., p. 405.

85. Williams, op. cit., pp. 69–70.

86. Cf. Williams, ibid., p. 69.

87. Pickthall, op. cit., pp. 300–301. In the Koran (4:3), Muhammad is recorded as urging the Muslims to marry the widows, up to four, of the men who had been killed at the battle of Uhud, and to care for their orphans.

88. Slave girls, however, are not to be forced against their will into prostitution (K 24:33).

89. Edward Atiyah, *The Arabs*, op. cit., pp. 27–28.

90. Muslim practice tended to revert, as previously noted, to a level below that of the Prophet and to be legally justified by various casuistical devices. Cf. Gibb, *Mohammedanism*, op. cit., p. 33.

91. Pickthall, op. cit., p. 405. Cf. Glubb, *The Life and Times of Muhammad*, op. cit., p. 359.

92. Williams, op. cit., p. 74.

93. Ibid., pp. 73, 70. The companion of the Prophet who reported the incident is said to have observed that if Muhammad had allowed the vow, "we would all have been castrated." The profound reverence for the Prophet, the force of his impact on the hearts and lives of men and women, are clearly revealed in this remark.

94. Williams, op. cit., pp. 74.

III

1. The translation here is from Kenneth Cragg, *The Event of the Quran* (London: George Allen & Unwin, 1971), p. 178. Cragg notes that *ajal* means "term" or "period" and that "book" may carry the added connotation of "destiny." Cf. Inam Musa al-Sadre, "Truth, Revelation and Obedience" in *Christian-Muslim Dialogue: Papers Presented at the Broumana Consultation*, 12–18 July 1972, S. J. Samartha and J. B. Taylor, eds. (Geneva: World Council of Churches, 1973), pp. 47–48.

2. Kenneth Cragg, *Muhammad and the Christian: A Question of Response* (Maryknoll, N.Y.: Orbis Books, 1984), p. 125.

3. Richard H. Drummond, "Toward Theological Understanding of Islam," *Journal of Ecumenical Studies* 9:4 (Fall 1972), p. 793. It is of con-

siderable significance that Fahmi Huwaidi, a journalist who is considered one of the leading thinkers of a Muslim reformist movement in contemporary Egypt, has written forcefully of the need for a mode of historical-critical methodology to be employed, especially with reference to the works of Muslim juridical scholars over the centuries. He suggests that even if certain texts are authentic, they should be read in light of the circumstances of their times. A particular text may be a response to a temporary situation and may offer no direction for the future. He goes on to say—presumably speaking of *hadith*, but possibly (?) implying certain passages in the Koran—that certain passages could have been pronounced by the Prophet "according to his human nature and that others concern the person of the Prophet alone, as in the case of his marriages with more than four wives." Waheed Hassab Alla, "Le Christianisme et les Chrétiens Vus par Deux Auteurs Arabes Musulmans," in *Islam and Christianity*, Jacques Waardenburg, ed. (Leuven, Belgium: Uitgeverij Peeters, 1998), pp. 200–201. The part of the last sentence in quotations marks represents my translation of Dr. Alla's French.

4. Kenneth Cragg, *Sandals at the Mosque* (London: SCM Press, 1959), p. 54.

5. The term for God used in the Arabic language from before the time of Muhammad—and specifically by Arabic-speaking Christians—was Allah. The word *Al-Ilah*, also meaning "the God," is used in the Koran to refer to the same unitary Creator God, though less frequently. The term *Allah* has neither feminine grammatical gender nor plural number and in the Koran is used only for the One God, Supreme over all, Creator and Judge of all.

6. Readers are reminded that verbatim quotations from the Koran are from the translation by A. J. Arberry, *The Koran Interpreted* (New York, Macmillan, 1955). The numbering of verses is also according to his version.

7. God is said to have created every animal out of water (K 24:44), humans from a blood clot (K 96:2), or from dust, and then from a drop of sperm, in the case of Adam, and "then He made you pairs" (K 35:12).

8. A. J. Arberry often uses the term "disbelieve," as does M. M. Pickthall, in preference to terms like "unbeliever" with their unfortunate historical associations of partisan rivalry. Muhammad evidently intended with the term to speak of an active disbelief, conscious rejection of the messengers of God and their revelations.

/. I am able to report confirmation of this point as a result of corre-
spondence a number of years ago (February 16, 1967) with the distinguished Islamic scholar Professor Edward J. Jurji of Princeton
Theological Seminary.

10. It is significant that the North African Christian theologian
Tertullian (ca. 150–222) in his work on prayer wrote how the birds soar
up to the sky in the morning and in place of hands spread their wings in
the shape of a cross, crying out something that seems like prayer (*De
Oratione* 29).

11. Cf. Edward J. Jurji, *The Great Religions of the Modern World*
(Princeton, N.J.: Princeton University Press, 1947), pp. 189–191.

12. Note in K 2:138 the statement that God has appointed the
Muslims to be a "midmost nation," that is, a mediatory people, a mis-
sionary people, witnesses to others even as Muhammad as Messenger of
God was witness to the Arabic-speaking peoples of his time.

13. It may be proper to note that belief in a process of divine compensation, or sowing and reaping, at work currently in this world—as
well as varied expectations of more complete fulfillment on the "Day of
the Lord"—exists as an assumption of faith in much of the Bible. It is a
conviction underlying the whole of the prophetic literature of the
Hebrew Old Testament, as of the faith and teaching of the Greek New
Testament (cf. Matt. 7:1–2; Luke 13:1–5; Gal. 6:7). Salvation, however
that term may be perceived and expressed in the Bible, is always a reality of ultimately divine origin at work in dynamic tension with this
process of sowing and reaping. The biblical vision of faith—in the context of Christian faith, the role of Jesus the Christ becomes singularly
effective as a divine-human reality—is that salvation is the final word.
Salvation will be ultimately victorious in the cosmos, yet not without
suffering, both divine and human (cf. Col. 1:24; 1 Pet. 4:13).

14. Kenneth Cragg, *The Mind of the Quran* (London: George Allen &
Unwin, 1973), p. 65.

15. I have already noted that in the Hebrew Old Testament both
Jeremiah (31:29–30) and Ezekiel (18:1–32) came to similar conclusions
regarding the affirmations of genetic continuity of moral guilt and divine
compensation cited in the Ten Commandments (Exod. 20:5–6). The
larger text of Jeremiah, however, reveals some inconsistencies (Jer. 2:9,
32:18).

16. Muhammad Zafrulla Khan, *Islam* (New York: Harper & Row,
1962), p. 196. The modern Qadiani Ahmadiya sect of Islam teaches that

punishment in hell is not everlasting. Cf. Alfred Guillaume, *Islam* (Baltimore, Md.: Penguin, 1962), p. 126; Annemarie Schimmel, *Islam* (Albany, N.Y.: State University of New York Press, 1992), pp. 85–86.

17. Kahn, *Islam*, op. cit., p. 196.

18. Tradition records that Muhammad had a fondness for honey. As we noted earlier, wine was at first allowed in moderation in the early Muslim community and then later forbidden.

19. It is worthy of note that among the great confessions of Christian faith in the age of the Protestant Reformation, the Belgic Confession of 1561 seems to have a comparable concept in its Article 37 on the Last Judgment. Here we read that "the thought of this judgment . . . is very pleasant and a great comfort to the righteous and elect, since their total redemption will then be accomplished."

20. This figure of a wall with a door between Paradise and Gehenna is given as part of Muhammad's imagined response on that Day on the part of the hypocrites, men and women, who ask to borrow the light of believers. They are told to go back and seek for a light themselves (K 57:13; cf. Matt. 25:8–10). This response, together with the imagery of a door, might seem to suggest some possibility of an alteration of human destiny after that Day. But nonesuch is forthcoming in this passage or the following (K 77:14; cf. Luke 16:26).

21. Cf. Herbert C. Alleman, *The Old Testament—A Study* (Philadelphia, Pa: United Lutheran Publication House, 1935), p. 183.

22. Muhammad seems to imply a certain divine reticence in revealing his person and nature, akin, as we may note, to certain passages in the Bible and in the history of Judeo-Christian spirituality (*Deus absconditus*). Cf. K 42:50–51; Exod. 33:20; John 1:18.

23. Cf. Geoffrey Parrinder, *Jesus in the Quran* (New York: Barnes & Noble, 1965), pp. 37–42.

24. Note the high appreciation of the persons and roles of angels in the cosmos in the later Muslim exegetical tradition as exemplified by Fakhr al-Din al-Razi (1149–1209). Cf. Kenneth Cragg, *The Mind of the Quran* (London: George Allen & Unwin, 1973), pp. 60–62.

25. The translation of N. J. Dawood seems preferable here to that of A. J. Arberry, in that Dawood translates the key term *furqan* as the distinction or criterion by which truth and right are distinguished from their opposites. Arberry's translation of the term as "salvation"—without explanation—is unduly vague.

26. Kenneth Cragg translates this last term as "the inviolate tablet."

The Mind of the Quran, op. cit., p. 42. Such language led to the later development in Islamic orthodoxy of the concept of the preexistent Koran, preexistent in the heavens from all eternity.

27. One may properly recall in this context that Muhammad's sense of the identity of his own Message with that of the Messengers of God who had preceded him seems to have been with reference to their essential content rather than in any minutely literal sense.

28. Cf. Parrinder, op. cit., p. 121.

29. This introductory section is found only in the Bodleian manuscript of the text and not in the more ancient Laurenziano manuscript that was published recently with an Italian translation by M. E. Provera (Jerusalem: Franciscan Printing Press, 1973). J. E. Peeters, who cites the text in full, believes that the item is indeed a scholion added by a copyist, *Évangiles Apocryphes* (Paris: Librarie Alphonse Picard et fils, 1914), p. 1. Cf. Neal Robinson, *Christ in Islam and Christianity* (Albany, N.Y.: State University of New York Press, 1991), pp. 19, 196–197. The English translation given here is cited as by Henry Sike, then professor of Oriental languages at Cambridge University, and published in 1697; Henry Sike, *The Lost Books of the Bible* (New York: Alpha House, 1926), p. 38.

30. Cf. Edgar Hennecke, Wilhelm Schneemelcher, *New Testament Apocrypha*, vol. 1 (Philadelphia, Pa.: Westminster, 1963), pp. 392–393.

31. Cf. Parrinder, op. cit., pp. 78, 146.

32. In this case, "the Book" would seem to refer to the heavenly preexistent Book of which the traditional Jewish Torah and the Christian Gospel are representations, essentially faithful but not necessarily inerrant.

33. Ahmad (the praised one) is one of the titles of praise historically given to Muhammad. This passage of the Koran has been widely believed by many Muslim scholars, as by less learned believers, to be the proper interpretation of the New Testament Johannine promise of the divine sending of a Comforter (John 14:16–17). Cf. Parrinder, op. cit., pp. 96–100.

34. Cf. Mohammed M. Pickthall, *The Meaning of the Glorious Koran* (New York: New American Library, 1961), p. 35, footnote 1.

35. The reference here is to a form of the Christian doctrine of the Trinity as it was perceived by at least some Arabs of the day. That is, Jesus and Mary are said to be the second and third persons of the Trinity in what is, of course, a misrepresentation of the ecumenical creeds of the Christian Church of the first six centuries.

36. As a continuation of this passage, we note one of the statements most critical of Jews in the entire Koran. Here the Jews are associated with idolators as "the most hostile of men to the believers [Muslims]." And those who are the nearest "in love to the believers are those who say 'We are Christians.'" Some of these are cited as priests and monks, and a primary characteristic is that "they wax not proud, and when they hear what has been sent down to the Messenger [Muhammad], thou seest their eyes overflow with tears because of the truth they recognize" (K 5:85–86). Some Christians, it appears, acknowledged Muhammad as an authentic Prophet of God recognizably in accord with their own tradition of faith. We do not know the locus of these Christians.

37. For a careful and persuasive treatment of this issue, see Parrinder, op. cit., pp. 105–125. It is significant that some contemporary Muslim scholars—most of whom, one must state, have lived long years in Western or Muslim-minority lands—claim that the Koran, in naming Jesus as Messiah, Prophet, and Servant of God and also insisting that he is not to be identified with God, does not mean that he is merely man (*bashar*). For example, Ali Merad, born in Algeria and teaching for a number of years at the University of Lyon in France and later at the Sorbonne in Paris, claims that the Koran, in affirming Jesus' miraculous birth from a virgin, his status as Word (*kalima*) of God and Spirit (*ruh*) from God, "should suggest a spiritual nature infinitely more eminent than ordinary natures." Merad adds, "Christ is placed above the ordinary level of the Envoys of God by virtue of the fact that he alone brings the dead to life. Christ is a dominant figure among the Envoys of God, an exceptional being, whose creation is given the same significance as that of Adam; for both represent unique points in the destiny of mankind on earth; Adam's creation indicates its beginning, that of Christ its spiritual consummation." This is to conclude, as does the East Indian Muslim scholar Syed Vahiduddin, that "Muslim and Christian are bound together by a shared devotion to Christ and to His Holy Mother." Hugh Goddard, "Christianity from the Muslim Perspective: Varieties and Changes," in *Islam and Christianity*, Jacques Waardenburg, ed. (Leuven, Belgium: Uitgeverij Peeters, 1998), pp. 243, 219.

Tarif Khalidi, professor of Arabic at Cambridge University, writes of the "singularity" of Jesus among the many prophets cited in the Koran. Tarif Khalidi, *The Muslim Jesus* (Cambridge, Mass.: Harvard University Press, 2001), p. 11. Khalidi also insists that the identification of Jesus in the Koran as the Word of God and as the Spirit of God is "absolutely central to the structure of his image" in the texts of the great mystical movement of Sufism in historic Islam. Ibid., pp. 41–42.

38. Tarif Khalidi, *The Muslim Jesus*, p. 121. A remarkable series of statements on this theme has been made by the contemporary East Indian Muslim scholar Syed Vahiduddin, who perhaps melds together somewhat the events of the resurrection and the ascension of Jesus Christ as recorded in the New Testament, but gives one of the highest Christological affirmations to be found in any Muslim interpreter. He writes: "What greater ignominy and disgrace could there be than that which Christ suffered. But it is here that Christ appears in all His glory, and the world and all it stands for is exposed in all its vanity . . . death is not allowed to prevail and Christ appears to be ascending to supreme heights defying death. Perhaps it is due to my Muslim background that what strikes me most is not the suffering through which he passes, but his triumph through suffering. What looks like defeat, subjection to mortality, the brute success of worldly power and of hard-headed priesthood lose their relevance [sic]. Death is vanquished once for all, and Christ's life serves as a beacon to all those who are laid low, who 'labour and are heavy laden' (Matthew 11:28)." Hugh Goddard, "Christianity from the Muslim Perspective: Varieties and Changes," in *Islam and Christianty*, Jacques Waardenburg, ed. (Leuven, Belgium: Uitgeverij Peeters, 1998), pp. 218–219.

39. Ibn Ishaq, *The Life of Muhammad*, with introduction and notes by Alfred Guillaume (New York: Oxford University Press, 1968), pp. 181–187. Three of these accounts refer to Muhammad's vision as including Abraham and Moses in heaven along with Jesus. Another account speaks of Jesus as in the "second heaven" along with his maternal cousin, "John, son of Zakariah." One of Ibn Ishaq's sources discusses Muhammad's, and other Prophets', experiences of receiving divine revelation and concludes that states of both waking and sleeping are equally authentic modes of human reception of divine revelation. For further discussion of the issue of the crucifixion of Jesus, see Neal Robinson, *Christ in Islam and Christianity* (Albany, N.Y.: State University of New York Press, 1991), pp. 106–141.

40. It should also be noted that similar language is used in the same passage to affirm that God sent down the Torah, "wherein is guidance and light" (K 5:48).

41. Guillaume, *Islam*, op. cit., pp. 13–14. Cf. Khalidi, op. cit., p. 44.

42. The favorable evaluation of Christian monks and priests in this

passage is to be compared with the criticism of monasticism as an institution that we have already noted (K 57:28).

43. Cf. Arend Th. van Leeuwen, *Christianity in World History* (London: Edinburgh House, 1965), pp. 218–219.

44. Charles Le Gai Eaton, *Islam and the Destiny of Man* (Albany, N.Y.: State University of New York Press, 1985), p. 2.

45. This passage contains some of the sharpest criticisms of the mind and practices of the Jewish community in Medina to be found in the entire Koran. With reference to the charge of Jewish belief in demons and idols, Muhammad was, of course, aware of the Jewish practice of exorcism and alleged "occult" (magical?) elements in the Jewish traditions of the time (cf. K 2:95–97). From an earlier period, one may recall the descriptions in the New Testament book of Acts 8:4–24, 13:4–12.

46. Cf. Guillaume, *Islam*, op. cit., pp. 186–192.

47. Mahmoud Mustafa Ayoub, "Jesus the Son of God: A Study of the Terms *Ibn* and *Walad* in the Quran and Tafsir Tradition," in *Christian-Muslim Encounters*, Yvonne Yazbeck Haddad, Wadi L. Haddad, eds. (Gainesville, Fla.: University Press of Florida, 1995), pp. 65–81. The same point is stressed by the Lebanese Shi-ite scholar Muhammad Hussein Fadlallad, who also suggests that the Koranic verses concerning this theme may refer to certain Christian views held in the seventh century, views that accord neither with the understanding of the early church nor with those of contemporary Christians. Waheed Hassab Alla, "Le Christianisme et les Chrétiens Vus par Deux Auteurs Arabes Musulmans," in *Islam and Christianity*, Jacques Waardenburg, ed. (Leuven, Belgium: Uitgeverij Peeters, 1998), pp. 172–173. Dr. Alla is an Egyptian Coptic Orthodox scholar now living in Lausanne, Switzerland.

48. The subsequent birth of human beings is denoted as by semen, described in Arabic as "an extraction of mean water" (M. M. Pickthall has "a draught of despised fluid." Cf. Pickthall's "a drop" of seed in K 23:14.

49. It is needful to note that original sin in the Augustinian sense of the genetic transmission of both moral guilt and sinful nature from Adam and Eve to all their descendants was not a doctrine held by the mainstream of the early Christian church. Cf. Roger L. Forster and V. Paul Marston, *God's Strategy in Human History* (Wheaton, Ill.: Tyndale House, 1974), pp. 270–272. Cf. Jer. 2:9, 31:29–30; Ezek. 18:1–32. One may note, however, that in another surah Muhammad uses the term

"weakness" to denote the physical weakness of early childhood and old age, as contrasted with the strength of physical maturity (K 30:53). Cf. Annemarie Schimmel, *Islam* (Albany, N.Y.: State University of New York Press, 1992), pp. 32–33.

50. Cragg, *The Mind of the Quran*, op. cit., p. 96.

51. It appears from a late Medinan surah that Muhammad believed growing knowledge of each other to be the basis for proper relationships among the races and tribes of humankind. The immediate context is proclamation of the creation of human beings as male and female (K 49:13).

52. Cf. Augustine, *Confessions* 1:1.

53. Muhammad's acceptance of slavery as an institution under divine approval—following general Middle Eastern mind and practice—needs to be set in the context of his proclamation of the setting free of a slave as among the highest of virtues. He taught the setting free of a believing slave as a significant element of penance for unwillful manslaughter (K 2:172; 4:93).

54. Cragg, *The Mind of the Quran*, op. cit., pp. 31–34. The meaning of *dhikr* seems to revolve around the two poles of a recollection in the human self of an original belonging to God and the practice of remembering the verses of the Koran, including systematic programs of memorization.

55. Alfred Guillaume translates this passage: When any prophet "allowed his own wishes to predominate, Satan interjected (words) into his desires." Guillaume, *Islam*, op. cit., p. 35.

56. One must recall that Khadijah was able to conduct her own business in Mecca as an independent, property-owning individual—at least for a time—before her marriage to Muhammad. Her proposal of marriage to Muhammad may, of course, have been partially motivated by the legal as well as social advantages of having a husband. There is no evidence that Muhammad ever beat Khadijah. One may properly note that, among the early Puritan settlers of New England, husbands were permitted by law to beat their wives, although not "too severely." Elizabeth Fox-Genovese, "Religion and Women in America," in *World Religions in America*, Jacob Neusner, ed. (Louisville, Ky.: Westminster/ John Knox, 1994), p. 262.

57. The language of this passage suggests that if wives, and other clients, are not wise in the management of their property, husbands have the right to take over the management thereof. But householders must

not only provide for the physical needs of those thus under their care, they must also "speak to them honourable words" (K 4:4). Bernard Lewis contends that "In Islam, unlike the ancient world, a slave was no longer a chattel but a person with a recognized legal and moral status. Women, though still subject to polygamy and concubinage, were accorded property rights not equaled in the west until modern times." Bernard Lewis, *The Middle East: A Brief History of the Last 2,000 Years* (New York: Scribner, 1995), p. 72.

58. Cf. Guillaume, *Islam*, op. cit., pp. 71, 177–184; Kenneth Cragg, *The Call of the Minaret* (New York: Oxford University Press, 1956), p. 168. There have been, moreover, Muslims in the twentieth century, like Sayed Ameer Ali of Pakistan or the Turkish poet Ziya Gok Alk, who have contended for monogamy in practice and equality in divorce. They have regarded the assumption of any inherent superiority of males over females as contrary to the spirit of Islam.

59. Sayed Ameer Ali, the Shi-ite Muslim whose work *The Spirit of Islam* has been one of the books most widely read by Muslims in the twentieth century, asserts that as absolute justice in such matters of feeling is impossible, the Koranic prescription of full equality of treatment among wives amounts in fact to a prohibition of polygamy. Sayed Ameer Ali, *The Spirit of Islam* (London: Christophers, 1946), p. 229. Tradition records, we should note, a statement by Muhammad's youngest wife, A'isha, that he practiced remarkably equal cohabitation among his wives. John Alden Williams, *Islam* (New York: Washington Square Press, 1963), p. 107.

60. Islamic custom has established that the Koranic prescription of "honourable provision" may be fulfilled by providing for the material needs of a wife for six months after the husband's first pronouncement of divorce. This is the time period normally required for the legal process to be completed. It is another question, however, whether this provision is "honourable" or suitable to human needs. Cf. Khan, op cit., p. 143.

61. Cf. Sayed Ameer Ali, op. cit., p. 244.

62. Cf. Guillaume, *Islam*, op cit., pp. 71, 159–160, 174, 183–185.

63. Khan, op. cit., p. 143; Mohamad Talbi, "Possibilities and Conditions for a Better Understanding between Islam and the West," *Journal of Ecumenical Studies* 25:2 (Spring 1988), pp. 166–168.

64. Khan, ibid., p. 133. Tradition also records Muhammad as having refused to let Uthman ibn Mazuh make a vow of chastity. Williams, op.

cit., p. 70. In the later practices of Muslim Sufi spirituality, we find instances of extended sexual abstinence for purposes of spiritual discipline and/or service, but apparently no cases of lifelong vows.

65. Previous to this time, Muslims had been forbidden to have intercourse with their wives throughout the month of Ramadan. "The Cow" is usually identified as an early Medinan collection, but various parts may be of later provenance. It is significant that this verse (K 2:183) follows immediately after the devotionally pregnant promise of God: "I am near to answer the call of the caller, when he calls to Me; so let them respond to Me, and let them believe in Me" (K 2:182). An initial call of God to persons seems also implied in this divine promise to hear and answer the prayers of believers.

66. Tradition records Muhammad as having ordered the stoning of a confessed adulterer. Williams, op. cit., p. 69. With reference again to the compassion of Muhammad, he forbade, with the authority of God, any Muslim to force a slave of his ownership into prostitution. If a Muslim should do such, God, it is promised, will be merciful and forgiving to the slave(s), but presumably not to their master (K 24:33).

67. Otherwise, Muslim males are forbidden to marry idolatresses, or Muslim females to marry idolaters, until they believe (K 2:220). We note that it is permissible for Muslims to marry—with full legality—a female slave who is a believer and "righteous" (K 24:32; 4:29). These passages, however, seem to imply that Muslims may own female slaves who are nonbelievers—an increasing possibility as the Islamic empire expanded—and also have sexual access to them.

68. Williams, op. cit., p. 70. Abdullah Yusuf Ali, in his translation of the Koran (with notes), understands 4:15–16 to mean prohibition of homosexuality whether among men or among women. *The Meaning of the Glorious Quran* (Cairo, Egypt: Dar Al-Kitab Al-Masri, 1938), pp. 183–184, ftn. 523.

69. Y. Toshihiko Zutsu, *Ethico-Religious Concepts in the Quran* (Montreal: McGill University Press, 1966), pp. 45, 251–252.

70. Abdullah Yusuf Ali, *The Meaning of the Glorious Quran* (Cairo, Egypt: Dar Al-Kitab Al-Masri, 1934), p. 17.

71. The term here translated as alms (*zakat*) came to be a state tax assigned at a fixed rate in proportion to the value of personal property owned. It was collected from people of means and distributed among the poor. Cf. Kenneth Cragg, *Sandals at the Mosque* (London: SCM Press, 1959), p.33. Cragg sees in the almsgiving of Islam the clue to its social

obligations, as "that acknowledgement of the right of God and of society in the possessions of the propertied which validates their ownership." Whether collected by the government or left to the conscience of persons, contemporary practice shows about 2.5 percent of personal wealth to be the norm for *zakat*-giving. Cf. R. Marston Speight, *God Is One: The Way of Islam* (New York: Friendship Press, 1991), p.38.

72. Cf. Speight, op. cit., pp. 60–62, for discussion of contemporary banking practices in predominantly Muslim lands.

73. Cf. Jeffrey Carlson, "Syncretistic Religiosity: The Significance of This Tautology," *Journal of Ecumenical Studies* 29:1 (Winter 1992), pp. 24–34.

74. Muhammad was instructed to say to prisoners of war who are not slaves that if God knows of any good in their hearts, that is, if they have intent to believe and participate in the Muslim community, God will forgive them and give them better than what they have lost. This was an invitation to become Muslims and share in both the spiritual life and the material goods of the community (K 8:71).

75. In a late Meccan surah, one notes a warning to believers that there are those among their women and children who are "an enemy to you" (K 64:14). The setting is generally conjectured to be resistance on the part of some Muslim wives and children to leaving Mecca for the *Hijrah* to Medina in 622 C.E. Muhammad, however, at once adds to this warning his sense that it is good to pardon and overlook such conduct. Human forgiveness is congruent with the All-forgiving, All-compassionate nature of God.

76. This is one aspect of the "countering independence" of Muhammad's respectful but discriminating posture toward both Judaism and Christianity, of which Kenneth Cragg writes. *The Mind of the Quran*, op. cit., p. 17.

77. One should note that, in a passage that seems to refer to believers coming to Muhammad for consultation more than once about the meaning of afflictions they had experienced, the Prophet suggests a deeper meaning than his usual directions to endure patiently whatever comes. This is that, even in the context of the overarching power of God, an affliction may come "from your own selves" (K 3:159).

78. Cf. Kenneth Cragg, *The Call of the Minaret* (New York: Oxford University Press, 1956), pp. 16–18; H. A. R. Gibb, *Mohammedanism, An Historical Survey* (London: Oxford University Press, 1950), pp. 104–105. With reference to the question of the possible loss of another severe

directive, the so-called Verse of Stoning, which *may* have been a genuine *hadith* of the Prophet or even a lost verse of the Koran itself, see Guillaume, *Islam*, op. cit., p. 191.

79. The affirmation of what came to be orthodox or historically dominant Christian faith is that Jesus Christ, as the supreme revelation of God the Father, was and is infallible as the channel of divine revelation. The flawed nature, however, of all human character at present on earth makes the reception of that revelation less than infallible.

80. Gibb, *Mohammedanism*, op. cit., pp. 88, 92.

81. Cragg, *The Call of the Minaret*, op. cit., pp. 47–48, 55–56.

82. Kenneth Cragg, *House of Islam* (Belmont, Calif.: Dickenson, 1969), p. 45. Cragg states that the term *Fiqh* "combines the twin ideas of directive and response, of God in command and man in surrender."

83. Cragg, *The Mind of the Quran*, op. cit., pp. 24, 31, 131, 169. Koranic passages are 15:6, 9; 16:45; 36:10; 38:8; 41:41; 68:51–52.

84. Cf. Dietrich Bonhoeffer, *Ethics*, E. Bethge, ed. (New York: Macmillan, 1965), pp. 248–249.

IV

1. We have also observed that the Koran itself frequently speaks of an internal Criterion of truth and goodness (*Furqan*) given to all humanity, a Criterion that for Muslims properly may be distinguished but never separated from the Koran.

2. Alfred Guillaume, *Islam* (Baltimore, Md.: Penguin, 1962), p. 160.

3. Marshall W. Baldwin, "The Crusades," in *The New Encyclopedia Britannica*, vol. 16 (Chicago: University of Chicago Press, 1990), p. 827.

4. We may note that the Mongols returned to the Middle East with even greater forces in the thirteenth century, destroying the city of Baghdad in 1258 and with it the religio-political rule of the sultan. This latter, to be sure, had for some time exercised a suzerainty more symbolic than real throughout the Islamic world, but the downfall of Baghdad marked the end of the formal unity of the Islamic Empire. It also coincided with the beginnings of a slow decline, in comparison with western Europe, of Muslim civilization and culture from their previous commanding heights.

5. V. L. Ménage, "The Islamicization of Anatolia," in *Conversion to Islam*, Nehemia Levtzion, ed. (New York: Holmes & Meier, 1979), pp. 54–59.

6. Note should be taken of the ethnic background of two elements

of the Muslim populations within present-day (former) Yugoslavia, Albania, and Macedonia. One element was the Turkic-speaking settlers who entered these lands after the Ottoman military victories and occupation. Another was the Bogomils, Christians of mostly Slavic ethnic and linguistic background who evidently had religious ties with the former Paulicians of Asia Minor. Both of these groups had experienced persecution severally from Eastern Orthodox Serbs and/or Roman Catholic Croats. It should be noted that there was a Muslim precedent to the institution of Janissaries. Already during the Abbasid dynasty, especially in the reign of the caliph al-Mutasim (833–842), Turkish slaves were brought from the eastern provinces of the Islamic empire and in increasing numbers trained for military service. They later became known as Mamluk and, in time, replaced their owners to become the Mamluk dynasty based in Egypt. Cf. Bernard Lewis, *The Middle East: A Brief History of the Last 2000 Years* (New York: Scribner, 1995), p. 87. For a helpful account of the rise and fall of the corps of Janissaries, see pp. 124–127.

7. Marilyn R. Waldman, "The Islamic World," *The New Encyclopedia Britannica*, vol. 22 (Chicago, Ill.: University of Chicago Press, 1990), p. 131. Perhaps it would be well in this context to mention the fact that it was the Janissaries (Christian boys levied from their parents in the Balkans by the Turkish Ottoman government to be trained for military and civilian service in the empire) who were evidently the predominant element in the military forces at two key battles between the Ottomans and European Christians. These two were the conquest of Constantinople by the Ottoman forces ending on May 19, 1453, and the decisive defeat of the Hungarians in 1526. Cf. Lewis, *The Middle East*, op. cit., pp. 110, 115.

8. Abrahaman H. Hartunian, *Neither to Laugh Nor to Weep: A Memoir of the Armenian Genocide*, translated from the original Armenian manuscripts by Vartan Hartunian (Boston: Beacon Press, 1968), p. 2. I may cite as an academically responsible and balanced book Christopher J. Walker's *Armenia: The Survival of a Nation* (New York: St. Martin's Press, 1980). See also Lewis, *The Middle East*, op. cit., pp. 326–340. A distinguished specialist in Armenian studies, Professor Richard G. Hovannisian of the University of California at Los Angeles, who graciously offered a critique of this chapter, disputed this account of alleged Armenian subversive activities behind the Turkish lines as having its origin in Turkish propaganda. He sees the true situation as "a fully

armed and mobilized state machinery against a largely unarmed civilian population." Personal letter dated November 25, 1995.

9. Hartunian, op. cit., pp. 10–23; Walker, op. cit., pp. 121–176. The most recent treatment of this subject is by the American author Samantha Power in her book *A Problem from Hell: America and the Age of Genocide* (New York: Basic Books, 2002), pp. 1–29. The term "genocide" was evidently coined by Henry Morgenthau Sr., American ambassador to the Ottoman Empire from 1913 to 1916, to denote what was then called "race murder."

10. Hartunian, op. cit., pp. 51–76; Walker, op. cit., pp. 177–240.

11. Walker, op. cit., p. 180.

12. Ibid., pp. 87–89, 125.

13. Ibid.; pp. 102–103, 142, 157–161, 167–168, 171, 202.

14. This statement was first published in the British Parliamentary papers, no. 31 (1916), pp. 638–639. It was later reprinted in Beirut in 1972 with the title "The Treatment of the Armenians in the Ottoman Empire." See Walker, op. cit., pp. 201, 238 (endnote 13).

15. Kenneth Caron Buss, "Turkey," *Encyclopedia Britannica*, vol. 22 (Chicago: University of Chicago Press, 1963), pp. 605–606. Cf. Feroz Ahmad, *The Making of Modern Turkey* (New York: Routledge, 1993), pp. 36, 46–47.

16. David B. Barrett, ed., *World Christian Encyclopedia* (Nairobi: Oxford University Press, 1982), p. 680; [no author], *Turkey: A Country Study* (Washington, D.C.: U.S. Government Printing Office, 1988), pp. 133–135. An editorial in the *Religion and Society Report* (12:1 [January 1995], p. 7) cites the change in the territory of modern Turkey as 32 percent Christian in 1900, 0.2 percent in 1995. It also states that of the Assyrian Christians long located in southeastern Turkey, "since the 1970s 150,000 have been forced to flee the country as a result of persecution." See also *The CIA World Fact Book* (Washington, D.C.: U.S. Government Printing Office, July 2000). I may add that a Greek historian of religions, Astérios Argyriou, has described the entire series of events of 1922 as "le catastrophe de l'Asie Mineure." He gives the count of Greeks living in Turkey in 1998 as only 4,000, with 120,000 Muslims living in the northeastern section of Greece with remarkable freedom for religious, linguistic, and cultural as well as political activity. Astérios Argyriou, "La Situation du Dialogue Islamo-Chrétien dans le Monde Orthodoxe et en Grèce," in *Islam and Christianity*, Jacques Waardenburg, ed. (Leuven, Belgium: Uitgeverij Peeters, 1998), pp. 101–102.

17. A noteworthy example of American "excesses" may be found quite outside the area of Christian-Muslim relations. I refer to the "Genocide by Transfer—in South Vietnam," the engineered—by the Saigon Military Mission created and controlled by the CIA—movement of over one million Tonkinese from North Vietnam to the South. See L. Fletcher Prouty, *JFK, The CIA, Vietnam and the Plot to Assassinate John F. Kennedy* (New York: Carol Publishing Group, 1992), pp. 70–80. For the situation in Bosnia-Herzegovina, see Adnan Silajdzic, "Musulmans et Judeo-Chrétiens Ensemble (L'expérience de Bosnie-Herzégovine)," in *Islam and Christianity*, Jacques Waardenburg, ed. (Leuven, Belgium: Uitgeverij Peeters, 1998), pp. 257–270.

18. *The 1994 Information Please Almanac*, 47th ed. (Boston, Mass.: Houghton, Mifflin, 1994), p. 412. These figures are a reprint from the *1993 Britannica Book of the Year* (Chicago, Ill: University of Chicago, 1993). They include data available from the former U.S.S.R.

19. Hans Küng, Josef van Ess, Heinrich von Stietencron, Heinz Bechert, *Christianity and the World Religions* (Garden City, N.Y.: Doubleday, 1986), pp. 440–443. Cf. Hans Küng, *Global Responsibility* (London: SCM Press, 1991).

20. Cf. Richard H. Drummond, "Is a Spiritual Renaissance Dawning?" *Venture Inward* 10:2 (March/April 1994), pp. 17–21.

21. The American Roman Catholic scholar (and editor of the respected *Journal of Ecumenical Studies*) Leonard Swidler, in a book as yet published only in a German translation, relates the whole area of praxis to the universal human quest for "salvation." This last term, σωτηρία in the original Greek of the New Testament, bearing etymological associations with "healing," properly points to wholeness, therefore also to a holy life. Mutual understanding and practical cooperation among all humans, even between theists and nontheists, may well emerge from this "soteriocentric" approach. Leonard Swidler, *Die Zukunft der Theologie im Dialog der Religionen und Weltanschauungen* (Regensburg, Germany: Verlag Friedrich Pustet, 1992), pp. 58–60.

22. Cf. ibid., pp. 21–26.

23. Karl Rahner, "Das Christentum und nichtchristlichen Religionen," *Schriften zur Theologie*, vol. 5 (Einsiedeln, Germany: Benziger Verlag, 1964), p. 153.

24. Karl Rahner, *Foundations of Christian Faith* (New York: Seabury, 1978), pp. 142–161, 311–321.

25. Raymond Panikkar, *The Unknown Christ of Hinduism* (London:

Darton, Longman and Todd, 1964), pp. 58–59. Cf. Heinz Robert Schlette, *Towards a Theology of Religions* (New York: Herder and Herder, 1966), pp. 71–76.

26. The prophet Jeremiah came to speak of a "new covenant," as that of a new, deeper relationship between God and the people of Israel. It was necessitated because they had broken the old covenant, and the emphasis of the prophet is on the interiority of the new. Nowhere, in the present text, however, does he speak of the abrogation of the older covenants in any structured sense, even though he proclaims the need for correction of certain popular understandings of God's ways (Jer. 31:31–34, 32:36–41; cf. Ezek. 36:26–28).

27. For example, Justin Martyr, *Dialogue with Trypho the Jew* 11.

28. The best manuscript evidence omits the adjective "new" from Jesus' mention of the covenant in accounts of the Last Supper in Mark and Matthew (Mark 14:24; Matt. 26:28). The shorter and better substantiated manuscript reading omits Luke 22:19b–20. There is, however, no problem of the "new" in the text of Paul (1 Cor. 11:25; 2 Cor. 3:6). In the Letter to the Hebrews, however, we have the sharpest rejection of the old covenant as something "growing old, near disappearance" (Heb. 8:13).

29. Paul Tillich, *The Future of Religions* (New York: Harper & Row, 1966), p. 81.

30. The translation given for John 1:9 is this author's choice of an alternative translation. See NRSV New Testament, p. 94, footnote b.

31. Justin Martyr, *The First Apology* 46; *The Second Apology* 13. In his *Dialogue with Trypho the Jew*, Justin is highly critical of Jews, but his chief complaint is alleged Jewish persecution of Christians and his appeal is that they repent, have the faith of Abraham, come to know "our Christ," be baptized with the baptism spoken of by Isaiah, and thus live lives free of sin (26, 44).

32. Irenaeus, *Contra Haereses* III 24; III 12–13; III 18, 1; IV 6–7, IV 20, 6 (Deus . . . Incognitus autem nequaquam); I 10, 3.

33. Clement, *Stromateis* VI 7; VII 2.

34. We must recall that the Creed of Chalcedon (451) was not acceptable to many Christians, especially of Semitic or Coptic ethnic background, in the eastern part of the Roman Empire. Cf. Williston Walker, *A History of the Christian Church*, Revised Edition (New York: Charles Scribner's Sons, 1959), pp. 138–145.

35. Cf. Russell Watson, "A Lesser Child of God," in *Newsweek* (April 4, 1994), pp. 53–54.

36. Michael G. Fonner, "Jesus' Death by Crucifixion in the Quran: An Issue for Interpretation and Muslim-Christian Interpretations." *Journal of Ecumenical Studies* 29:3–4, (Summer-Fall, 1992), pp. 432–449. Cf. K 14:18–19; 37:171–172; Rom. 6:4, 8:11; 1 Cor. 1:23–25, 6:4, 15:24–28; 2 Cor. 2:14, 4:16; Gal. 1:1; Eph. 1:20; Phil. 2:8–9; Col. 2:12–15; 1 Thess. 1:10. Fonner observes that "the Koran is not interested in reconstructing the historical Jesus. This is in line with how the Koran looks at other historical figures." Ibid., p. 436; cf. William Montgomery Watt, *Muslim-Christian Encounters, Perceptions and Misperceptions* (London: Routledge, 1991), pp. 125–129, 137–151.

37. Daud Rahbar, "Muslims and the Finality of Jesus Christ in the Age of Universal History," *Ecumenical Review* 17:4 (October 1965), p. 364.

38. *Lumen Gentium* II, 16.

39. To cite only a few of his many books: Kenneth Cragg, *The Call of the Minaret* (New York: Oxford University Press, 1956); *The House of Islam* (Belmont, Calif.: Dickenson, 1969); *The Mind of the Quran* (London: George Allen & Unwin, 1973); *Muhammad and the Christian* (Maryknoll, N.Y.: Orbis, 1984); *Jesus and the Muslim: An Exploration* (London: George Allen & Unwin, 1985).

40. Richard H. Drummond, "Toward Theological Understanding of Islam," *Journal of Ecumenical Studies* 9:4 (Fall 1972), p. 795. I should add here P. Xavier Jacob's article: "Christians in Turkey and Their Relations with Moslems," *Studies in Interreligious Dialogue* 4:1 (1994), pp. 42–61. Father Jacob is a Roman Catholic theologian stationed in Ankara, Turkey. It is gratifying to me that this article with its data is in substantial agreement with my own data and interpretation. For a fair assessment of Muhammad as a person, see W. Montgomery Watt, *Muhammad: Prophet and Statesman* (London: Oxford University Press, 1961), pp. 229–240.

BIBLIOGRAPHY

Ali, Abdullah Yusuf, *The Meaning of the Glorious Quran* (Cairo, Egypt: Daval-Kitab Al-Masri, n.d.).

Ali, Sayed Ameer, *The Spirit of Islam* (London: Christophers, 1946).

Alla, Waheed Hassab, "Le Christianisme et les Chretiéns Vus par Deux Auteurs Arabes Musulmans," in *Islam and Christianity*, Jacques Waardenburg, ed. (Leuven, Belgium: Uitgeverij, Peeters, 1998).

Alleman, Herbert C., *The Old Testament—A Study* (Philadelphia, Pa.: United Lutheran Publication House, 1935).

Amnesty International Report 2000 (London: A1 Publications, 2000).

Arberry, A. J., *Sufism* (London: Allen & Unwin, 1963).

Argyriou, Astérios, "Le Situation du Dialogue Islamo-Chrétien dans le Munde Orthodoxe et en Grèce," in *Islam and Christianity*, Jacques Waardenburg, ed. (Leuven, Belgium: Uitgeverij Peeters, 1998).

Armstrong, Karen, *Muhammad: A Biography of the Prophet* (San Francisco: HarperCollins, 1992).

Atiyah, Edward, *The Arabs* (Harmondsworth, Middlesex, U.K.: Penguin, 1958).

Attar, Fahid al-Din, *Muslim Saints and Mystics* (Chicago: University of Chicago Press, 1966).

Aydin, Mahmut, "Religious Pluralism: A Challenge for Muslims—A Theological Evaluation," *Journal of Ecumenical Studies* 38:2–3 (Spring-Summer, 2001).

Ayoub, Mahmoud Mustafa, "Jesus the Son of God: A Study of the

Terms *Ibn* and *Walad* in the Quran and Tafsir Tradition," Yvonne Yazbeck Haddad, Wadi Z. Haddad, eds., *Christian-Muslim Encounters* (Gainesville, Fla.: University Press of Florida, 1995).

Bell, Richard, *The Origin of Islam in its Christian Environment* (London: Macmillan, 1926).

Blauw, Johannes, *The Missionary Nature of the Church* (New York: McGraw-Hill, 1962).

Bonhoeffer, Dietrich, *Ethics*, E. Bethge, ed. (New York: Macmillan, 1965).

Carmichael, Joel, *The Shaping of the Arabs* (New York: Macmillan, 1967).

The CIA World Fact Book (Washington, D.C.: U.S. Government Printing Office, July 2000).

Cook, Michael, *Muhammad* (Oxford: Oxford University Press, 1983).

Cragg, Kenneth, *The Call of the Minaret* (New York: Oxford University Press, 1956).

———, *Sandals at the Mosque* (London: SCM Press, 1959).

———, *The Event of the Quran* (London: George Allen & Unwin, 1971).

———, *The Mind of the Quran* (London: George Allen & Unwin, 1973).

Cuttat, Jacques-Albert, *The Encounter of Religions* (New York: Desclée, 1960).

Dawood, N. J., *The Koran* (Harmondsworth, Middlesex, U.K.: Penguin, 1966).

de Franch, Ramon Sugranyes, "The Springtime of Missions in the Thirteenth Century," in *History's Lessons for Tomorrow's Mission*, Philippe Maury, ed. (Geneva: World Student Christian Federation, 1960).

The Europa Year Book, 1943, vol. 2 (London: Europa Publications).

Fregosi, Paul, *Jihad in the West* (Amherst, N.Y.: Prometheus, 1998).

Gibb, H. A. R., *Mohammedanism* (London: Oxford University Press, 1950).

———, "Islam" in *The Concise Encyclopedia of Living Faiths*, R. C. Zaehner, ed. (New York: Hawthorne, 1959).

Glubb, John Bagot, *The Life and Times of Muhammad* (New York: Stein and Day, 1970).

Goddard, Hugh, "Christianity from the Muslim Perspective: Varieties and Changes," in *Islam and Christianity*, Jacques Waardenburg, ed. (Leuven, Belgium: Uitgeverij Peeters, 1998).

Grant, Frederick C., ed., *The Interpreter's Bible*, vol. 7, George Buttrick, ed. (New York: Abingdon-Cokesbury, 1951).

Guillaume, Alfred, *New Light on the Life of Muhammad* (Manchester, England: Manchester University Press, 1960).

———, *Islam* (Baltimore, Md.: Penguin, 1962).

Haines, Byron L., and Frank L. Cooley, eds., *Christians and Muslims Together: An Exploration by Presbyterians* (Philadelphia, Pa.: Geneva Press, 1987).

Hitti, Philip K., *History of the Arabs* (London: Macmillan, 1953).

Hodgson, Leonard, *Sex and Christian Freedom: An Enquiry* (London: SCM Press, 1967), quoted in *Church Missionary Society Newsletter* 304 (May 1967).

The Holy Bible, New Revised Standard Version (New York: Oxford University Press, 1989).

The Holy Bible, Revised Standard Version (New York: Thomas Nelson & Sons, 1952).

Hunter, Archibald M., *Introducing the New Testament* (Philadelphia, Pa.: Westminster Press, 1957).

Ibn Ishaq, *The Life of Muhammad*, with introduction and notes by Alfred Guillaume (London: Oxford University Press, 1968).

Izutsu, Toshihiko, *Ethico-Religious Concepts in the Quran* (Montreal: McGill University Press, 1966).

Jeffery, Arthur, *Islam: Muhammad and His Religion* (New York: Liberal Arts Press, 1958).

Jurji, Edward J., "Islam," in *The Great Religions of the Modern World*, Edward J. Jurji, ed. (Princeton, N.J.: Princeton University Press, 1947).

Katsh, Abraham J., *Judaism in Islam* (New York: New York University Press/Bloch, 1954).

Kellerhals, Emanuel, *Der Islam* (Basel, Switzerland: Basler Missionsbuchhandlung, 1945).

Kerr, David A., "'He Walked in the Path of the Prophets': Toward Christian Theological Recognition of the Prophethood of Muhammad," in *Christian-Muslim Encounters*, Yvonne Yazbeck Haddad, Wadi Z. Haddad, eds. (Gainesville, Fla.: University Press of Florida, 1995).

Keyserling, Count Herman, *The Travel Diary of a Philosopher*, vol. 1 (New York: Harcourt, Brace, 1925).

Khalidi, Tarif, *The Muslim Jesus* (Cambridge, Mass.: Harvard University Press, 2001).

Khan, Muhammad Zafrulla, *Islam* (New York: Harper & Row, 1962).

Khoury, Théodore, "Manuel II Paléologue," in *Entretiens Avec un Musulman* (Paris: Les Editions du Cerf, 1966).

Kitagawa, Joseph M., *Religions of the East* (Philadelphia, Pa.: Westminster, 1960).

Kitamori, Kazo, *Kami no Itami no Shingaku* (Tokyo: Shinkyo Shuppansha, 1958), English edition, *The Theology of the Pain of God* (Richmond, Va.: John Knox, 1965).

Kraemer, Hendrik, *World Cultures and World Religions* (Philadelphia, Pa.: Westminster, 1960).

Kretzmann, Martin L., "Analysis of the Encounter to Date," *International Review of Missions* 4:220 (October 1966), quoting the April 1966 *Bulletin* from the Henry Martyn Institute of Islamic Studies in Hyderabad, India.

Lewis, Bernard, *The Arabs in History* (London: Hutchinson University Library, 1960).

———, *The Middle East: A Brief History of the Last 2,000 Years* (New York: Scribner, 1995).

———, *What Went Wrong? Western Impact and Middle Eastern Response* (New York: Oxford University Press, 2002).

Lukacs, John, *At the End of an Age* (New Haven, Conn.: Yale University Press, 2002).

Maimonides, Moses, *The Guide of the Perplexed*, Shlomo Pines, ed., (Chicago: University of Chicago Press, 1963).

ben Maimun, Rabbenu Mose, *Iggeret Teman* (Philadelphia, Pa.: Jewish Publication Society, 1950).

Mujeeb, M., *The Indian Muslims* (Montreal: McGill University Press, 1967).

Nasr, Seyyed Hossein, *Three Muslim Sages* (Cambridge, Mass.: Harvard University Press, 1964).

Omar, Irfan A., "Islam and the Other: The Ideal Vision of Mawlana Wahiduddin Khan," *Journal of Ecumenical Studies* 36:3–4 (Summer-Fall, 1999).

Parrinder, Geoffrey, *Jesus in the Quran* (New York: Barnes & Noble, 1965).

Peers, E. Allison, *Mother of Carmel* (New York: Morehouse-Gorham, 1948).

Peters, F. E., *Muhammad and the Origins of Islam* (Albany, N.Y.: State University of New York Press, 1994).

Pickthall, Mohammed Marmaduke, *The Meaning of the Glorious Koran* (New York: New American Library, 1961).

Power, Samantha, *A Problem from Hell: America and the Age of Genocide* (New York: Basic Books, 2002).

Rahbar, Daud, "Muslims and the Finality of Jesus Christ in the Age of Universal History," *Ecumenical Review* 17:4 (October 1965).

Rahman, Fazlur, *Islam* (Garden City, N.Y.: Doubleday, 1968).

———, *Major Themes of the Quran*, 2d ed. (Minneapolis, Minn.: Bibliotheca Islamica, 1994).

Robinson, Neal, *Christ in Islam and Christianity* (Albany, N.Y.: State University of New York Press, 1991).

Schmidt, Wilhelm, *The Origin and Growth of Religion* (New York: Dial, 1935).

Schwartz, Stephen, *The Two Faces of Islam* (New York: Doubleday, 2002).

Silajdzic, Adnan, "Musulmans et Judeo-Chrétiens Ensemble" (L'expérience de Bosnie-Herzégovine), in Jacques Waardenburg, ed., *Islam and Christianity* (Leuven, Belgium: Uitgeverij Peeters, 1998).

Smith, Margaret, *The Sufi Path of Love* (London: Luzac, 1954).

Speight, R. Marston, *God Is One: The Way of Islam* (New York: Friendship Press, 1991).

Spencer, Robert, *Islam Unveiled* (San Francisco: Encounter Books, 2002).

Stanton, H. U. Weitbrecht, *The Teaching of the Quran* (London: Society for the Promotion of Christian Literature, 1969).

Talbi, Mohamad, quoted in R. Marston Speight, "Some Bases for a Christian Apologetic to Islam," *International Review of Missions* 54:214 (April 1965).

Taylor, Vincent, *The Gospel According to St. Mark* (London: Macmillan, 1952).

Teipen, Alfons, "The Word of God: What Can Christians Learn from Muslim Attitudes toward the Quran?" *Journal of Ecumenical Studies* 38:2–3 (Spring-Summer 2001).

Toynbee, Arnold J., *The Treatment of Armenians in the Ottoman Empire, 1915–1916* (London: Her Majesty's Stationery Office, 1916).

Troll, Christian W., SJ, "Changing Catholic Views of Islam," in *Islam and Christianity*, Jacques Waardenburg, ed. (Leuven, Belgium: Uitgeverij Peeters, 1998).

Valiuddin, Mir, "Love in its Essence: The Sufi Approach," *Studies in Islam* 3:1–2 (January–April, 1966).

van Leeuwen, Arend Th., *Christianity in World History* (London: Edinburgh House, 1964).

von Grunebaum, Gustave E., *Medieval Islam* (Chicago: University of Chicago Press, 1962).

Waardenburg, Jacques, ed., *Islam and Christianity: Mutual Perceptions since the Mid-Twentieth Century* (Leuven, Belgium: Uitgeverij Peeters, 1998).

Watt, W. Montgomery, *Muhammad: Prophet and Statesman* (London: Oxford University Press, 1961).

Wiedenmann, Ludwig, *Missions und Eschatologie* (Paderborn, Germany: Verlag Bonifacius-Druckerei, 1965).

Williams, John Alden, *Islam* (New York: Washington Square Press, 1963).

Wollcombe, Kenneth J., "The Pain of God," *Scottish Journal of Theology* 20:2 (June 1967).

Ye'or, Bat, *The Decline of Eastern Christianity under Islam* (Madison, N.J.: Fairleigh Dickinson University Press, 1996).

INDEX

Index

Index

ABOUT THE AUTHOR

 Richard Henry Drummond is an author with a broadly cosmopolitan cultural background. A linguist, he was born in San Francisco and raised in Hollywood and North Hollywood, California, graduating from U.C.L.A. with highest honors in Latin. He received a Ph.D. in classics from the University of Wisconsin with a dissertation on the historical thinking of the Latin Christian writers. He taught New Testament Greek and Theological German at the Lutheran Theological Seminary, Gettysburg, PA.

Dr. Drummond met his wife, Pearl in Alberta, Canada while serving as pastor of English and German-speaking churches. With his wife he served eighteen years as a Christian field and educational missionary in Japan. He became professor of Christian Studies and Classical Languages at Meiji Gakuin University and Tokyo Union Theological Seminary.

As a longtime professor at the University of Dubuque Theological Seminary, Dr. Drummond became the first incumbent of the Florence Livergood Warren chair of comparative religions. He is the author of several books and many articles; some